Issues in Historiography

The Debate on the American Civil War Era

Issues in Historiography

The Debate
on the American Civil War Era

HUGH TULLOCH

MANCHESTER
UNIVERSITY PRESS
MANCHESTER AND NEW YORK

Published by Manchester University Press
Oxford Road, Manchester M13 9NR, UK
and Room 400, 175 Fifth Avenue, New York, NY 10010, USA
www.manchesteruniversitypress.co.uk

Distributed exclusively in the USA by
Palgrave, 175 Fifth Avenue, New York NY 10010, USA

Distributed exclusively in Canada by
UBC Press, University of British Columbia, 2029 West Mall,
Vancouver, BC, Canada V6T 1Z2

British Library Cataloguing-in-Publication Data
A catalogue record for this book is available from the British Library

Library of Congress Cataloging-in-Publication Data
A catalog record for this book is available from the Library of Congress

ISBN 0 7190 4938 5 paperback

First edition published 1999 by Manchester University Press

First digital, on-demand edition produced by Lightning Source 2006

CONTENTS

GENERAL EDITOR'S FOREWORD

History without historiography is a contradiction in terms. No historian writes in isolation from the work of his or her predecessors nor can the historian stand aloof from the insistent pressures, priorities and demands of the present. Though historians address the past they always do so in ways that are shaped – consciously or unconsciously as the case may be – by the society and systems of their own day and they communicate their findings in ways that are intelligible and relevant to a reading public consisting of their own contemporaries. For these reasons the study of history is concerned not with dead facts and sterile, permanent verdicts but with dialogues, disagreements, and controversies among its presenters, and with the changing methodologies and discourse of the subject over time. *Issues in Historiography* is a series designed to address such matters by means of case studies.

The American Civil War ranks as the most traumatic experience in that nation's history. An anticipation of the kind of total war that did not afflict Europe until the twentieth century, its complex political, social, racial, and psychological legacies have painfully lingered long after the original upheavals and battle carnage ended. Hugh Tulloch's book shows how successive generations of historians have tried to make sense of slavery, abolitionism and their place in the causes, course, and consequences of the Civil War. The changing reputations of key figures such as Lincoln, Jefferson Davis, Sherman and Robert E. Lee are examined as, more generally, are the ways in which the changing vantage points provided by Reconstruction, Depression, the two World Wars, the Cold War, the Civil Rights Movement and Vietnam have caused the troubled decade of the 1860s in American history to be viewed and explained very differently. In starkly obvious ways American historians (and others) have gone on both re-fighting and atoning for the Civil War – not just conducting academic debates with each other; this past just refuses to fade! The differing contributions of a host of American historians – including Turner, Beard, W.E.B. Du Bois, Richard Hoftsadter, Allan Nevins, John Blassingame, and Kenneth Stampp – are brought into focus here. So are commentaries from 'outsiders' as various as Karl Marx, Lord Acton, Pieter Geyl and Marcus Cunliffe. Historian-turned-politician Woodrow Wilson finds a place here as do Griffith's epic film *Birth of a Nation* and the Klu Klux Klan. This period in America's past,

and its central issues of slavery and the outcomes of the war, still rever-
berates strongly in the present. *The Debate on the American Civil War
Era* shows why.

R.C. Richardson
September 1999

ACKNOWLEDGEMENTS

I should like to express my gratitude to Hugh Brogan and Anne Merriman, whose help, whether by correction or encouragement, was invaluable. I should also like to thank Anne Griffiths, Paula Warburton and Heather Hernandez for their secretarial assistance.

Fellow citizens, *we* can not escape history. We of this Congress and administration will be remembered in spite of ourselves. No personal significance or insignificance can spare one or another of us. The fiery trial through which we pass will light us down in honor or dishonor to the latest generation ... We, even *we here*, hold the power and bear the responsibility. In *giving* freedom to the *slave* we *assure* freedom to the *free* – honorable alike in what we give and what we preserve. We shall nobly save or meanly lose the last, best hope of earth.

(Abraham Lincoln)

INTRODUCTION

The Civil War is, without doubt, one of the central, formative events in American history. During the war itself, and thereafter, politicians and historians have been constantly engaged in explaining its causes and exploring its ramifications, and their writings have been characterised by deep engagement and the search for a 'usable' past. Even today, some 130 years after it ended, the war retains its significance and its unprecedented hold over the American spirit. In 1998, for example, a major furore broke out on the Harvard campus when attempts were made to add the names of Confederate alumni to the college's Memorial Hall, which commemorates only the Union dead. Throughout the South the Confederate flag is still unfurled with pride and a sense of defiance. Fundamental questions of equality and race, unresolved by the Civil War, continue to trouble the souls of Americans today.

It is these questions of equality and race which distinguish the middle years of nineteenth-century America and which, at the same time, hold this period inextricably together. During the preceding years America was absorbed in the difficult transition from the elitist republican politics of the founding fathers to the mass participatory politics of Jacksonian democracy. Here the political battles were fought over the vestiges of eighteenth-century privilege – be it the Bank of the United States or the college which indirectly elected the President – but it was a politics which demanded equal representation for white male Americans only. Andrew Jackson, symbol of that age, was both a Tennessee slave holder and a notorious exterminator of Indians. Likewise, with the ending of Reconstruction in 1877, the question of race was tacitly dropped and the South was left to deal with its racial problem as it saw fit as America began to meet the fresh challenges of industrialisation, urbanisation and mass immigration. Informally disfranchised and segregated, the black all but vanished from the political scene. One of the first executive acts of that Progressive and Southern President, Woodrow Wilson, was to segregate his Washington bureaucracy, white from black.

It was only during the tumultuous years of the mid nineteenth century that race became of paramount importance, culminating in a bloody conflict of unparalleled proportions, the imposition of military rule on the South and the passing of the three Civil War amendments to the Constitution which gave the black freedom, equal citizenship and the vote. Very few white Americans – the abolitionists were the exception – wanted to raise the troubling and divisive issue of race: it confronted the North starkly with its own negrophobe assumptions and threatened to subvert and revolutionise the entire Southern social order. Yet the issue emerged, irrepressibly, for all that and touched the lives of every American during this eventful period.

Abraham Lincoln, for example, caught up in the maelstrom of these middle years, insisted that he was controlled by events and was unable to control them himself. As a young man he travelled on a flatboat down the Mississippi to New Orleans, where he witnessed scenes of brutal injustice to slaves. He bit his lip and said nothing. Personally he abhorred slavery: if slavery was right, he insisted, then nothing could be wrong. In so many ways a typical product of his age, he entertained serious doubts about the capacity of blacks and was not an abolitionist. As an astute politician who had to win votes, he was acutely aware of his Northern constituency's underlying racism, and that any challenge to the peculiar institution of slavery in the South could lead to bitter, wholesale conflict. When he argued against Stephen A. Douglas for the non-extension of slavery in the senatorial race in Illinois in 1858, he was arguing in favour of preserving Illinois for the white man under the banner of 'Free soil, free labor, free men'. In the same year, however, in his 'House divided' speech, he ventured to suggest that a house divided against itself could not stand, and that the institution of slavery must be set on the path of ultimate extinction. Yet in 1861, as President of the United States as well as leader of the Republican party, and with the South already seceding, he was prepared to guarantee the institution of slavery for all time under a constitutional amendment. He made it clear, time and again, during the early stages of the war, that he was fighting to reunite the Union, not to abolish slavery. Yet the ultimate military offensive against the South became slowly and inexorably an offensive against slavery, and in January

1863 Lincoln issued his Emancipation Proclamation. Lincoln did not live to witness the passing of the Civil War amendments which flowed from his proclamation and his Gettysburg address of 1863, 'dedicated to the proposition that all men are created equal', but their spirit continued to inform the Republican party in its Reconstruction policy, led to a bitter constitutional crisis between Congress and the new President, Andrew Johnson, and not until 1876, when the Democratic party came within a whisker of capturing the presidency, did the Republican party relinquish its strategy of directly aiding the Southern freedmen.

Lincoln's evolving attitude to slavery and race is a conspicuous example, but each and every American, however obscure and forgotten, was caught up, whether he or she wished it or not, in the climactic events of those years, and was compelled by the force of events to confront, individually, the same questions the President confronted. And it is this thread of race and justice which gives the era its distinctiveness and its unity. As Allan Nevins expressed it: 'The main cause of the conflict ... was the problem of slavery with its complementary problem of race-adjustment. It was a war over slavery and the future position of the Negro race in North America.'

This book's organisation works on two levels. The first, chapter by chapter, follows the events of the Civil War era: the existing slave order in the South, the Northern abolitionist crusade against that order, the swelling of the Republican ranks which opposed the extension of slavery, elected Lincoln and triggered off the secession crisis of 1860–61, the military struggle itself, and the attempt at Reconstruction which followed the military defeat of the South. In Chapter 5, on the Civil War itself, I partly depart from this scheme. Because of the complexity and interrelatedness of the sectional struggle (temporary victory for the Confederacy lowered Northern military and civilian morale, for example, and vice versa), I have treated the conflict, initially, as a single phenomenon, before looking separately at North and South.

The second level of chronology, within each chapter, traces the evolution of historical perspective from direct participants reflecting upon the events of their time up to the latest scholarly reappraisal of this era by the historical profession. To set the scene and help make sense of what follows, I have attempted in Chapter 1 to link these two separate chronologies and to show how, just as the actors of the Civil War stage were shaped by the pressure of events, so historians studying that era were similarly entangled in the presuppositions of their own time.

To repeat: I take the central cause and consequence of the war to be a recognition of, and attempt to adjust, the racial question in America to conform to the principle of the Declaration of Independence that 'all men are created equal'. This moral dimension lies at the heart of the historiographical debate and, just as one group of historians has attempted to play down the moral significance of race and slavery, so another has insisted on its paramount importance.

What I have attempted to do is to analyse each historian's attitudes and assumptions and to suggest that each writer's perspective was partly determined by the dictates of time and place. What I hope will emerge is the endurance of racial assumptions following the failure of the first Reconstruction (1865–77) and the profession's gradual emergence from it with the launching of the second period of Reconstruction which recommenced in the 1950s. It was not until the 1940s, for example, that Richard Hofstadter questioned the benign character of antebellum slavery depicted by Ulrich Bonner Phillips, not until the 1950s and 1960s that historians like Martin Duberman questioned the conventional depiction of abolitionists as crackpot extremists.

Dwight Macdonald, the journalist, once wrote that there were only three literary genres in the United States: fiction, nonfiction and Civil War studies, the last combining elements of the first two. The amount of material on the era is immense (there are over 50,000 books covering the period and the Lincoln bibliography alone is over 1,000 pages in length), and any attempt at comprehensiveness would merely result in a tedious annotated bibliography. Instead I have been highly selective in this survey and if, at times, an inordinate amount of space has been given to controversial studies – such as Stanley Elkins and Robert Fogel and Stanley Engerman on slavery – it is partly because these writers employ novel historical methodologies and spark off interesting and constructive debate. One of the main aims of the book is to suggest that historiography, far from being otiose and irrelevant, is highly pertinent and central to our sense of how we interpret the world around us. History, in the words of the late Victorian historian Lord Acton, is 'a narrative told of ourselves, the record of a life which is our own, of efforts not yet abandoned to repose, of problems that still entangle the feet and vex the hearts of men'.

1

The American historical profession

The American historical profession is to the American past what
the Supreme Court is to the Constitution: that is, its primary task
is to guard and interpret a living legacy much as the associate
justices guard and interpret the Constitution. But historians do
not live outside or apart from history any more than the justices
of the Supreme Court are immune to the currents of contemporary judicial concern. The Constitution, Chief Justice Hughes
once boldly asserted, is what the judges say it is but, at the same
time, the brethren are forced to keep a keen eye upon public
opinion and the latest electoral returns. The same can be said of
American historians: they strive to establish as authoritative an
interpretation of the past as possible while, at the same time,
inevitably reflecting the shifting assumptions – or prejudices? – of
their time. Here, all too faithfully, some historians have
succeeded in giving voice to and legitimising an all but endemic
racism which has distorted, and even diametrically opposed, the
professional quest for objectivity.

To put the matter with disarming crudeness – and it can be –
with the fundamental presumption of black racial inferiority
assumed by most white historians, the historiography of the Civil
War era between 1877 and, say, 1945, falls neatly into place.
Slavery, once justified on grounds of social control, was now
conceded to be an evil and Southern secession was likewise
conceded to be an error, because the Union was sacred and indis-
soluble. Because the South lost the Civil War, the war was
deemed by Southern historians to be a bad thing and, therefore,
needless and avoidable, and blame for its outbreak was attached

to the hyperbolical fanaticism of Northern abolitionists. But it was the abolitionists who, together with radical Republicans, gave racialist historians their easiest victory. To free the slave was right and proper; to go further and press for racial equality during Reconstruction patently was not. On this matter, at least, both Northern and Southern historians could agree and could forge a national consensus. James Ford Rhodes, writing in 1928, was the main symbol and spokesman of this consensus. 'So long as Southern reasoners maintained that the Negro race was inferior to the Caucasian their basis was scientific truth, although their inference that this fact justified slavery was cruel as well as illogical.' As in the political sphere, so in the historical profession, a new consensual history was forged at the expense of the freedmen. The era was now depicted in terms of a tragic but noble struggle from which the reunited Union emerged, ultimately, strengthened and purified. And this strategy of vindication operated even on a microscopic level. When, for example, Rhodes turned his attention to the vexed question of 'Who burned Columbia?' in South Carolina towards the end of the Civil War, he found neither the Southerner, Wade Hampton, nor the Northern commander, Sherman, responsible, but, instead, a combination of marauding Confederate soldiers, escaped convicts and Northern prisoners.[1]

This consensus was also duplicated by the Supreme Court. Piece by piece in 1873 (*Slaughterhouse*), 1883 (*Civil Rights cases*) and 1896 (*Plessy v. Ferguson*), the court undercut the federal commitment to racial equality embodied in the three constitutional amendments which emerged from the crusade of the Civil War and Reconstruction. This allowed the Southern states to impose peonage upon the freedmen along with disfranchisement and segregation in the name of white supremacy, while the North looked on indifferently. It was this tacit collaboration of North and South which rendered the black, in Ralph Ellison's potent phrase, invisible politically, economically, culturally and historically.

And this historical invisibility was not unimportant for, as Eugene Genovese has written, there is no future without the past, and the black was essentially denied his past. It was no coincidence that the eminent historian of abolitionism, David Brion

Davis, was given the racist writings of U.B. Phillips to read, when he embarked on a PhD at Harvard in the late 1930s and then went on to find himself fighting in a segregated US army in the Second World War. Insistence upon greater visibility and the writing back of blacks into the national history was an explicit and essential part of the civil rights movement. As Herbert Aptheker wrote in 1964 in the aftermath of *Brown* v. *Board of Education of Topeka* (1954), 'Part of the effort to cleanse the United States of racism is to cleanse its educational system of that blight. Certainly, an anti-racist educational system cannot have racist history books; integrated schools require integrated texts.'[2]

It was natural for nineteenth century American historians to adopt racial assumptions because they were both academically and scientifically respectable. In the last quarter of the nineteenth century the predominant school of American graduate research was centred at Johns Hopkins University under Herbert Baxter Adams. It propagated a genetic theory of historical continuity: the task of the historian was to trace Americans' roots back to their Teutonic origins and chart their ineluctable progress through time in those institutions and constitutions which were created for carrying forward the specifically Anglo-American characteristics of orderly self-government. This school's methodology was deterministic – the sunflower seed could only grow into a sunflower – and racial too, in that it identified a specifically Anglo-Saxon mission to expand and progress at the expense of other races, of whatever colour, red or black. James Ford Rhodes found it extraordinary that Senator Charles Sumner could be both a friend of Louis Agassiz, the pre-eminent scientist of his day, who biologically confirmed the inherent superiority of the white race over the black, and yet still persisted in urging black civil rights after the Civil War. The general concept of white manifest destiny was vague enough to enable it to expand beyond the American hemisphere and, at the turn of the century, America engaged in its own splendid little war and acquired the Philippines as a consequence. Whatever mixture of motives it was that thrust the United States into the Spanish American War of 1898, this fatal imperial venture was justified and underpinned by an ideology of racial superiority which required it to act as ward and trustee for the lesser breed of little brown brothers.

There were stirrings against this overwhelming racial consensus. Franz Boas, an anthropologist at Columbia University, having accumulated a vast array of data from his study of Pacific North West Indians, rejected biological for cultural and linguistic criteria in his 1911 *The Mind of Primitive Man*, and patiently argued that there were greater variations within biological groups than there were between them. His pupil, Melville Herskovits, in his 1941 study *The Myth of the Negro Past*, more specifically refuted the lax assumption that the black was both intellectually inferior and devoid of his own unique Afro-American culture. But this ground-breaking research by social scientists only slowly filtered through to their colleagues in history faculties throughout the country. During this period it was left to black historians to write blacks back into American history and if, at times, they concentrated excessively on black achievement and black contribution, it can be excused on the grounds of their having to throw their own weight against an almost entirely white history written by white historians for a white audience. 'I do not for a moment doubt that my Negro descent and narrow group culture have in many cases predisposed me to interpret my facts too favourably for my race; but there is little danger of long misleading here, for the champions of white folks are legion,' wrote W.E.B. Du Bois.[3] Carter Woodson established the Association for the Study of Negro Life and History and, in 1916, the invaluable *Journal of Negro History*. He was the author of over eighteen books including, in 1922, *The Negro in our History*, but on his death in 1950 he received only a seventeen-line obituary in the pages of *The American Historical Review*, compared with a longer appreciation of an obscure and forgotten English medieval historian in the same issue. W.E.B. Du Bois (1868–1963) was the outstanding Afro-American scholar of his generation and the first to receive a PhD (from Harvard in 1895), but his political activism, his seminal influence in creating the National Association for the Advancement of Colored People, his growing Marxist sympathy for Soviet Russia and his advocacy of black nationalism and anti-imperialism led to his being generally ostracised by the historical establishment. In 1951 he was arrested and imprisoned briefly on charges of treason and in 1961, thoroughly disillusioned, he emigrated to Ghana, where he died. Du Bois received only a

9

one-line obituary in *The American Historical Review* though his long-neglected *Black Reconstruction* is now recognised as a pioneering masterpiece.

There were exceptions to this wide ostracism. J. Franklin Jameson, the editor of *The American Historical Review,* published some of Du Bois's research on Reconstruction and Herbert Bushnell Hart of Harvard nurtured and encouraged him and got him to speak at American Historical Association conventions in 1891 and 1909. But this was exceptional, for Du Bois was exceptional and broke all established rules. As he stated in his introduction to *Black Reconstruction in America* (1935), 'I am going to tell this story as though Negroes were ordinary human beings, realising that this attitude will from the first seriously curtail my audience.'[4] Du Bois was right: this major work was never reviewed in *The American Historical Review.*

Meanwhile, in stark contrast to this small peripheral band of black scholars and a sprinkling of white supporters, there was an all-pervasive and immensely potent pro-Southern bias which dominated the profession entirely until the middle years of the twentieth century. Why, having surrendered at Appomattox courthouse, did the South go on to win the historiographical war? Defeat and failure have, themselves, something to do with this. In America Civil War buffs prefer to wear the grey colours of the defeated Confederacy rather than the blue of the victors. There is a heady scent and a bitter sweetness in loss, an evocation of an adamic innocence and a prelapsarian paradise: a sense that the lost cause was the better cause and all the more potent because irrevocably lost. William Yancey, a Southern fire-eater, impressively captured this mood on the eve of the Civil War when he wrote, 'Our poetry is our lives; our fiction will come when truth has ceased to satisfy us; and as for our history, we have made about all that has glorified the United States.'[5] Prescient too, was the veteran who, following the Civil War, advised his fellow Southerners to hang on to their worthless Confederate currency, for it would eventually appreciate in value. Well into the twentieth century the myths surrounding the Civil War, *the* war, continued to exert their spell: on Robert Penn Warren, for example, who spoke of history in general as 'the big myth we live, and in our living, constantly remake' and of the Civil War era in particular as 'the great single event of our history. The Civil War is our only felt history – history lived in the national imagination.' As William Faulkner, the Mississippian and Nobel Prize winner, aptly noted *à propos* the Southerner, 'the past is never dead. It's not even past.'[6]

In the early years of the twentieth century, Ulrich Bonner Phillips dominated the field of research into ante-bellum slavery and W.A. Dunning in Reconstruction studies. Dunning was a Northerner, born in New Jersey in 1857, and was primarily concerned with political theory, but settling at Columbia he established a highly prestigious and influential school of researchers, whose state-by-state studies of the South during Reconstruction were almost all predicated on the assumption that congressional interference by radical Republicans who sought to bring about a revolution in race relations in the South was a national disaster, happily brought to an end by Southern 'redemption', white supremacy and 'home rule' for that section by 1877. Dunning was a political independent, or a mugwump as they were then called, who deplored the endemic corruption of the Republican party ascendancy which had rocked President Grant's two administrations and spread a similar web of corruption on the carpetbag governments of the South. It was Dunning who, for all his scholarship, perpetuated and reinforced the caricature of 'carpetbaggers' from the North, of 'scalawag' collaborators from the South, and of ignorant blacks who all came together to despoil and exploit the prostrate South. Dunning's pre-eminence grew and grew, his loyal research students churned out studies which confirmed the view of their professor, whom they reverently referred to as the 'old chief', and in 1913 he was elected president of the American Historical Association at the same time that the first Southerner to be President since the Civil War, Woodrow Wilson, entered the White House. The South had indeed returned with a vengeance.

U.B. Phillips, a Southerner from Georgia, wrote principally on the institution of slavery but also on the defining characteristics of Southern sectionism. What, he asked, in his 'Central theme of Southern history', made that region so different from the rest of the United States? It was not, as many historians believed, the predominant agrarianism of the South: the Northern Mohawk valley was as rural as the Southern Roanoke: wheat was a staple crop of the Dakotas as cotton was of Alabama. Nor was it the Southerners' unique dedication to state rights. John Calhoun, senator from South Carolina, had at one stage been as nationalist as President Andrew Jackson himself and, after his split with the President and the debacle over the nullification crisis of 1832, had attempted, in vain, to establish a United Southern Republic. No, the defining characteristic of the South was its 'common resolve, indomitably maintained, that it shall be, and remain, a white man's country'. That current resolve dictated that the usable and selected past conformed to the dictates of the present. As William Dodd wrote (he was himself a Southerner, though settled at the University of Chicago), 'The Confederate veteran works almost as great a havoc in the field of history as does the US veteran in the neighbourhood of the US Treasury. Time alone can work a cure in this respect.'[7]

But the cure was a long time in coming. Curiously enough, while the progressive school of historians identified conflict and change as the essence of American history, their writings, collectively, tended to play down the moral significance of the Civil War era. For Frederick Jackson Turner (1861–1932) the sectional conflict was relatively insignificant in comparison with the all-shaping impact of the moving western frontier. For Turner the South had a frontier and was, therefore, *echt* American and democratic. For Charles Beard (1874–1948) the South was predominantly rural and, therefore, likewise symbolic of Jeffersonian democracy. The Civil War did constitute a 'Second American Revolution', but that revolution was economic, not moral. Vernon Louis Parrington (1871–1921), like Turner and Beard, was a Mid Westerner and a fervent admirer of rural grass-roots democracy, who discerned in the South a tradition of sectional pride which defiantly and valiantly opposed the inexorable rise of Northern big government and big business. As he wrote of Calhoun, that great advocate of Southern nationalism: 'He erected a last barrier against the progress of middle class ideals, consolidation in politics and standardisation in society; against a universal cash-register evaluation of life; and the barrier was blown to bits by the guns of the civil war.'[8]

In the 1920s and 1930s the South experienced an extraordinary literary renaissance which did much to buttress the region's unique view of itself in the eyes of a wider English-speaking public. Centred on Vanderbilt University in Nashville, Tennessee, the group included writers such as Allen Tate and Robert Penn Warren, and historians such as Frank Owsley, all united by the common purpose of reaffirming the distinctiveness and significance of Southern civilisation. For far too long the South had been made to feel inferior and irrelevant to mainstream Yankee culture: just as in the mid nineteenth century Emerson had asserted with an insufferable air of superiority that the South displayed only temperament, not thought, so H.L. Mencken in the twentieth century, the humorist from Baltimore, dismissed the South as the philistine Sahara of the Bozarts. The notorious monkey trial in Dayton, Tennessee, once more displayed the South as crude, unscientific and backward, with William Jennings Bryan making a last-ditch stand for cracker-barrel creationalism and the rock of ages against Clarence Darrow, the sharp, fancy-talking lawyer from Chicago, arguing the case for scientific Darwinism and the age of rocks. The agrarian school, in its 1930s manifesto *I'll Take my Stand*, chose not to measure itself by Northern standards but rather distanced itself from the increasingly overwhelming values of urbanism, industrialism and frenzied capitalism. The Southern writers postulated an imperishable Southern counter-culture rooted in soil, race and community. Despite its military and political defeat in 1865 the South continued to stand firmly against a predominant culture of urbanism, centralisation, Hamiltonian economics, atomic economic relations, mindless materialism, relentless consumerism, science, industry, big corporations and cultural modernism. In its place they attempted to reaffirm older traditions and impalpable folk ways – localism, organic social relations, order, hierarchy, economic self-sufficiency and, above all else, agrarian values harking back to the lost arcadian world of Jefferson. They evoked 'the culture of the soil which is the best and most sensitive of vocations' and which created, in turn, 'the social exchanges which reveal and develop sensibility in human affairs'.[9]

Heady and intoxicating stuff as all this was, it is worth bearing in mind that the manifesto was aimed, in part, against the

South itself, which, in the eyes of this group of writers, was only too willing to join the mainstream and succumb to the common lure of American materialism. Moreover, the importance which the school attached to sensibility in human affairs tacitly affirmed the unique biracial structure of Southern society. Robert Penn Warren, for one, initially opposed desegregation strongly and, in private, Allen Tate wrote that social order must always take precedence over social justice and that miscegenation – sexual intercourse between races – was always wrong because 'moral symbolism requires that the source of life shall not be polluted'.[10]

Historical rehabilitation played a crucial part in this elaborate evocation of a Southern pastoral. It is no coincidence that Tate's first publication was an uncritical biography of *Stonewall Jackson* (1928) and Warren's a critical life of *John Brown* (1928). Frank Owsley was the court historian of this movement, and in a revealing and rather cynical letter to Allen Tate he defined his role in the agrarian movement. 'The purpose of my life,' he wrote, 'is to undermine by "careful" and "detached", "well-documented", "objective" writing, the entire Northern myth of 1820 to 1870.'[11]

But while the agrarians looked back to a lost Arcadia that had never existed, history moved forward: readjustments and fresh reappraisals questioned their last-ditch stand. The Southern mystique had placed the agrarian anti-slavery Jefferson at the centre of its sectional history, but perhaps Calhoun, the staunchly pro-slave fire-eater, was more typical? Clement Eaton, himself a Southerner from Winston Salem, North Carolina, traced the descent into illiberal intolerance and authoritarianism in his *The Freedom of Thought Struggle in the Old South* (1940) and John Hope Franklin, a black historian from Oklahoma, similarly depicted a rabidly, intolerant, honour-obsessed society in *The Militant South* (1956). In his *Age of Jackson* (1944), Arthur Schlesinger Jr located the essential Jacksonian democratic impulse neither in the South nor in the west (Andrew Jackson was a slave owner from Nashville, Tennessee) but in the nascent trade unionism and liberal intelligentsia of New England. Richard Hofstadter, in his influential *Age of Reform* (1955), depicted the South as the seat of populist racism, nativism and rampant anti-semitism, all that was most suffocatingly irrational and anti-intellectual in the American political tradition. David Potter, a Southerner from Georgia, brilliantly exploded the precious myth of Southern agrarianism: the South, he suggested, was traditionally wedded not to Jefferson's vision of a self-sufficient yeoman-farmer republic, but to agri-business, commerce and a hard cash-crop monoculture dedicated to increasing profit margins. Southern society was hierarchical and stratified and bi-racial: its typical rural workers were black sharecroppers or poor white landless labourers. The image of a stark, irreparable gulf between industrial North and rural South in 1860 was untenable: both sections were predominantly rural, and the small dirt farmer, not the slave-owning aristocrat or the industrial business-men, was more representative of both sections. But Potter aimed not merely to dismantle the Southern mystique, but to achieve a more balanced sectional view. If North and South held to a common constitution, party system and religion, they also shared a common negrophobia. The South might hold blacks as property, but the North was incapable of extending equal civil rights to blacks. The South, a numerical minority by 1860, was compelled to fall back on state rights as a form of defence for their peculiar institution, while Lincoln and the Northern majority could deftly and decisively capture the banner of Unionism and nationalism for their own sectional cause. Coner Vann Woodward, a historian from Arkansas, also urged a more balanced picture. Born in 1908, he attended Emory University in Atlanta, and did his doctoral research at Chapel Hill, North Carolina, then a liberal centre of the region, dominated by two forward-looking sociologists, Rupert Vance and Howard Odum. Though a staunch civil libertarian, Vann Woodward, acutely aware of the tragedy of the South's racial past, felt that that section had, for far too long, been the sole repository of collective guilt and sin. 'The south has long served the nation in ways still in great demand. It has been a moral lightning rod, a deflector of national guilt, a scapegoat for stricken consciences. It has served the country much as the Negro has served the White Supremacist – as a floor under self-esteem.'[12] The historical uniqueness of the South, he suggested, lay not in its peculiar racism but in its un-American chronicle of loss, failure and defeat. As a historian he was incapable of carrying out a pre-frontal lobotomy on that tragic past, but a sustained engagement with it ought not to lead to a Freudian fixation on past traumas but serve, instead, as a form of liberation from psychic bondage. The injustice of Southern segregation had its Northern counterpart in the crowded misery of numberless Northern black urban ghettoes, and the South, the New South, was changing. Atlanta, the city now too busy to hate, had taken the initiative in desegregation. James Silver, delivering his presidential address before the Southern Historical Association in Asheville, North Carolina, in 1963, unleashed an excoriating attack upon 'Mississippi: the closed society', a state mired in historical romanticism, religious fundamentalism and a states rights theory which served to underpin white supremacy. Mississippi was a state where 'the search for historical truth has become a casualty ... where neither the governor nor the legislature, in their hot pursuit of interposition, indicate any awareness that Mississippians were Americans before they were southerners, or that Magnolia State politicians once stood firm against nullification and secession.'[13] The South was changing and entering the mainstream of American history.

Events, both internal and external, contributed to this change. The dramatic collapse of the American economy after 1929 encouraged the pragmatic experimentalism of the New Deal years. F.D. Roosevelt could do little for black rights because, paradoxically, his extraordinary and unrepeatable four terms in office still depended upon the support of the Democratic lily-white regimes of the unreconstructed South. But one result of the Depression was a widespread diaspora of blacks from the Southern heartland to the Northern urban centres, which turned a hitherto exclusively Southern problem of race relations into a general, national problem. The New Deal witnessed, too, the increasing extension of federal activity to every area of American life, and an enlarged bureaucracy began to address itself to social problems such as urban poverty and unemployment, unionisation and the recognition of statutory labour rights. The Supreme Court, after a failed attempt to pack it by F.D.R. in 1936–37, became more attuned to constitutional innovation and social engineering. The unprecedented depression of the 1930s forced America to jettison its old Jacksonian *laissez-faire* principles and begin to challenge acceptance of the *status quo* for a more radical commitment to change.

The domestic crisis became a global crisis when the United States entered the Second World War in 1941, and the struggle for the survival of Western democratic values became also a struggle against totalitarian tyranny based on pernicious racial theories which terminated in the unexampled horrors of Belsen and Dachau. As in the Civil War, blacks were recruited into the army, and, as in the 1860s, the question was asked: if blacks could die for the Union should they not also enjoy equal citizenship in that Union? It seemed increasingly anomalous, to Du Bois and others, that a so-called army of liberation should also be a racially segregated army, and President Truman moved swiftly to desegregate after the end of the war. The war against godless fascism turned rapidly into a war against godless communism, and most historians were recruited, consciously or unconsciously, into the ideological Cold War which ensued. In this grimmer, uncertain age, indifference or pacifism seemed fond memories which could no longer be indulged. In a climate of crisis, with the ever-present prospect of mutual destruction, the Harvard historian, Arthur Schlesinger Jr, challenged the romanticism of those in the profession who had argued for the needlessness of the Civil War: there were times – 1861 was one, 1941 was another – when men had to be prepared to go to war to defend enduring moral values and die for them if need be: isolation or neutrality were no longer feasible options.

Continuing external crisis triggered domestic crisis and the McCarthy era of enforced anti-communist conformity was both the best of times and the worst of times for the academic profession. Intellectual witch hunts and the ferreting out of past communist sympathisers were the order of the day on campuses, and some academics sacrificed free intellectual thought and succumbed to the oppressive weight of majoritarian tyranny. Daniel Boorstin, the pre-eminent historian of the 'consensus' school which flourished in the 1940s and 1950s, gave evidence before the House Un-American Activities Committee (HUAC) and named the names of communist associates with whom he taught in the Harvard history faculty. Having conceded that the committee had in no way impinged upon his own academic freedom, he went on to insist that communists should not teach in universities. His own personal opposition to communism had taken two forms:

First, the form of an affirmative participation in religious activities, because I think religion is the bulwark against Communism ... The second form of my opposition has been an attempt to discover and explain to students, in my teaching and in my writing, the unique virtues of American democracy. I have done this partly in my Jefferson book ... and in a forthcoming book called *The Genius of American Politics*.[14]

In that book he argued persuasively for a consensual tradition, marked by the absence of sharp ideological conflict or indigenous radicalism, which made for a unique American exceptionalism: 'We do not need American philosophers, because we already have an American philosophy, implicit in the American Way of Life ... Why should *we* make a five-year plan for ourselves when God seems to have had a thousand-year plan ready-made for us?' He even managed, though it was not easy, to fit the Civil War into his consensual, self-celebratory theme, which led Richard Hofstadter to respond ironically: 'A Reb and a Yank meet in 1865 to survey the physical and moral devastation of the war. "Well," says one to the other consolingly, "at least we escaped the ultimate folly of producing political theorists."'[15] Professor Boorstin was rewarded in time, with the prestigious librarianship of the Library of Congress. Along with sociologists like Daniel Bell and Nathan Glazer, Richard Hofstadter of Columbia University, New York, horrified by the excesses of McCarthyism (he had himself briefly been a Communist party member), began systematically to probe the historical roots of American anti-intellectualism – the visceral sources of nativism, racism and populism which rocked, from time to time, the dominant liberal consensus in the American psyche. In retrospect Hofstadter wrote that McCarthyism 'instead of provoking a radical response, aroused in some intellectuals more distaste than they had ever thought they would feel for popular passions and anti-establishment demagogy. The populism of the right inspired a new skepticism about the older populism of the left.' In 1948 Hofstadter's hugely influential *The American Political Tradition* appeared. Like Boorstin, he believed that the progressive historians had over-emphasised conflict in America at the expense of an underlying consensus. Hofstadter's research convinced him of 'the need for a reinterpretation of our political traditions which emphasises the common climate of American opinion. The existence of such a climate of opinion has been much obscured by the tendency to place political conflict in the foreground of history ... Societies [such as America which] are in such good working order have a kind of mute organic consistency.' But, unlike Boorstin, his intention was not to canonise an American past: 'I have no desire to add to a literature of hero-worship and national self-congratulation which is already large.'[16] On the contrary, his collection of brief, brilliant biographies was often critical and subversive of established reputations. Against a McCarthyite background, Hofstadter was acutely aware that consensus could only too easily turn into stultifying majoritarian tyranny. His essay on Wendell Phillips, for example, rehabilitated and praised the abolitionist precisely because he stood out against the preponderant moral indifference of the majority of his contemporaries.

But there was, happily, another side of the Cold War that was not simply a bipolar war of big battalions and thermonuclear warheads. It was also a cultural struggle of words and of propaganda for the hearts and minds of the undeveloped world. The United Nations headquarters in New York saw an amazing proliferation of Third World sovereign states struggling for full status and recognition while abroad, in Africa, Asia and Latin America, proxy wars were being fought, communism versus capitalism, in a bid to harness a vociferous post-colonial nationalism to one side or the other of the global struggle. America knew that its values were superior to those of soulless Marxist–Leninism. Yet the Soviet explosion of an atomic bomb in 1949 and the 'loss' of China to communism in the same year (it took a British observer, Denis Brogan, to point out that China was not theirs to 'lose' in the first place) suggested that Americans were not winning the struggle hands-down. And this recognition partially contributed to the launching of a second Reconstruction to achieve what the first, following the Civil War, had failed to accomplish. As with the nineteenth-century civil rights movement, motives were mixed – but then, pure, unsullied altruism is generally absent from history. If Howard Beale, as president of the American Historical Association, and himself a distinguished historian of the first Reconstruction, argued for the abandonment of racial stereotypes and insisted that the association meet only in desegregated cities in future, it was, in part at least, to prove that domestic racial equality was one way of winning the ideological Cold War.

The civil rights movement was launched by the Supreme Court's unanimous decision in *Brown* v. *the Board of Education of Topeka* (1954). In that epoch-making case, Chief Justice Warren, along with his associate justices, unanimously struck down the Constitution's acquiescence in southern 'Jim Crow' segregation laws in education. In 1896, in the case of *Plessy v. Ferguson*, the Supreme Court had sustained the principle of separate but equal facilities for the black race. Warren, probing the potential for educational, psychological and social harm which could be suffered by blacks in segregated schools, insisted that separation was inherently unequal and that national desegregation must proceed with due and deliberate speed. In sustaining its case for change, the Chief Justice relied heavily upon the distinguished black NAACP lawyer, Thurgood Marshall, who, in turn, had been supplied with voluminous historical briefs by the young black historian John Hope Franklin.

Franklin had grown up in Tulsa, Oklahoma, and in 1915 had vivid recollections of being ejected along with his mother from white buses in that city and of his father's property being burnt in race riots. He remembered, too, that in 1931, at Fisk University, a black student while cycling had accidentally struck a white child and slightly injured him. As a consequence of this minor incident the black student had been lynched by a white mob. Moving north to pursue postgraduate research at Harvard, he had been appointed associate professor in the history faculty but not made a teaching assistant: it was considered inappropriate for a black to mark and grade white students' essays. In 1956 he was the first black to be appointed head of a history faculty with tenure at a white university, Brooklyn College, but he recalls the extreme difficulty of finding accommodation in a predominantly white neighbourhood. He joined in the great freedom marches under the banner of Martin Luther King from Selma to the outskirts of Montgomery, Alabama, along with some thirty other historians. He vividly recalls: 'I was afraid, yes, frightened out of my wits, by the hate-filled eyes that stared at me from the sidewalks.'[17]

Coner Vann Woodward was a companion-in-arms in these

terrifying incursions into the Southern heartland. Vann Woodward had studied at Emory, Atlanta, along with David Potter and had met such black luminaries as the poet Langston Hughes and Du Bois. He had become embroiled in political activism when defending Angelo Herndon, a black student expelled from the Georgia Institute of Technology for his communist sympathies, who was on trial for inciting insurrection. The white Vann Woodward and the black Franklin were among those who injected a new liberal and humane understanding into the historical profession. American history was not, could not be, a merely otiose and antiquarian concern. It was a study charged with direct relevance and obvious significance which made it all the more important to pursue the subject in as detached and disinterested a manner as possible and not stoop to propaganda and agitation. The racial disparities lingered, despite Chief Justice Warren's call for a colour-blind society. S.E. Morison and H.S. Commager's *Growth of the American Republic* (1930), perhaps the most popular and widely read textbook of the period, continued to depict slavery as a benign institution, a transitional stage between barbarism and civility for the black. Another widely available textbook by Thomas Bailey, *The American Pageant* (1961), repeated the tired stereotypes of freedmen during reconstruction who 'insolently jostled the whites off the sidewalks, into the gutter'. In 1968 Bailey delivered his presidential address before the Association of American Historians arguing for detachment from the stirring events of the day. 'How many of us can march in Mississippi one week and teach history with reasonable objectivity the next?'[18] The answer from the majority of the profession was that current engagement and commitment gave their research deeper meaning and understanding. The civil rights movement galvanised the profession and unleashed an extraordinary intellectual vitality into its writings. Many young, middle-class liberal academics, marching along the dusty roads of the South, organising endless meetings and marches, defying the local authorities, attacked by police truncheons and savage dogs, began to gain a fresh appreciation of the difficulties, tribulations and sacrifices made by the abolitionists of the 1830s or the radical Republicans of the 1860s. They started to understand why the abolitionists couched their speech in such harsh, unremitting terms; began to sympathise with the Freedmen's Bureau in its largely failed attempt to assist the ex-slave in such a fundamentally hostile Southern environment. Other radical historians – Howard Zinn, for example, and Staughton Lynd – stayed some time in the South and taught in black colleges. Deep engagement with the present led to greater engagement with the past and a deeper analysis of the historical roots of current conflict. John Hope Franklin, for example, turned to study the closing of the Southern ante-bellum mind and the growth of intolerance, bigotry and insularity in his *Militant South*; he traced the complex military and political forces which led ultimately to the freeing of his race in the midst of civil war in his *Emancipation Proclamation* (1963); he revised historical stereotypes which dogged reconstruction history and found an honourable place for his own race in their fight for post war freedom in *Reconstruction* (1961). But his approach was not insular: here, as elsewhere, he insisted upon analysing North as well as South, white as well as black. He wrote a textbook on black history, *From Freedom to Slavery*, and in 1985 a biography of an all but forgotten black historian, George Washington Williams, who, in 1882, had written the first history of his race and in 1887 had recorded its contribution of black troops to the Union effort (in which he himself had served). 'History,' Lord Acton once wrote, following Michelet, 'was resurrection': it was also, he insisted, 'restitution', and Franklin played an honourable role in rescuing black America and black historians from the general condescension of the profession.

Vann Woodward's chosen field of research was the post-Reconstruction New South, but this Gilded Age epoch was itself rooted in the South's tragic past. An early work, *Reunion and Reaction* (1951), traced the collapse of Reconstruction idealism and the cynical political and economic manoeuvres which restored home rule to the South in 1877. His *Origins of the New South* (1951) and *Tom Watson* (1938) echoed the writings of Du Bois, in depicting a nascent biracial alliance of poor blacks and poor whites foundering on the rocks of racism, a racism which, after the bloody struggles of Reconstruction, took the form of strict segregation traced in his *Strange Career of Jim Crow* (1955).

In the 1960s, race riots proliferated in the Northern urban

centres in the wake of civil rights legislation: Boston, the old centre of the abolitionist crusades, suffered severe disruption while Atlanta remained relatively calm. The Supreme Court's *Brown* decision unleashed a domestic revolution in America of unparalleled proportions. Alexis de Tocqueville, the perceptive nineteenth-century French commentator on America, had observed that initiating a revolution was far easier than either controlling it or stopping it before it became self-destructive and devoured its own children: that once the snow of winter began to melt the torrents of spring could wreak havoc and flood. This revolution's springtime augured well. In 1957, three years after the *Brown* decision, Kenneth Stampp brought out his *Peculiar Institution*, the first major study of slavery in over thirty years, which for the first time depicted that institution as almost wholly cruel and malign. In its preface, Stampp stated his firmly held belief and credo that blacks were merely white men with black skin: no more, no less. Stanley Elkins's study of *Slavery* followed in 1959, depicting a uniquely closed and psychologically damaging institution. And this severe damage was, to a large extent, permanent and irreparable, much as the destruction of the family unit under slavery was permanent and irreparable. When in 1965 the Harvard sociologist, Daniel Moynihan, wrote his *Negro Family: The Case for National Action*, he quoted directly from Elkins's severe indictment of slavery. Elkins's study was cited as an historical explanation for the current deprivation of dysfunctional one-parent families in the ghettoes of the North and South. Armed with this evidence, Moynihan urged immediate action by President Johnson and his Great Society programme to end, once and for all, this legacy of 'ancient brutality, past injustice and present prejudice'.[19] The Great Society programme was the high point of 1960s American liberalism. Born into the impoverished Panhandle of rural Texas, Johnson, for all his political complexity and tragic flaws, was a true son of New Deal optimism and held the conviction that direct federal action and federal cash could eliminate the long history of racial grievance. Taking up the liberal banner from the martyred Kennedy, he launched an all-out war on black poverty north and south, racial discrimination and disenfranchisement. But then, somehow, notoriously, the liberal dream began to unravel: the snow began to melt and turn into a torrent. Johnson, with his belief in deals and negotiations, escalated the war in Vietnam in order to bring the Vietcong to the negotiating table. American hubris made retreat unthinkable. Unthinkable, too, was the prospect of the defeat of the unassailable US military by mere guerrilla bands. Had not the vast Union army and Northern industry ensured the conquest of the South in 1865? To the crusade for civil rights was now added the growing army of anti-war protest. America's imperial arrogance and its contempt for the Vietcong – dehumanised to the status of expendable 'gooks' – paralleled the earlier racial arrogance of American soldiers crushing Filipino independence at the beginning of the century. Jane Fonda and Mary McCarthy received perhaps greater publicity in their pilgrimage to Saigon and Hanoi, but two radical historians, Herbert Aptheker and Staughton Lynd, also made the journey. The year 1968 saw the culmination of the nightmare. Disenchanted, Johnson proclaimed that he would not run for re-election. Widespread rioting flared up in urban centres all over the country. At the Democratic convention in Chicago that year Mayor Richard Daley unleashed his police force upon anti-war demonstrators. Martin Luther King and Robert Kennedy were assassinated.

Eugene Genovese, the Marxist historian, then at George Williams University in Montreal, emotionally recaptured the madness and turbulence of those years. He wrote of pseudo-Freudian passion plays, of nihilist perversions and of black reactionaries masquerading as revolutionaries. Current conflict and turmoil intruded brutally into the calm of the academic study. Professors' rooms were trashed; revolutionary cabals met and talked endlessly; established courses were ignored: students would formulate their own; an intoxicating drama – part millenialist, part destructive – was in the ascendant. In the wake of general disillusionment, black demands for integration gave way increasingly to a more radical insistence upon black history and black nationalism. A new class of black intellectuals – Julius Lester, Leroi Jones, Eldridge Cleaver and others – insisted upon separatism as the only escape route from endemic white racism. History had to be totally rewritten by blacks, for blacks, to meet urgent current black demands. Vincent Harding wrote in his introduction to There is a River, 'I know that my first commitment was not to the ambiguous abstractions of objectivity or scholarship, but to the lively hope and faith of a people in struggle for a new chance to be whole. ... We seek for control of our own story.' Another, Sterling Stuckey, wrote that black history 'must become a searchlight flashing over the terrain of the American night, illuminating hidden horrible things'. The hopes of historical as well as political integration appeared to founder. Stampp, in later editions of his *Peculiar Institution*, had to add as a rider: 'I do not, of course, assume that there have been, or are today, no cultural differences between white and black Americans. Nor do I regard it as flattery to call Negroes white men with black skins.'[20] White historians were attacked for encroaching upon black history. Eric Foner at Columbia, August Meier at Kent State and Robert Starobin at Wisconsin were subjected to verbal assaults. Starobin, a left-wing supporter of the Black Panthers and historian of industrial slavery in the antebellum South, delivered a paper at a conference at Wayne State in 1969. One black in the audience walked out: another mocked his reading out of black letters and another attacked him for presuming to write black history in the first place. Julius Lester recalls: 'He had to be attacked and I did so. All too often we let ourselves be history's willing victims, and, that day, history demanded I treat another human being as a category and I, not without hurting inside, acceded.'[21] Lester soon re-established cordial relations with Starobin but Starobin committed suicide a year later. Other, calmer, voices called the profession back from the abyss of terminal confusion. Vann Woodward in his Association of American Historians presidential address of 1969, 'Clio with soul', called for calm and mutual toleration, and Genovese alluded to the logical absurdity of historical separatism: should he, a scholar who had devoted himself to the study of the old South, be forced, because of his personal background, to study and teach only Italian immigrant history, about which he knew nothing?

There were further painful splinterings. Many Jewish historians, nurtured by socialism in the 1930s Depression and who identified with racial grievances, such as Aptheker, Philip Foner, Gilbert Osofsky, Herbert Gutman and Ira Berlin, were dismayed by the strain of antisemitism in the ranks of black nationalism.

There were fissures, too, within the ranks of the left: mainstream Marxist historians like Genovese and Aileen Kraditor distanced themselves from those who, like Staughton Lynd, identified and studied a home-grown radicalism – individualist, agrarian, anarchic, milder – which countered the theoretical dialectic of the European Marx and Gramsci with America's Henry Thoreau and Henry George.

The effervescence of America in the 1960s was perfectly reflected in the historical writing of the decade, after which things began to calm down. No longer the first fine careless rapture, but a degree of historical balance had been achieved at a cost. The simultaneous collapse of American arms in Vietnam and the moral collapse of Watergate at home ushered in a period of introspection and a retreat from larger idealistic agendas. President Reagan's specific aim and achievement was to convert this sense of trauma and introspection into an effective conservative coalition by retreating to narrower ground from which to assert a new national pride and self-confidence. Neo-conservative rhetoric (it was no more than that) insisted that government was the cause, not the cure, of America's outstanding problems. The call for a general reduction of taxes, for example, boded well for the rich (who would be taxed less) but ill for the poor, who had been the main beneficiaries of redistributive taxation. Now unemployment and disparities in income became greater than ever before and the predominantly poor blacks suffered disproportionately. California, as ever the shaper of things to come, voted overwhelmingly in favour of a referendum on Proposition 13, which drastically cut taxes and deregulated the state's economy. In 1996 California set another trend by supporting Proposition 209, which struck down affirmative action taken on grounds of race or sex with regard to hiring staff, state contracts or admission to state colleges. Thurgood Marshall, the architect of *Brown* v. *Topeka*, had argued in *Fullilove* v. *Kluznick* (1980) that quotas might be set for racial minorities in the field of federal contracts for construction work on the grounds that 'the consideration of race is relevant to remedying the continuing effect of past racial discrimination'. Or, as he had argued similarly in *Bakke*, 'It is because of a legacy of unequal treatment that we must now permit the institutions of this society to give consideration to race in making decisions about who will hold the positions of influence, affluence, and prestige in America.'[22] Ironically, Marshall's replacement on the Supreme Court, Clarence Thomas (himself a beneficiary of affirmative action), was nominated by President Bush in part because of his opposition to positive discrimination. He was among a growing class of prosperous middle-class blacks (whose percentage rose from 11.6 in 1970 to 21.2 in 1996, measured in terms of a minimum $50,000 income per annum) who had escaped the urban ghettoes. But what of the remaining 80 per cent, locked into a cycle of deprivation, one-parent families, drugs, violence and crime in the inner cities? One black youth in three is currently in jail, on probation or awaiting trial. As in the 1870s, so now in the 1990s, a large majority of Americans seem to have grown disillusioned and bored by the interminable and unresolved question of race.

Other factors contributed to this growing indifference. The Republican party, Lincoln's party, now holds the white South as its heartland and is not averse to playing the racial card. North Carolina's senior senator, Jesse Helms, was re-elected with the help of a television advertisement in which a white hand held a rejection slip and a voice-over insidiously intoned, 'You needed that job, but they gave it to a minority.' A powerful Southern League has emerged in the new prosperous South unfurling the flag of the Confederacy, opposing the erection of a statue to the black tennis player, Arthur Ashe, in Richmond, Virginia, among the grave faces of forgotten Confederate generals. Like the agrarian movement of the 1930s, its members, who include Grady McWhiney, the distinguished historian at Texas Christian University, and Clyde Wilson, editor of the Calhoun papers at the University of South Carolina, called for the return to a pre-civil rights culture of hierarchy where black and white once more know their place. A new sociobiology, of which Charles Murray and Richard Hernnstein's *The Bell Curve* (1995) is the starkest example, once more links genes with intelligence and attempts to prove statistically that average blacks are intellectually inferior to either white or Asian and therefore incapable of being helped: instead they are doomed to become a permanently unassimilable 'underclass'. These sentiments, clothed in the guise of austere scientific language and graphs, echo similar sentiments expressed during the Reconstruction era concerning the permanent degradation of a particular race. As President Clinton expressed it in his second inaugural address, 'Race continues to be America's constant curse,' and set up a committee of inquiry into the matter under the chairmanship of John Hope Franklin.

The American historical profession has contributed immeasurably to eliminating that curse. During the middle years of the twentieth century the profession purged itself of the racial presumptions which, often unconsciously, distorted its interpretative understanding of the past. Because Phillips and Dunning wrote the black out of American history, they necessarily presented a false history. The achievement of scholars thereafter was to readjust the distortion and replace the image of the black as passive victim with one of the black actually shaping, as far as possible, his own destiny. The Civil War era has always attracted the attention of America's finest scholars despite all the excesses, the overly audacious theorising, the special pleading and desperate searches for an all too usable past. The dust has settled, leaving a more complex and nuanced history. Classic works stand out as monuments to this perpetual modification and shifting assessment. One such is David Potter's *The Impending Crisis*, which places the moral issue of slavery at the centre of the unfolding movement to civil war; another is Eugene Genovese's *Roll, Jordan, Roll*, a brilliant evocation of the world the slaves made for themselves. James McPherson's *Battle Cry of Freedom* in the *Oxford History of the United States* is a balanced synthesis of the entire era, and Eric Foner's *Reconstruction* presents a huge and comprehensive canvas which once and for all destroys the crude stereotypes of the era.

Without succumbing to the late Victorian optimism of Lord Acton, it is possible to affirm, despite its vicissitudes, the progressive nature of historical research. It is also possible, while avoiding Acton's obsessional desire to pass judgement, to see the era in terms of a great moral drama. After the failure of Reconstruction, historians colluded in eliminating or playing down this element of the narrative. Americans take their history very seriously, much as they take their constitutional rights seriously. The profession has been, traditionally, deeply committed and engaged. For historians the past is not dead or merely of antiquarian concern: it is very much alive and living, shaping both present and future. Controversies abound in academia: in the 1960s it was civil rights and opposition to the Vietnam War: now it is political correctness, gender issues, affirmative quotas and the debate on postmodernist deconstruction. A historian of historiography has no need to be reminded of relativities and contextualisation; this is the very essence of his studies: facts dissolve, orthodox explanations evaporate, nothing remains entirely solid or substantial. But if advances have been made in reconstructing a more comprehensive explanatory picture of the Civil War era – and I believe they have – they have not been won by means of total detachment and scientific indifference to the materials of history. On the contrary, this greater understanding has been reached with the aid of emotional engagement, imaginative recreation and a fuller empathy. Contrary to Thomas Bailey, the rich narrative of American history has been added to by marching in Mississippi. As Benjamin Quarles, the distinguished black historian, once wrote: 'For blacks, it is a new way to see themselves. For whites it furnishes a new version of American history, one that uneasily challenges our national sense of smugness and self-righteousness and our avowal of fair play.' An article by another distinguished black writer, Du Bois, was once rejected on the grounds that there was too much history in it. Du Bois simply replied, 'Don't you understand that the past is present; that without what was, nothing is?'[23] Let us look, then, at what was and what is.

Notes

1 Rhodes quoted in Robert Fogel, *Without Consent or Contract* (New York, 1989), p. 155. Rhodes's article 'The burning of Columbia' was published in 1902 and reprinted in his *Historical Essays* (New York, 1909).
2 Herbert Aptheker, *Essays in the History of the American Negro* (New York, 1964), p. vii.
3 Du Bois quoted in Rayford Logan (ed.), *W.E.B. Du Bois: A Profile* (New York, 1971), p. 252.
4 W.E.B. Du Bois, *Black Reconstruction in America, 1860–1880* (New York, 1969), in his preface 'To the reader'.
5 Yancey quoted in Charles Sellers Jr (ed.), *The Southerner as American* (Chapel Hill, N.C., 1960), p. 3.
6 Warren quoted in Daniel Aaron, *The Unwritten War* (Oxford, 1973), p. 308;

and in John Rosenberg, 'Towards a new Civil War revisionism', *American Scholar* (38:2, 1969), p. 459. Faulkner quoted in C. Vann Woodward, *The Burden of Southern History* (Baton Rouge, 1974), p. 36.

7 Phillips's 'Central theme of Southern history' is reprinted in U.B. Phillips, *The Slave Economy of the Old South: Selected Essays in Economic and Social History* (Baton Rouge, 1968). Dodd quoted in Peter Novick, *That Noble Dream* (Cambridge, 1988), pp. 78–9.

8 Parrington quoted in Staughton Lynd, *Class Conflict, Slavery and the U.S. Constitution* (Indianapolis, 1967), p. 431.

9 Louis D. Rubin Jr (ed.), *I'll Take my Stand* (New York, 1962), pp. xxix, xxv.

10 Tate quoted in Aaron, *The Unwritten War*, p. 299.

11 Owsley quoted in Novick, *That Noble Dream*, p. 238.

12 Vann Woodward quoted in Marcus Cunliffe and Robin Winks (eds), *Past Masters* (New York, 1969), p. 392.

13 Silver in George Tindall (ed.), *The Pursuit of Southern History* (Baton Rouge, 1964), p. 466.

14 Boorstin's testimony quoted in Novick, *That Noble Dream*, p. 328 n. 13.

15 *Ibid.*, pp. 333, 355 n. 53

16 Richard Hofstadter, *The American Political Tradition* (London, 1962), pp. xi, xii, xv.

17 John Hope Franklin, *Race and History* (Baton Rouge, 1989), p. 288.

18 *Ibid.*, p. 390. Grady McWhiney, *Southerners and other Americans* (New York, 1973), p. 183.

19 Johnson quoted in *Commentary* (60, 1975), p. 41.

20 Harding quoted in August Meier and Elliott Rudwick, *Black History and the Historical Profession, 1915–1980* (Urbana, 1986), pp. 284, 288.

21 Lester quoted in Novick, *That Noble Dream*, p. 476.

22 Marshall quoted in Richard Hofstadter (ed.), *Great Issues in American History*, III (New York, 1982), pp. 486, 487.

23 Quarles quoted in William Cartwright and Richard Watson Jr (eds), *The Reinterpretation of American History and Culture* (Washington, D.C., 1973), p. 54; Du Bois in Benjamin Quarles, *Black Mosaic* (Amherst, Mass., 1988), p. 88.

Selective bibliography

Aptheker, Herbert, *Essays in the History of the American Negro* (New York, 1964).

Brock, William (ed.), *The Civil War* (New York, 1969).

Cartwright, William, and Watson Jr, Richard (eds), *The Reinterpretation of American History and Culture* (Washington, D.C., 1973).

Crowe, Charles (ed.), *The Age of Civil War and Reconstruction, 1830–1900* (Homewood, Ill., 1975).

Cunliffe, Marcus, and Winks, Robin (eds), *Past Masters* (New York, 1969).

Donald, David, *Lincoln Reconsidered* (New York, 1969).

Escott, Paul, and Goldfield, David (eds), *Major Problems in the History of the American South*, I (Lexington, KY. 1990).

Fehrenbacher, Don, *Lincoln in Text and Context* (Stanford, CA. 1987).

Fehrenbacher, Don, *Prelude to Greatness: Lincoln in the 1850s* (Stanford, 1962).

Fitzhugh, George, *Cannibals All, or, Slaves without Masters* (Cambridge, Mass., 1960).

Foner, Eric, *Politics and Ideology in the Age of the Civil War* (Oxford, 1980).

Foner, Eric, *Reconstruction: America's Unfinished Revolution, 1863–1877* (New York, 1988).

Franklin, John Hope, 'Afro-American history: state of the art', *Journal of American History* (74, 1988).

Franklin, John Hope, *Race and History* (Baton Rouge, 1989).

Frederickson, George, *The Arrogance of Race* (Middletown, Conn., 1988).

Freehling, William, *The Reintegration of American History: Slavery and the Civil War* (Oxford, 1994).

Garraty, John (ed.), *Interpreting American History* (London, 1970).

Gatell, Frank, and Weinstein, Allen (eds), *American Themes: Essays in Historiography* (London, 1968).

Genovese, Eugene, *In Red and Black* (New York, 1972).

Genovese, Eugene, *Roll, Jordan, Roll* (New York, 1976).

Genovese, Eugene, *The Southern Tradition: The Achievement and Limitations of an American Conservatism* (Cambridge, Mass., 1996).

Grob, Gerald, and Billias, George (eds), *Interpretations of American History: Patterns and Perspectives*, I (New York, 1972).

Higham, John (ed.), *The Reconstruction of American History* (London, 1972).

Hofstadter, Richard, *The Progressive Historian* (New York, 1970).

Kraus, Michael, and Joyce, Davis, *The Writing of American History* (Norman, Okla., 1983).

Leopold, Richard, Link, Arthur, and Coben, Stanley (eds), *Problems in American History*, I (Englewood Cliffs, N.J., 1966).

Link, Arthur, and Patrick, Rembert (eds), *Writing Southern History* (Baton Rouge, 1965).

Lynd, Staughton, *Class Conflict, Slavery and the U.S. Constitution* (Indianapolis, 1967).

McPherson, James, 'Slavery and race' in *Perspectives in American History* (3, 1969).

McPherson, James, *Abraham Lincoln and the Second American Revolution* (Oxford, 1991).

McPherson, James, *Battle Cry of Freedom* (Harmondsworth, 1988).

McPherson, James, *Drawn with the Sword* (Oxford, 1996).

McPherson, James, *The Struggle for Equality: Abolitionists and the Negro in the Civil War and Reconstruction* (Princeton, 1964).

Meier, August, and Rudwick, Elliott, *Black History and the Historical Profession, 1915–1980* (Urbana, 1986).

Novick, Peter, *That Noble Dream: The 'Objectivity Question' and the American Historical Profession* (Cambridge, 1988).

O'Brien, Michael, *The Idea of the American South, 1920–1941* (Baltimore, 1979).

Potter, David, *History and American Society* (Oxford, 1973).

Potter, David, *The Impending Crisis, 1848–1861* (New York, 1976).

Potter, David, *The South and the Sectional Conflict* (Baton Rouge, 1968).

Potter, David, 'The South and the Sectional Conflict', in Charles Crowe (ed.), *The*

Age of Civil War and Reconstruction, 1830–1900 (Homewood, Ill., 1975).
Quarles, Benjamin, *Black Mosaic* (Amherst, Mass., 1988).
Rose, Willie Lee, *Slavery and Freedom* (Oxford, 1982).
Rubin, Louis Jr (ed.), *I'll Take my Stand* (New York, 1962).
Sellers, Charles Jr (ed.), *The Southerner as American* (Chapel Hill, 1960).
Swierenga, Robert (ed.), *Beyond the Civil War Synthesis* (Westport, Conn., 1975).
Wish, Harvey, *The American Historian* (New York, 1960).
Woodward, C. Vann, *American Counterpoint* (New York, 1971).
Woodward, C. Vann, *The Burden of Southern History* (Baton Rouge, 1974).

2

Slavery

On 1 January 1863 Lincoln signed the Emancipation Proclamation, a decision confirmed by the Thirteenth Amendment to the Constitution, passed by Congress on 1 February 1865 and ratified (by three-quarters of the states) on 18 December 1865. The slaves' day of jubilee, fervently hoped for and long prayed for, had arrived. On this issue the South wearily conceded defeat. Indeed, some historians, such as Kenneth Stampp, have suggested, rather implausibly, that Southern guilt over the peculiar institution had demoralised the Confederate war effort from the very beginning, and that by 1865 the South was heartily relieved to be rid of the incubus of the peculiar institution. The passing of the Fourteenth and Fifteenth Amendments, which granted the freedmen equal civil liberties and the right to vote, was, however, vigorously opposed by the majority of Southern whites, and while these amendments formally remained, along with the federal commitment to maintain them, the withdrawal of the last Northern troops from the South in 1877 informally ended the period of active reconstruction, and granted that section 'home rule', which amounted, in practice, to acknowledgement that the South could deal with its race problem as it saw fit and without further interference.

Ulrich Bonner Phillips was born in 1877, that year of 'redemption', as the white South called it, at La Grange in Georgia, and grew up steeped in the legacy of the Civil War. The legacy, for example, of the lost cause: 'The memories of its heroism are a pride; the thought of its loss is a sorrow.' He appears to have had an idyllic childhood, recalled in the glow of richly embroidered memories. 'In happy childhood I played hide-and-seek among the cotton bales with sable companions; I heard the serenade of the katy-dids while tossing on a hot pillow, somehow reconciled to the night's heat because it was time for the cotton crop.' He came increasingly to evoke a lost paradise which was tantalisingly never to be regained, of a harmonious old South, in which slavery and the plantation system in particular played a crucial, almost mystical, role. 'For him ... who has known the considerate and cordial, courteous and charming men and women, white and black, which that picturesque life in its best phases produced, it is impossible to agree that its basis and its operation were wholly evil.'[1]

Such richly nostalgic feelings underlay Phillips's *American Negro Slavery* (1918) and *Life and Labour in the Old South* (1929) both of which exerted a remarkable hold on the historical profession into the middle years of the twentieth century. Phillips spent most of his career in the North: at first at the University of Wisconsin as a colleague of Frederick Jackson Turner, then, in his most productive years, at the University of Michigan (1911–29), before settling at Yale, where he taught another Southern historian, David Potter, and where his textbooks on slavery were required reading – indeed, the only reading available on the peculiar institution. Phillips owed his extraordinary ascendancy to a potent combination of serious scholarship combined with attitudes and assumptions perfectly attuned to the time in which he wrote, wrapping both in a language of lush, almost suffocating, romanticism. In his preface, for example, to *American Negro Slavery*:

> For twenty years I have panned the sands of the stream of Southern life and garnered their golden treasure. Many of the nuggets rewarding the search have already been displayed in their natural form; and this now is a coinage of the grains great and small. The metal is pure, the minting alone may be faulty.

Only a generation away from the African practice of polygamy, human sacrifice and cannibalism, the black was transported to America as a slave, but remained entirely untouched by American culture and civilisation, for 'the wrench from Africa and the subjection to the new discipline while uprooting his ancient language and customs had little more effect upon his temperament than upon his complexion'. With the invention of the cotton gin, and the intensive cultivation of cotton in a plantation setting, the South had evolved a unique form of labour relations based on slavery: but this Southern form of labour relations was essentially social, not economic; benign, not exploitative. Because the black was essentially a child, he had to be protected both from himself and from others, and the master's role was essentially paternal. Without slavery the black would either lapse into African savagery, and bring about a devastating race war in the South, or die out. It was because of this that the cardinal test of the Southerner and the central theme of Southern history was 'a common resolve, indomitably maintained, that it shall be and remain a white man's country'. Phillips subtitled his *American Negro Slavery* 'A survey of the South, Employment and Control of Negro Labour as Determined by the Plantation Régime' and in his *Life and Labour in the Old South* he posed the social question in the following terms: 'Slaves were also persons presumably dangerous to the social order, for they were deprived of the privileges and ambitions which commonly kept freemen self-restrained. On that score, as well as because of the contrasts in race and culture, a distinctive system of police was developed'.[2]

Northerners, and the abolitionists in particular, had no conception of the subtle social tissues which held black, white and master–slave relations in delicate balance. Their abstractions, their arrogance and their ignorance of the South had led them to caricature the complexities and positive features of the peculiar institution. This rancorous abolitionist strain had unfortunately entered into the mainstream of American historical writing, and Phillips was resolved to destroy it. 'The history of the United States,' he wrote, 'has been written by Boston and largely written wrong.'[3] Phillips had met Turner during his brief spell at Wisconsin and had admired his historical revisionism, which decisively rejected the predominant Boston Brahmin interpretation of American history to stress, instead, the vital contribution of the western frontier to the making of the national character. Phillips would do the same for the South, and dethrone the old arrogant New England ascendancy. The New Englanders could admire the black race as an abstract whole and wish, in a philanthropic,

idealistic manner, to assist it, but they were constitutionally incapable of developing an intimate and cordial relationship with an
individual black man as a Southerner intuitively could.

Phillips's own attitude and tone towards the black can be
gauged in his preface to *American Negro Slavery*:

> My sojourn in a National Army Camp in the South while this book
> has been going through the press has reinforced my earlier convic-
> tion that Southern racial asperities are mainly superficial, and that
> the two great elements are fundamentally in accord. That the
> harmony is not a new thing is evinced by the very tone of the camp.
> The men of the two races are of course quartered separately; but it is
> a daily occurrence for white Georgian troops to go to the negro
> companies to seek out their accustomed friends and compare home
> news and experiences. The negroes themselves show the same easy-
> going, amiable, serio-comic obedience and the same personal
> attachments to white men, as well as the same sturdy light-hearted-
> ness and the same love of laughter and of rhythm, which
> distinguished their forebears. The non-commissioned officers among
> them show a punctilious pride of place which matches that of the
> plantation foremen of old; and the white officers who succeed best
> in the command of these companies reflect the planter's admixture
> of tact with firmness of control, the planter's patience of instruction,
> and his crisp though cordial reciprocation of sentiment. The negroes
> are not enslaved but drafted; they dwell not in cabins but in
> barracks; they shoulder the rifle, not the hoe; but the visitor to their
> company streets in the evening hours nevertheless enters a planta-
> tion atmosphere. A hilarious party dashes in pursuit of a fugitive,
> and gives him lashes with a belt 'moderately laid on'. When ques-
> tioned, the explanation given is that the victim is 'an awnrooly
> nigger', whose ways must be mended.[4]

This stifling condescension and a sense of effortless superiority Phillips extended to the slave owners of the ante-bellum
South, who were 'talented', 'benevolent', 'well-bred', 'ruled by a
sense of dignity, duty and moderation', who 'schooled multi-
tudes, white and black, to the acceptance of higher standards' and
who 'wrought more sanely and more wisely than the world yet
knows'. Their treatment of their slaves was governed by a high
sense of gentlemanly conduct and benign despotism, 'a despotism
in a majority of cases benevolent but in some cases harsh and
aggressive, a despotism resented by some ... but borne with light-

heartedness, submission and affection by a large number of the blacks'.[5]

The plantation setting which Phillips idealised was a microcosm of a larger, harmonious hierarchical order. In a chapter entitled 'Life in thraldom' from his later *Life and Labour in the Old South* each paragraph begins with sentences which, cumulatively, have the effect of making one feel envious of the slave's happy condition. 'The plantation force was a conscript army, living in barracks and on constant fatigue.' 'But the plantation was also a homestead, isolated, permanent and peopled by a social group with a common interest in achieving and maintaining social order.' 'The plantation was a school.' 'The civilising of the Negroes was not merely a consequence of definite schooling but a fruit of plantation life itself. The white household taught perhaps less by precept than by example.' 'The plantation was a parish, or perhaps a chapel of ease.' 'The plantation was a pageant and a variety show in alteration.' 'The plantation was a matrimonial bureau, something of a harem perhaps, a copious nursery and a divorce court.' 'The home of a planter or a well-to-do townsman was likely to be a magnificent Negro boarding-house.'[6] And so forth.

So bedazzled was Phillips by the myth of the plantation that in 1904 he argued strenuously for its reintroduction. Freed and left to congregate in large cities, the blacks become depraved and unhappy, irksome to the white population. Slavery was indeed an evil: but a controlling hierarchic, rural order was wholesome. But did this consummate expert on Southern racial history ever think of asking the black what he wanted instead of being sure that he knew? With the ending of slavery, the blacks were universally determined, above everything, never to return to the plantation system. And what of education? Again Phillips recalls setting off as a young child to school, burdened by the thought of a long day of dull reading, writing, arithmetic and the prospect of a future which would be dully responsible, while his 'sable companion' was able to play, irresponsibly, the livelong day. Did he not know that, after the desire to possess land, the blacks desired education? The answer was no, because he had never asked them.[7]

Throughout, Phillips maintained that the slave owner carried the greater burden of slavery. It was not a system of economic exploitation: the institution was unprofitable, and its main aim was not to make fortunes, but men. Those laws which enforced the institution reduced people to the status of property, were admittedly harsh and had to be, but the letter killeth and the rigid harshness of the Black Codes was rarely enforced. And punishment? It was mildly applied and invariably beneficial to the recipient, for 'the law forbade cruel treatment or the destruction of life and limb except when meeting resistance or by mishap in the course of "moderate correction"'.[8] Slave marriages? They were formally forbidden under the Southern legal codes but allowed in practice. If both partners sued for informal annulment (Phillips quotes from a plantation which made systematic provision for just such an event), both would receive 100 lashes each, and separated, not allowed to remarry for a period of three years.

Without going into lurid detail, Phillips obviously considered the slave population to be sexually promiscuous and gives an example of one slave mother bearing forty-one children. Miscegenation between the races – there were half a million mulattoes in 1860, about 12 per cent of the total Southern black population – is barely touched on and it does not appear in the index at all, while the taking of a black mistress by the white owner is referred to as 'not merely ... making black women subject to white men's wills but [also] promoting intimacy and weakening racial antipathy'.[9] Phillips invariably skirts such tragic issues deftly by means of euphemism and a light, innocuous touch. The master's taking of a black mistress promotes good race relations. The severity of the Southern Black Codes is likened to the Volstead Act, which forbade the sale of alcohol during the Prohibition era: that is, they are universally breached. Holding property in the shape of other human beings sounds less serious when ironically likened to the alimony a husband has to pay his divorced wife.

What is so extraordinary in retrospect is how long this insidious nonsense and historical duplicity held sway as a textbook. Edward Channing's influential five-volume *History of the United States* (1905–25), suggested that 'It is by no means improbable, as a Southern writer has intimated, that the slaves were often happier than their masters.' Not until 1944 in an article by Richard Hofstadter in the hospitable pages of the *The Journal of*

Negro History were the assumptions and contents of the Phillips books questioned. 'Let the study of the old South,' Hofstadter wrote, 'be undertaken by other scholars who have absorbed the view point of modern cultural anthropology, and who have a feeling for social psychology.' On the basic level of archival investigation, Phillips's research was highly selective and most untypical. His records were derived from some 200 plantations, but these were very large plantations with over 100 slaves which represented only 1 per cent of the slave-owning class and were drawn exclusively from the deep South. Both from personal predisposition and from the limitations of his material, Phillips saw the institution exclusively through the eyes of the slave-owner. Much has been made of his highly selective use of contemporary sources, culled from Sir Charles Lyell, Charles Eliot Norton, Basil Hall, Frederick Olmsted, William Russell and Harriet Martineau, all of whom are selectively revealed making highly positive statements about slavery. He even recruits a twentieth-century 'critic' (Howard Snyder in *The Atlantic Monthly*) to his cause and quotes him: 'In some ways the Negro is shamefully mistreated – mistreated through leniency.'[10] He makes particular reference to Olmsted's *Seaboard Slave States* when he writes of a Louisiana sugar planter distributing a small sum to his slaves as a Christmas bonus but omits a number of horrendously sadistic encounters and whippings described by the same Northern traveller.

Here then are sins, both of omission and of commission, and the invidious *a priori* conviction that slavery was a beneficial means of social control salutary for both black and white. Because this assumption distorts everything he writes it is puzzling that a younger Marxist historian, Eugene Genovese, has been such a stout defender of his reputation. It is true that Genovese gained in critical insight from Phillips's emphasis on the reciprocity of master–slave relations; that, as Phillips wrote, 'The general regime was in fact shaped by mutual requirements, concessions and understandings, producing reciprocal codes of conventional morality.'[11] But Genovese goes further and suggests that Phillips just falls short of greatness as an historian. Short, because Phillips's racism blinds him to the full horrors of the system. But if racism infuses and distorts all his writings and is integral to his historical purpose, can Phillips claim such high respect? He remains useful for his insights into the mind of the slave master's paternalistic rationale, but such insights are commonplace enough and endlessly repeated in the pro-slavery writings of Thomas Dew, George Fitzhugh and other defenders. Phillips's bias made for false history and this, surely, is inexcusable.

At the time the only criticisms levelled against *American Negro Slavery* came from black historians. Du Bois referred to the onesided obtuseness of Phillips's survey, which had 'no adequate conception of 'darkies', 'niggers' and 'negroes' (words liberally used throughout the book) or making a living mass humanity with all the usual human reactions.' Similarly, Carter Woodson pointed to Phillips's total inability to fathom the black mind because the book 'deals primarily with the slaves as property in the cold-blooded fashion that the Southerners usually bartered them away. Very little is said about the blacks themselves, seemingly to give more space to the history of the whites, who profited by their labour.'[12]

Kenneth Stampp's *The Peculiar Institution* (1956) appeared two years after the *Brown* Supreme Court decision, and was the first sustained assault upon Phillips. In his preface Stampp acknowledged the pioneering work of Phillips as a preliminary to demolishing its structure, stone by stone. Stampp frankly acknowledges the impact of current concerns on his study, concerns which informed his own re-reading of slavery.

> With the historian it is an act of faith that knowledge of the past is the key to understanding the present. In this instance I firmly believe that I must know what slavery meant to the Negro and how we reacted to it before I can comprehend his more recent tribulations. Yet there is a strange paradox in the historian's involvement with both present and past, for his knowledge of the present is clearly a key to his understanding of the past. Today we are learning much from the natural and social sciences about the Negro's potentialities and the basic irrelevance of race, and we are slowly discovering the roots and meaning of human behaviour.[13]

Stampp dismissed the underlying determinism of Phillips – the assumption that somehow slavery just happened to the South along with the cotton gin – which had served to justify Phillips's theory of social control. 'Let us begin,' Phillips had written, 'by discussing the weather ... the chief agency in making the Southern distinctiveness'. But it was nonsense, Stampp retorted, to assume that whites were incapable of working in such high temperatures and that the climate made black slavery inevitable. It was false to deny that slavery had been constructed deliberately by human agency, built, 'little by little, step by step, choice by choice, over a period of many years ... Not the Negro but slavery was the old South's great affliction – the root of its tragedy.' Stampp went on to strike down Phillips's self-serving assumption that slavery was unprofitable: that non-economic factors – status, paternalism, a sense of *noblesse oblige* – had motivated the slave holder and sustained the system. The classical school of economists – Adam Smith, for example, and John Cairnes – had been co-opted by the abolitionists in their crusade against slavery. The theological assumption that an immoral system could not yield profit was reinforced by Adam Smith's insistence that, lacking incentives and pay, slavery was not, and could not, be efficient. Lord Cairnes insisted that, under slavery, 'fear is substituted for hope as the stimulus to exertion. But fear is ill-calculated to draw from a labourer all the industry of which he is capable.' A slave mistress in Texas, for example, complained about her domestic slave, who persistently tracked in mud through the kitchen without wiping her shoes. All very tiresome. But 'What do they care?' she reflected. 'They'd just as lief clean the mud after themselves as [do] anything else – their time isn't any value to themselves.'[14] Stampp argued, however, that slavery was an inherently inefficient system, not an unprofitable one, because of the countervailing forces of widely available land as the black cotton belt spread ever westward, the high price of cotton, its well nigh monopoly position in supplying the textile industries of Europe and the North, and the self-reproduction of a labour force which was compelled to work hard without being paid. By 1860 the total slave population was of the order of 4 million. The ending of the slave trade in 1808 had raised the price of slaves, which continued to rise up to 1860, but this also reflected the buoyancy of the slave economy. Even so, slave labour was cheap compared with free white labour, even though it depressed white wages in the South. Slaves, if temporarily hired out, were paid 20–50 per cent less than white labour, while, comparatively,

Northern workers earned $505 per annum on average as against $145 per annum by their Southern counterpart. It was precisely because slavery was profitable that the Southern black codes, which enforced the institution, were tightened, and there was a highly lucrative domestic trade in which the tidewater states, such as Virginia and Maryland, sold off slaves to the expanding Cotton Belt of the Southern frontier.

For slavery, Stampp emphasised, was also a highly mobile labour system. As ever, Phillips depicted this mobility in benign terms. 'Ancestral halls were fewer than ancestral servitors, for a planter's migration would vacate the house but carry the personnel.'[15] But this sentence muffles one of the major iniquities of the system: slave marriages had no legal status and families, or parts of the family, could be sold down the river to the slave traders of Natchez and New Orleans. Slaves lived in ever present terror of this prospect and hoped that their master might flourish, anything, rather than face the sickening eventuality of separation. The abolitionist, Theodore Weld, in his *Slavery As It Is: Testimony of a Thousand Witnesses* (1839), sifted through a huge number of Southern newspapers collecting advertisements placed in them offering rewards for the return of runaway slaves. A large proportion of them concerned runaways attempting to reunite with their separated families. One such, reprinted from *The Richmond Compiler* (Virginia) of 8 September 1837, is a gem of moral obtuseness: 'Runaway from the subscriber, Ben. He ran off without any known cause, and I suppose he is aiming to go to his wife, who was carried from the neighbourhood last winter.'[16] Like Weld, Stampp considered this aspect of the peculiar institution as especially damning.

Phillips wrote on the Southerner's paranoid fear of slave insurrection, but was incapable of imagining why contented slaves might possibly want to rebel against their condition in the first place. When Herbert Aptheker's pioneering study of slavery rebellion appeared in 1943, Stampp was compelled to rethink the stereotype of the contented slave, for 'it appears that many not-so-docile "Old Black Joes" tucked numerous exploiting "massas" in the cold, cold ground'.[17] In fact Aptheker's analysis of some 250 slave revolts was grossly exaggerated and was based predominantly on white fears and rumours, which were rife, but Stampp could agree with Aptheker that slaves, being white men with black skins, did not remain submissive under such conditions. But Stampp refined this concept and spoke rather in terms of a 'troublesome property', sullen and disruptive, who frequently internalised his feelings with day-to-day forms of resistance such as sabotage, stealing, arson and self-mutilation. He noted the evidence of psychological trauma and buried hostility; of stuttering and stammering and of eating dirt. Throughout, Stampp tried to avoid rarefied theorising and concentrated on concrete, almost mundane, explanations. Theoretically, for example, there was little incentive for the slave to work harder in order to enrich his master. More practically, if slave workers displayed that idleness of which Phillips spoke so eloquently, it was due in part to dietary deficiencies such as scurvy, beri-beri and pellagra, which had an enervating effect. And, more mundanely still, having often worked from sun-up to sundown, some sixteen hours, in harsh and often unpleasant conditions, what could be more tempting than idleness after a long, tiring work day?

Stampp also corrected Phillips's distortions concerning large plantations. Half the Southern male population, much like their Northern counterparts, were yeoman farmers, three-quarters of whom had no connection with slavery whatsoever: 88 per cent of owners held fewer than twenty slaves and only 1 per cent, admittedly the social and political elite of Southern society, owned over 100 slaves. He also readjusted Phillips's selective use of contemporary sources. In place of Olmsted's reflections on the benign nature of slavery he quotes a comment made to Olmsted by a farmer in Mississippi: 'I'd rather be dead than be a nigger on one of these big plantations.'[18]

The first major reappraisal since Phillips, Stampp's study, with its sanity and balance, its concern with particularities rather than grand theorising, has endured the test of time. On its appearance Hofstadter suggested that the book was too coldly objective; David Donald thought that it was too *engagé*. This suggests that Stampp got the balance about right, and that these two reviewers saw separate facets united in the same book. The prose is calm and measured, yet informed by a deep sense of indignation. Stampp has been criticised for following Phillips too closely and using, in general, the same sources that Phillips used;

for the fact that Phillips's categories – food, shelter, policing, medical care – were the categories that Stampp followed. But that was because Stampp wanted to demolish Phillips, chapter and verse, at each and every juncture and affirm that 'cruelty was endemic in all slave holding communities'. In this he may at times have gone too far. Given the absence of stable family units, he depicted the slaves inhabiting a cultural void, a twilight world between their lost African roots and alien American values. Subsequent studies suggest that it was not so. Stampp tended to use traditional literary sources rather than quantify, and literary sources can at times be misleading and unrepresentative. Masters tended to recall periods of epidemic or unusually severe illness. Fogel and Engerman, two cliometricians, have taken the account books of Southern plantations to tabulate an average morbidity rate of 1.9 days per man per year and paint a less gruesome picture than Stampp. They accuse Stampp of concentrating on superficial tangibilities rather than directing his attention to the deeper underlying racist denial of education and the opening of the professions to talented blacks. But surely, under involuntary servitude, such wider considerations did not arise, and it is these deep intangibilities which are surely beside the point? But the greatest criticism levelled against Stampp, again by Fogel and Engerman, is that, in following a neo-abolitionist strategy, he perpetuated a racist myth of black incompetence. 'What,' they ask, 'of black achievement under slavery? A world in which good work is synonymous with betrayal and in which evasion, deception, and sabotage are the objectives to which to aspire, leaves scant room for black achievement.'[19] But this is to misread Stampp, who never accused blacks of incompetence, only of simply lacking the incentive to work harder for the further enrichment of their masters. Given that slavery was not a system that they had made but one which, rather, they had been involuntarily forced into, and given that the regime was highly coercive, the slave, unable to rebel openly and outwardly, could only sabotage to some extent from within and carry out minor acts of limited resistance and protest.

In his pathbreaking critique of Phillips in 1944, Hofstadter had called for an historical revolution that would see the institution of slavery through the eyes of the slave and not through those of the master. Stanley Elkins, a pupil of Hofstadter's, set out to do this is in his highly controversial *Slavery: a Problem in American Institutional and Intellectual Life* of 1959. For all his virtues, Elkins believed that Stampp had, however unconsciously, bestowed contemporary white feelings upon the slave's ante-bellum condition and, in his determination to destroy Phillips, was caught up in a relentless polemical cycle which had essentially remained unchanged since the Civil War period. But to reimagine the world the slave had made would require consider-able ingenuity and a revolution in historical methodology, because the slave remained, in many ways, the most silent of all America's minorities. Education had been proscribed and 90 per cent of slaves were illiterate. Diaries and letters were sparse, the reports of Northern travellers tended to be biased, as were slave narratives and autobiographies written up and tailored to meet the requirements of a Northern white abolitionist audience. There was the vast repository of the Works Progress Administration archives in the 1930s: a series of some 120,000 interviews conducted among ex-slaves who had survived into the New Deal era. But these documents had to be handled with extreme care. Over two-thirds of those interviewed were over eighty and their recollections of childhood, before the full rigours of the work system came into play, could be overly rosy and, interestingly, black interviewers elicited a grimmer picture than white interviewers (7–9 per cent recollected harsh conditions with white interviewers, compared with 25 per cent with black interviewers) and the entire enterprise was distorted by the vague rumour that those who painted a benign picture were more likely to receive federal hand-outs.

Elkins had a brilliant mind; sharp, highly original, intelligent. The prose fizzes and ideas take wing: throwaway bravura refer-ences to Sarah Bernhardt, *Hamlet*, Turgenev and Edmund Burke add to the general air of intellectual virtuosity. He, more than the average mundane historian, felt entirely at home in the world of ambitious theorising, abstract ideas and fresh, innovative method-ologies culled from psychology, anthropology and sociology. He was struck, from the first, by what he took to be a fundamental paradox concerning slavery. Stampp and others had revealed an institution of great cruelty and degradation, and yet open, large-scale revolt was conspicuous by its absence. Apetheker's misguided attempts to conjure up heroic resistance were dismissed out of hand. Of those rebellions which had occurred, two had been led by free black preachers (Gabriel Prosser in 1800 and Denmark Vesey in 1822), and the other, the infamous Nat Turner uprising in Southampton County, Virginia, in 1832, by an educated slave who had been taught to read by a kind master. Why? Elkins had read the pioneering works of Frank Tannenbaum and Gilberto Freyre on hemispheric and Brazilian slaves, which revealed, in contrast, the further paradox of milder systems of enslavement in which widespread rebellion did occur. Latin America had inherited a Roman legal system which encompassed the status of slavery. However circumscribed or limited, slaves enjoyed certain contractual rights, such as marriage, ownership of plots of land, a large number of religious holidays, the ability to save money in order to buy eventual manumission, all of which fell short of total ownership. Then again, the Crown and the Catholic Church were powerful institutions which served to mitigate the full rigours of local slavery. In the United States it was far otherwise. The thirteen colonies had inherited the English common law tradition, under which human slavery had no legal recognition and therefore, paradoxically, slaves were reduced to the status of mere property, a status reaffirmed by the Supreme Court in the Dred Scott case of 1857. From the start, the colonies had been commercial enterprises, concerned with profits, royal control from the metropolitan centre being lax and all but non-existent. Comparative studies revealed slavery in the United States to be uniquely oppressive and starkly caste-ridden – both physically and mentally a 'closed system'. Contemporary accounts also seemed to suggest that the Southern black was uniquely childlike, submissive and docile – the ubiquitous 'Sambo' personality. This too was surprising, for the anthropological research of Melville Herskovits revealed an extraordinarily rich and sophisticated native West African culture whence the slave had originated. 'We are tempted ... to wonder how it was ever possible,' Elkins concluded, 'that all this native resourcefulness and vitality could have been brought to such a point of utter stultification in America.'[20]

At this point, and with increasingly audacity, Elkins plunged into the treacherous shallows of psychological analogies. He looked, for example, at Sigmund Freud's work on the authoritarian father and the way in which he shaped the growing child; he read Anna Freud's studies of child psychology and the way the infant coped with early physical and psychic threats by introjection – that is, by internalising the threat and taking on the personality of the threatening mother or father. He looked at Harry Stack Sullivan's study of 'significant others' whom the young child sought desperately to emulate and to replicate in his own developing psychology. In looking at writings on the harrowing psychological consequences of existence in Nazi concentration camps Elkins is at his most daring, but it proved a practical laboratory of extremity where intense and overwhelming psychological damage could be practically measured. Elkins was much criticised for using this analogy, but he never intended Auschwitz exactly to parallel the plantations of the old South – only to serve as a proposal, an illumination, an extreme test case of absolute power and absolute powerlessness. The analogy also assisted his strategy of moving the debate away from race in America. The evidence of Bruno Bettelheim, a concentration camp survivor and psychologist, was not only of significant value in itself, it also separated the universal consequences of powerlessness from the specific question of the black race.

What Bettelheim had survived to relate was precisely what Anna Freud had observed in her young charges: that, under massive threat, the real personality, the authentic psychology of the individual, was wiped out and replaced by total identification with the authority figure. In the concentration camp the inmates came to emulate and even to admire their sadistic Kapo guards who became grotesque father figures. Did the same acute depersonalisation occur between master and slave? The black African captured and marched in irons to the coast, shipped in appalling conditions through the notorious middle passage to America, underwent the double trauma of shock and detachment. Once in America, the slave was cast into lifelong bondage in which his entire survival, both physical and psychological, was dependent upon the whim of the authoritarian master. Under such traumatic conditions the slave took refuge in regression and infantilisation. 'The Negro was to be a child forever.'[21] 'Sambo' was not the rationale of the master class but the slaves' true self. The absence of family structure, of a strong father figure (black children were raised by, and took the surname of, their mothers, in part to spare the master's embarrassment in acknowledging his mulatto offspring), served to complete the process of emasculation which only left the male with the role of either 'boy' or 'uncle'. Paradoxically, while totally condemning the system, Elkins had ended by depicting Phillips's passive child slave. The book was more damning than any abolitionist critique of the peculiar institution, yet, at the same time, an entirely unheroic portrayal of the black as 'Uncle Tom' accommodationalist finally emerged.

Elkins's thesis was illuminating, dramatic, high-pitched, self-consistent and apparently seamless: indeed, it had only one flaw – it was all entirely wrong, and each and every work on the subject thereafter serves only to confirm its fundamental fallacies. Genovese wrote tellingly that Elkins's greatest weakness as an historian was that he could brook no contradiction, while his own Marxism encouraged a dialectical process which could postulate both one truth and its unfolding opposite simultaneously. Take, for example, Elkins's crucial hemispheric comparison, which served to emphasise the unique severity of North American slavery. It was true that the caste system in Brazil was less rigid, that miscegenation was more commonplace, that blacks' talent and money served to 'whiten' their skin in the eyes of society. By 1860, 50 per cent of Brazil's black population was free, while in the United States only 10 per cent were freedmen. But Genovese, David Brion Davis, Carl Degler and others undermine the benign picture of Latin American slavery depicted by Gilberto Freyre and Frank Tannenbaum on which Elkins heavily relied. While the Spanish Crown did exert an ameliorating, if distant, influence, the Portuguese Crown was less effective. The Catholic Church was shown to be deeply involved in the Angolan slave trade and used trading to fund its missionary work. Locally the priest was more likely to collaborate with the slave owner than with his distant bishop or yet more distant monarch. Herbert Klein had compared the rigours of slavery in Virginia to Cuba to the disadvantage of Virginia but at a time in Cuba before the full impact of intense capitalist sugar production made the system infinitely harsher. There was, too, a stark demographic figure which refused to go away. While Latin America and the Caribbean required the continuous influx of fresh slaves to sustain the slave system, the Southern US slave population, constituting only 4.5 per cent of the total Atlantic traffic, was self-sustaining. The slave population in the United States increased at the rate of 20 per cent per decade, roughly the same as the white population, amounting to a total population of 4 million by 1860. How did this square with the unique horrors of the closed system depicted by Elkins?

And the absence of slave revolts? Again, more practical and commonplace explanations were offered. In Latin America the plantations tended to be vast, there was far less policing, there were frequently black majorities – many of them armed volunteers – and large runaway maroon communities surviving in largely uncontrolled mountain and swamp areas. Leaders of revolts tended to be newcomers rather than settlers or Creoles (what to make here of Elkins's stress on the trauma of the middle passage?) while the high ratio of male to female and a general absence of established fixed family units, encouraged rebellion. What to make of Elkins's stress on the absence of such revolts in the United States? Rebellion in the ante-bellum South, Genovese starkly concluded, was tantamount to committing suicide. There was an overwhelming white majority which controlled all arms and ammunition, the South had blocked most escape routes, and posses and patrols and white vigilantes enforced their dominion.

What to make of Elkins's Sambo character, which he argued made rebellion impossible in the first place? Sambo existed wherever slavery existed and was by no means unique to the United States. In Brazil he became 'Banzo' and in Jamaica 'Quashee'. Sambo was not only universal in slave societies: he could easily change into Nat the insurrectionist. Sambo was endemic in Haiti, for example, until the greatest slave rebellion in history occurred. Sambo was, in short, the tractable, accommodating mask presented to the slave owner as a means of day-to-day survival. Elkins was provided with any number of clues which he perversely chose not to follow up. Harry Stack Sullivan, one of his principal psychological sources, had written of 'dissociation' as well as of 'significant others', of psychological plasticity, split personalities and manipulation of the significant authoritarian other. All sorts of false selves might come into play: the acting out of required roles, the donning of false disguises, all to aid the primary psychic task of preserving the true self relatively inviolate. But Elkins had typically argued himself into a corner. Only during the ensuing onslaught on his book did he modify his position – concede 'something less than absolute power produces something less than absolute dependency', that there was survival as well as damage, and a 'broad belt of indeterminacy between mere acting and the true self'.[22] Elkins offered the concentration camp analogy as a 'proposal' but one, nevertheless, which he thought worked, as is made clear in an appendix to the book entitled 'Analogy as Evidence'.[23] His strategy was to postulate a psychic death analogous to that of the camp inmate – yet his primary source, Bruno Bettelheim, who was required to carry so much of the weight of his thesis, patently survived, physically and psychologically. As ever, Elkins was incapable of moderation. His own service in the army, he wrote, had made a man of him but had made a boy of him also. Would not personal empirical experience have been more useful than grandiose psychological theorising? And if one was looking for institutional parallels wouldn't prison, schools, borstals or even the authoritarian structure inherent in every family be more apposite?

Elkins's ingenuity had terminated in the image of a slave that held little appeal to a black audience or to liberal America, but he had taken up and extended Stampp's insistence on the unparalleled brutality of the institution of slavery. The most conclusive refutation of Elkins came in a series of more measured studies. These, collectively, depicted a slave society, much of it hidden from white society, which was alive and vibrant and positive, with a culture and a personality which survived and endured.

In 1974 a book appeared, *Time on the Cross*, written by two eminent cliometricians, Robert Fogel and Stanley Engerman, which was to turn Elkins on its head and cause a similar uproar in the profession. Initially reviewers such as Vann Woodward were puzzled and bemused by what seemed to emerge from its dense two volumes. Volume I summarised the authors' findings; Volume II was an all but incomprehensible appendix given over to methodological procedures, complex econometric equations and dense statistical tables. For what was depicted was an essentially benign institution. One review in the *New York Review of Books* was entitled 'The jolly institution', another 'Slavery without tears', and a cartoon appeared in which an overseer was reassuring a field hand with the words 'You may take comfort in the knowledge that some day a revisionist historian will make all of this seem like it didn't exist.'

The question of the profitability of slavery was a perennial historical chestnut. The abolitionists had argued that the institution was economically inefficient as well as morally repugnant. Phillips, coinciding with the abolitionists for once, agreed that slavery was not ultimately sustained by and for the slavemasters' profits. Stampp disagreed, and in 1958 A.H. Conrad and J.R. Meyers had written a seminal if unreadable paper which sought to prove that the marginal efficiency of slave capital was high-yielding and commensurate with railroad investment in the North and with dividend returns on the New York stock exchange. Already in this influential article can be detected the characteristics of the cliometric revolution: vast lists of raw numerical data and a cold, depersonalised language such as 'Each prime field wench produced five to ten marketable children during her lifetime.'[24] But this new method was to reach its grotesque apotheosis in *Time on the Cross*.

The book curiously combined austere scientific methodological claims with stinging invective. Provided with a $333,000 grant from the National Science Foundation, and armed with a battery of research assistants and computers, Fogel and Engerman set out to investigate 'Factor productivity in American agriculture'. Their academic agenda was made quite explicit: 'The re-examination of slavery is part of a more ambitious effort to reconstruct the entire history of American economic development on a sound quantitative basis.' Previous studies of slavery had mainly relied on literary sources, which were fragmentary and impressionistic: 'highly intelligent and perceptive' historians would continue to be misled until they fully recognised 'the role of mathematics and statistics in historical analysis'.[25] They could not entirely ditch words for figures, but prose had to be rigorously pure and scientific and buttressed throughout by numbers.

'As we use the words, "ideology" means a system of beliefs, "belief" means an unverified proposition which is held to be true, and "knowledge" refers to propositions which have been verified according to a set of objective criteria such as those employed in statistics or in various fields of science.'[26] For which, decoded, read: 'ideology' equals traditional myths concerning slavery; 'belief' equals erroneous conclusions all historians before Fogel and Engerman reached on the basis of unreliable, non-quantifiable subjective material; 'knowledge' equals the operationalised facts issuing from Fogel and Engerman's overworked computer system. Here we are pitched back remorselessly into the dreary world of the dismal science, its votaries Adam Smith's classical profit-maximising market model and Gradgrind's dogged, unimaginative obsession with facts. Here numbers – cold, impersonal, platonic, austere – alone are real, and individuals mere robots in a neoclassical market world of profit maximisation and input–output ratios or, as our authors would have it, 'geometric indices of total factor productivity'. Averaging out and counting heads is all-important, and what cannot be counted does not really count at all. Arthur Schlesinger, the American historian, once wrote that, on the contrary, that which can be counted never really ultimately counted. It is surely possible to find middle ground here, but Fogel and Engerman definitely did not seek middle ground: they demanded stark, unconditional surrender. With each new computer print-out they became more intoxicated. At first they held that, while free labour was more profitable than Southern slave labour, the peculiar institution was far from inefficient. But, with each new operational assumption factored in, they were amazed to discover, finally, that slavery was 35 per cent more efficient than free Northern farms.

The intellectual chronology of their enterprise is important. First the surprising econometric conclusion, followed by the *a priori* application of the macroeconomic result to the microeconomic level of the plantation, and then the extrapolation of a slave model to fit the figures. To the dazzling innovation of their method was added a powerful, polemical purpose. If slavery was profitable, where did that leave the slave? Stampp had taken his cue from Adam Smith:

> The experience of all ages and nations, I believe, demonstrates that the work done by slaves, though it appears to cost only their maintenance, is in the end the dearest of any. A person who can acquire no

property, can have no interest but to eat as much, and to labour as little, as possible. Whatever work he does beyond what is sufficient to purchase his own and maintenance can be squeezed out of him by violence only, and not by any interest of his own.[27]

But how could the slave be a troublesome, intractable property when cotton profits were so buoyant and *per capita* income grew 30 per cent more in the South than in the North between 1840 and 1860? Smith's market economics would in any case suggest that slavery would long since have been abandoned by the Southern profit maximiser had it not been profitable, but then Smith's economics presumed freedom, contract and choice. Did slaves have a choice? Fogel and Engerman implicitly assume they did: that the slave chose to work hard and co-operate in return for a system which essentially offered him incentives in place of force and coercion.

Fogel and Engerman wrote with the fervent moral tone of the abolitionists, although they anathematised the abolitionists and neo-abolitionists such as Stanley Elkins and Kenneth Stampp who perpetuated the racist myth of black incompetence. The highly emotive title of their book was reflected in the outrage of their hubristic prose. 'We were lured,' they wrote,

by the desire to contribute personally to the resolution of one of the great issues of American history. How often are scholars presented with an opportunity to untie a Gordian knot as massive, as urgent, and as deeply entwined in the moral trauma of a nation as the racial issues that have tortured America for most of its history?

Together they would untie the racist knot, 'strike down the view that black Americans were without culture, without achievement and without development for their first 250 years on American soil'.[28] That achievement, pre-eminently, was to be hard workers: imbued with the Protestant work ethic and singlemindedly dedicated to the profitability of Southern agriculture.

To reinforce this revolutionary method they set up straw dogs, as reviewers recognised, and dismissed views which had long since been revised or rejected by the profession. Their supposedly original view that plantation slavery had been adapted to industrial slavery, for example, had already been thoroughly explored by Frederic Bancroft and Robert Starobin's study of slave labour in the Tredegar Iron Foundry in Richmond, Virginia. As already mentioned, they accused Stampp of perpetuating the racist myth of black incompetence when, in fact, Stampp was referring to slave labour, not black labour, as such. In fact Fogel and Engerman perpetuated this muddle themselves when they wrote indiscriminately of 'superior black labour' interchangeably with 'superior slave labour'.

Response from reviewers was resoundingly hostile. Their methodology was judged to be highly unscientific. Having started by establishing the high profitability of slavery they were forced to conjure up, deductively, a phantom co-operative slave worker. Most science works by means of hypothesis, conjecture and induction. A hypothesis is held only as long as it is consistent and viable, and dropped when evidence refutes it. But Fogel and Engerman's starting point was itself fundamentally flawed, for profitability and efficiency are not the same thing or directly interchangeable. A Massachusetts farmer, for example, might seek to emulate the Southern farm and cultivate cotton but, however efficiently he worked, climatic conditions would render the pursuit profitless. Making sandbags in Egypt or ice blocks in Iceland might require little skill yet still bring profitable returns. Profitability is essentially a measure of value, the margin between costs and the price charged for the product: efficiency is, in turn, a physical measure of input factors – land, labour and capital – and output: the physical product which results. Take, for example, the hypothetical case of an export-dependent British industry such as whisky or cars. The government devalues the currency by, say, 10 per cent, the export becomes cheaper by 10 per cent and more competitive, and profits rise. But this is not the same as saying the British car or whisky industry has become more efficient overnight. Southern cotton was in an analogous position in the 1850s. Demand for raw cotton was almost inexhaustible and the South, providing 80 per cent of cotton for the British market and a third of the world's total, was in a highly favourable monopolistic position. Cotton prices were high and this, in turn, was reflected in the high price of slaves. Indeed, so buoyant was the market, it was generally believed that the South's 'King Cotton' strategy during the Civil War, which was intended to starve Britain of cotton and force it to come to the aid of the South, would work miracles.

How did these misunderstandings shape Fogel and Engerman's image of the slave? Essentially the slave must have been a happy slave who was offered an array of incentives in the form of extra income, private garden plots and a varied and open occupational pyramid from overseer (79 per cent of whom were black) down, a highly nutritious diet, comfortable accommodation, inculcation of the Victorian values of hard work and self-help, support for the family unit and the encouragement of prudish rather than promiscuous sexual behaviour. Contented and supremely adapted to the proto-industrial methods of the gang system, the rationalised rhythm of field work and economies of scale were achieved within a supportive framework of cradle-to-grave social welfare.

This high proportion of black slave overseers, 79 per cent, was reached by means of what the authors called the 'disappearance method', that is to say, if there were no free overseers counted in the census, it was assumed, firstly, that there must be one and, secondly, that it had to be a slave. But on the vast majority of plantations, which were small, the master or the son usually doubled as overseer, and the census did not mention overseers unless they were living in the same house as the master – an unlikely occurrence. Happy families made happy workers; only 10 per cent of these families were separated and sold down the river, and less than 2 per cent suffered the breaking up of a marriage. But a critic, himself a cliometrician, reworked these figures from scratch on the basis of New Orleans slave market records between 1804 and 1862 and revealed that they were erroneous owing to the authors' failure to do long division. Good morals made good workers, and probate records yielded the fact that the average female slave was 22.5 years of age when she gave birth to her first child. But the records listed only the first surviving child, which, in an age of high infant mortality for both black and white, could be highly misleading, and the age of female slave conception was probably closer to eighteen years. Accommodation, according to Fogel and Engerman, was relatively spacious – in fact, superior to that enjoyed by workers in New York in 1893. But here again further investigation revealed that Fogel and Engerman had enlarged the average size of slave cabins by 50 per cent and their comparison was based on a New

York City survey carried out among immigrant slums in the depths of a major depression. Diet was good and slaves ate well (here there is much on the nutritional value of sweet potatoes) but then the slave required a high calorific intake in order to carry out highly arduous physical duties.

There is an inordinate amount of space given over to whipping, which might seem odd but for the fact that an emphasis on incentive rather than punishment was crucial to the authors' strategy. The vast pyramid of assumptions which add to the final figure of 0.7 per cent whippings per hand per year was based on the records kept over a period of two years on one single plantation, that of Bennet Barrow in Louisiana. As expressed the figure of 0.7 per cent does not sound so awful; put another way, it amounts to a public whipping every four days. Herbert Gutman and Richard Sutch in a reappraisal returned to these records and found that, during this time, there were in fact 175, not 160, whippings as Fogel and Engerman maintained; that the authors had overestimated the number of hands on the plantation (they put it at 200, because they had based it on an inventory of 1854, thirteen years following the record of whippings); that a recalculation of the figures revealed the master wielding his whip every four days to serve as a deterrent in front of other slaves, sixty of those punished being women; that only 22 per cent of the work force, not 50 per cent, as Fogel and Engerman suggested, remained unwhipped, and that the corrected figure was not 0.7 but 1.19 whippings per hand per year. Further literary evidence, no longer considered impressionistic when it supported their case, was shown to undermine rather than buttress it. Concentration on whippings ignored the multiplicity of punishments Barrow heaped upon his slaves. Some were chained, others were jailed, threatened with death, shot at and beaten with a stick, or humiliated by Barrow making his male slaves dress up in women's clothes or sacking – and this from a master whose biographer says he treated his slaves reasonably well by local standards. And overwhelmingly, as Gutman and Sutch proved, punishment was meted out for bad work. The authors did not quote the following extract from Barrow's diary: 'The better you treat them the worse they are, Big Lucy, the leader, corrupts every young Negro in her power.' What was selectively quoted was this, of 15 October 1840: 'My Negroes have their name up in the neighbourhood for making more than anyone else & they think whatever they do is better than anybody else.' But placed in context it is clear that Barrow is being ironic and our cliometricians are seemingly deaf to its nuances. What they do not quote is a diary entry of two days earlier, 13 October. 'I think my hands have Picked cotton worse this year than in several years picked it very trashy & not better weights nor as good as common, intend Whipping them straght.'[29]

It was fellow cliometricians, armed with the requisite expertise, who questioned the figures and conclusions of the book, not the traditional literary historians. A conference was held at Rochester where *Time on the Cross* was subjected to withering criticism, and the resulting collection of critical essays edited by Paul David, *Reckoning with Slavery* (1976), left precious little standing. Not only had Fogel and Engerman started from an erroneous conclusion and insidiously distorted their material at every stage to fit this conclusion, they had become bewitched by the seeming certitude of numbers. Fogel had already strayed into the perilous waters of counterfactual analysis in writing *Railroads and American Economic Growth* (1964), where he conjured up an imaginary American world of 1890 without railroads, placing them back on their tracks again, and then concluding that rails contributed only 5 per cent to gross national production during this period. This book, too, was subjected to devastating criticism by fellow cliometricians. Fogel and Engerman were adept at playing games with numbers: it all depended on how you expressed it. One such figure crucial to their strategy was that only 1.92 per cent of slaves were sold per year, which meant, in practice, that every slave in his or her lifetime had a fifty–fifty chance of being sold along with eleven members of his or her immediate family. Numbers can mislead just as readily as words can, and Fogel and Engerman's use of numbers was highly impressionistic. To achieve the overall 35 per cent efficiency of the plantation economy, for example, the misleadingly solid figure of superior Northern soil fertility of 2.5 per cent was fed into the overall assumptional pyramid. Language could not be more impressionistic than this notional figure. And their writing could be vague and indistinct. Kenneth Stampp found sixty-three examples of such loose writing – 'most', 'may', 'sometimes', 'often', 'few', etc, – in fourteen pages, between pages 109 and 126 in their text adding up, on average, to 4.5 times a page. *Touché.* Lack of information compelled Fogel and Engerman to speculate recklessly. The whipping figures, as we have seen, derived from one plantation: their figures on the slave occupational hierarchy from only thirty plantations in a highly untypical sugar and rice parish of Louisiana. Similarly literary sources were used selectively to confirm their thesis. They quoted Olmsted describing a disciplined gang of slaves working with an overseer, omitting the following lines where Olmsted described a tall powerful black cracking his whip and shouting, 'Shove your hoe there.' (But here, as Peter Parish, the English historian, points out in his *Slavery,* 1989, Fogel and Engerman's critics themselves distort the case by omitting the following line – 'But I never saw him strike anyone with the whip.'[30]) Parish also draws attention to the all-pervasive economic euphemisms in their writing. Even if whites had been offered 50 per cent above their average earnings, Fogel and Engerman write, they would still not have worked in labour gangs. This 'negative non-pecuniary income' is a euphemism for very nasty and unpleasant work. Likewise the fact that two-thirds of the black race were in the work force as opposed to only one-third of the white is referred to as 'the extraordinary high participation rate of blacks', as if they had a choice and enjoyed their work. Here, as elsewhere, Fogel and Engerman assumed free market contracts which did not exist. A study of slave profitability had, of necessity, to revolve around the profitability of the master class, with the black labourer essentially absent. Ironically, as Stampp concluded, 'Two cliometricians who want to restore to blacks their true history in slavery have written a book which deprives them of their voice, their initiative, and their humanity.'[31]

Eugene Genovese's *Roll, Jordan, Roll* appeared in the same year as *Time on the Cross.* Born in 1930 into a family of Italian immigrants in Brooklyn, Genovese became a Marxist and a radical. His involvement in the politics of the period made him so critical of government policy both at home and abroad ('For radicals the success of imperialism abroad remains inseparable from the success of imperialist-generated moral decay at home') that

President Nixon tried to get him fired from his teaching post at Rutgers.[32] Though he became a leading authority on the ante-bellum South his historical writing has always been informed by his Marxist contempt for conventional bourgeois values and the conviction that bourgeois hegemony is far from benign. 'In bourgeois democratic society the hegemony of the bourgeois masks its dictatorship.' His Marxism was reinforced by reading such English historians as Christopher Hill, Eric Hobsbawm and E.P. Thompson, but his own brand is far from the crude home-grown material determinism of a Charles Beard. Shaped by the Italian Marxist, Antonio Gramsci, Genovese is fascinated by the infinitely subtle modes by which a master class exerts its control – by assumptions, values and attitudes, both materially and in the world of ideas. There is, throughout his writings, an ambivalence born of his understanding of the dialectic as it operates in concrete historical reality. The ante-bellum South offers a classic case study of a master class in full ascendance, appealing to a common interest of both white and black with an ideology so powerful that it compels consent and kills any nascent class opposition. Against such an omnipotent ideology struggle seems hopeless. As Gramsci wrote, 'Where an order exists, it is more difficult to decide to replace it with a new order.'[33]

Genovese had already published *The Political Economy of Slavery* (1965) and *The World the Slave Holders Made* (1969). The subject of *Roll, Jordan, Roll* was a world the slaves made with 'their demonstration of the beauty and power of the human spirit under conditions of extreme oppression ...'. And yet the book has a good deal to say about master and overseer, mistress and poor white, too, because, rejecting the simplicities of 'bottom up' history, his approach is holistic and held together by mutual reciprocities and by the unifying concept of paternalism. It seems at first sight strange that a radical Marxist should be turning to Phillips's central concept, yet Genovese handles it with far greater subtlety and ambivalence. There is no apologetic here. 'The reception accorded by white America to the black people brought here in chains and raised in slavery and under racist oppression has, first and foremost, provided a record of one of history's greatest crimes.' But Genovese's primary aim is to understand, not to pass judgement. Paternalism for him becomes the bridge which reconciles intolerable contradictions, the abyss between power and powerlessness, in a form of compromise between the enslaver's ideology and a bargaining counter for the enslaved. Genovese never forgets that both master and slave were human, trapped in the matrix of their time. If paternalism was a white pro-slavery rationale it was also a means whereby slaves set limits to their dehumanisation and imposed a complex set of mutual obligations, one on the other. 'The South was made up of one people but also two races, indissolubly linked but separate too.' 'The fate of master and slave was historically intertwined, and formed part of a single social process; each in his way struggled for autonomy – struggled to end his dependence upon the other – but neither could wholly succeed.' For the master paternalism required fatherly protection as well as stern admonition: it allowed the master to believe the slave happy and when, in 1865, the mask of 'Sambo' slipped, and hegemony came to an abrupt end, the master class was traumatised. 'They had been moulded by their slaves as their slaves had been moulded by them ... And they wallowed in those deformities which their slaves had thrust upon them in the revenge of historical silence.'[34] Paternalism compelled the slave to be a child, but children could be submissive or fractious, and Genovese's initial title for his book was *Sambo and Nat Turner*. Either way, this particular form of property remained troublesome. A slave stole from another slave but took from his master. The master insisted that the slave lacked gratitude – but dependence excludes gratitude, which implies equality, freely given and freely taken.

Everywhere in Genovese there is dialectical ambivalence and the continuing unfolding of contraries resulting in uncertain and unstable compromises. Economically slavery was pitched somewhere between a peasant society and a factory. Genovese's early writing parallels to some extent the writings of John Cairnes on the economic backwardness of slave societies: the rapid exhaustion of soil under cotton monoculture, the low level of labour productivity, the technological retardation, even the light weight of Southern hogs, all suggested a pre-capitalist semi-feudal order. There was not, and could not be, an industrial revolution in the South. Up to 1860 the South continued to provide a primary staple for the mills of New England and of Europe. The South could boast only two large cities, Baltimore and New Orleans, and few towns with a population over 15,000. Influenced by the writings of Marx and the English economist Maurice Dobb, Genovese depicted the South as a merchant capital venturer, buying and selling produce but not hiring labour in the market place to provide those products. Herbert Gutman, a one-time colleague at the University of Rochester, convinced Genovese of the profitability of slavery in the bourgeois market place of mid-nineteenth-century America, but high profitability was not incompatible with general economic retardation. Like India in the nineteenth century or Saudi Arabia in the twentieth, the South was both inside and outside the capitalist mould: it advocated free trade but not free labour; it operated in a highly competitive market but the world of the market slave was a quintessentially non-market relationship. Genovese distinguished between three types of capitalism. The first, exemplified by the United Fruit Company in the Caribbean, consisted of informal economic penetration of a country. The second, typified by the British West Indies, was that of a colonial plantation economically and politically subservient to the mother country. The third was the independent slave economy of the South. 'The plantation society that had begun as the appendage of British capitalism ended as a powerful, largely autonomous, aristocratic civilisation, although it was tied to the capitalist world by bonds of commodity production.' It was because the mature capitalism of wage labour in the North was 'a revolutionary solvent of social relations' that the pre-eminent pro-slave advocate of the South, George Fitzhugh, attacked it so vehemently. Appealing to Filmer's *Patriarcha*, against the atomic rational contract theory of Locke, Hobbes and Jefferson, Fitzhugh rejected the economics of *laissez-faire*. 'If all men had been created equal,' he wrote, 'all would have been competitors, rivals and enemies.' In the South the patriarch did not claim his authority over wife, child and slave by means of consent. The South's organic social culture clashed inexorably with the atomistic economics of Northern capitalism. 'Only a Herculean suspension of disbelief,' Genovese concluded, 'could cast them as rational capitalist entrepreneurs.'[35]

The hegemonic power of Southern legal codes reflected a similar ambivalence. The rational bourgeois law of contract and tort assumed an equality of labour in the market place which was directly contradicted by the institution of slavery. As in economics, Southern law had, somehow, to graft patriarchal ideas of property and power on to a rationalist jurisprudence of contract. If the slave was property he constituted a very odd form of property indeed. Judge Green of the Tennessee Supreme Court declared in 1846 that 'A slave is not in the condition of a horse. He has mental capacities, and an immortal principle in his nature that constitute him equal to his owner, but for the accidental position in which fortune has placed him.' But how did this statement square with Judge Thomas Ruffin of North Carolina's judgement of 1829?

> The end [of slavery] is the profit of the master, his security and public safety; the subject, one doomed in his own person, and his posterity, to live without knowledge, and without the capacity to make anything his own, and to toil that another might reap the fruits ... Such services can only be expected from one who has no will of his own, who surrenders his will in implicit obedience to that of another. Such obedience is a consequence only of uncontrolled authority over the body. There is nothing else which can operate to produce the effect. The power of the master must be absolute to render the submission of the slave absolute.[36]

The Black Codes never resolved this dichotomy of 'human property', and once more Genovese illustrates how paternalistic jurisprudence could operate to the advantage of the slave. The codes insisted that no black could offer testimony against a white man in court. In practice this meant, as a case in 1840 in Louisiana showed, that a white man who incited slaves to revolt had to be acquitted because black depositions were inadmissible in a court of law.

Likewise in his rich exploration of black religion Genovese depicts slaves conquering the religion of those who conquered them. Like Marx, Genovese holds that religion is both an opiate and 'the heart of a heartless world'.[37] It offered spiritual if not political strength. The slave moulded his own unique body of faith by which to attest and affirm his autonomy. Unlike the quietistic otherworldly religion whites attempted to impose upon the slave, with its promise of rewards stored up in heaven, the blacks' religion was firmly of this world: 'God is not the God of the dead but of the living' (Matthew). They were God's oppressed but chosen people, waiting, like the Hebrew captives in Egypt, for Moses to lead them out of Pharaoh's bondage into the land of Canaan. As Moses would deliver his people, so Jesus would save their souls. They were being tested, not punished, for the crucifixion of Christ was followed by his resurrection and by the resurrection of the world. Nor were they gulled. Their intense understanding of divine authority put human authority into perspective. They would render to God, as Jesus admonished, those things which were God's and would not serve Caesar alone. Divine providence would ultimately right the wrongs of their unjust temporal enslavement. 'Be not deceived; God is not mocked; for whatsoever a man soweth, that shall he also reap' (Galatians).

In all matters of black culture, such as the particular role of house mammy and the ambivalent status of overseer, Genovese writes with intelligence and insight, reconstructing a complex human tapestry. *Roll, Jordan, Roll* is, without doubt, a masterpiece and the finest single work on the slave world. There was also a hidden agenda: although black religion was essentially prepolitical, Genovese saw the roots of black nationalism in the common religion forged by the black slave community. Just as Genovese accused Fogel and Engerman of espousing an integrationist model of master and slave collaboration effectively to maximise profits, so Genovese was accused by David Donald of being the 'house honky'. David Brion Davis, in a review of *Roll, Jordan, Roll*, suggested that 'his professed Marxism may no longer provide protective coloration against the charge of sentimentalising and romanticising slavery'. On a less serious level, Vann Woodward suggested that had Genovese grown up in the South he would not have waxed so lyrical over the culinary joys of homminy grits, and Kenneth Lynn has written a critical piece on him irreverently entitled 'Smelling the magnolias with Massa Gene'.[38]

Much of this was unfair. In one sense Genovese had taken interpretations from previous historians to weld a new and persuasive understanding of the peculiar institution: from Phillips the crucial unifying concept of paternalism; from Elkins, shorn of his extremism, the recognition that bondage had resulted in some degree of psychological damage; from Fogel and Engerman the appreciation that, with the ending of the slave trade and the emergence of the cotton boom, the slave enjoyed comparatively good material standards. Genovese's ideology combined with his empirical research made him stand back from the image of the 'Teflon' slave – a positive depiction of slave culture untouched and unaffected by any negative influences – and here Genovese was to have harsh words about Herbert Gutman's study of the slave family, which depicted that nuclear institution as essentially self-contained and distinct, untouched by the crushing weight of the master class. Genovese's own study of the slave family was in terms of hegemonic control – that stable families tended to make compliant slaves – but to which could be added the ultimate threat of separation to compel submission.

Genovese has always displayed a profound ambivalence about the world the slave owner made.

> The inhumanity they condemned must still be condemned; and the values for which they fought still have something to offer. How easy ... for us to judge them as cynics who rationalised a system of exploitation, or as rusty windbags who talked nonsense, or as thoughtless reactionaries of no account. They were all of these, but none. However guilty they may have been on each count, they did nonetheless stand for a world different from our own that is worthy of our sympathetic attention. The questions they asked are still with us.

David Brion Davies is on firmer ground when he tackles Genovese's growing infatuation with the South. Genovese has become increasingly critical of northern neo-abolitionists, who, he maintains, fail to understand or empathise with the South: Northern victory in 1865 ended a distinctly Southern mode of interpreting America and a predominant Southern critique of liberalism. This is odd, given the Southern domination of Civil War studies until mid century: it also comes perilously close to saying that the Yankee is disqualified from any serious worthwhile criticism and that the South has been wise in matters of race. This, ironically, is not dissimilar to black nationalist attacks on Genovese and their insistence that he should stick to Italian immigrant history – a suggestion which Genovese rightly took exception to. In *The Southern Tradition* (1996) and *The*

Slaveholders' Dilemma (1992) Genovese returned to the abrasive pro-Southern arguments of J.H. Hammond, Thomas Dew, Edmund Ruffin and George Fitzhugh, and argued that, shorn of slavery and racism, their searing critique of liberal capitalist tendencies still holds good. Throughout his long career Genovese has entertained a strong dislike of the sterile corporate America of endless individual consumerism and a fragmented, alienated society. Just as Fitzhugh depicted slavery as a form of benign communitarian hierarchy in opposition to the vicious exploitative and soulless wage labour of the North, so Genovese's nostalgia harks back to the coarser anti-capitalism of the 1930s agrarian school. In an odd, roundabout way Genovese, like Fitzhugh, has become the 'Marx of the master class'. He is now settled in Atlanta, Georgia, and admits to Southern partisanship: 'Get your heart in Dixie or get your ass out.' He continues to argue against judging the planter class but passes endless moral judgements on contemporary American capitalism. He argues unfailingly for academic courtesy and dispassion, then excoriates those on the left who dare to part company with him. He remains an engaging and controversial historian. As Genovese himself has written, 'While opposed to ideological history and presentism, I've never written a line that has not been, in George Rawick's phrase, "a political intervention".'[39]

Genovese's colleague at Rochester, Herbert Gutman, had written extensively on the nineteenth and twentieth-century culture of immigrant labour before turning his attention to the slave family. *The Black Family in Freedom and Slavery* (1976) resulted from a provocation. What provoked Gutman was what he took to be the flawed historical assumptions underlying Daniel Moynihan's *The Negro Family – The Case for National Action*. Investigations by his own research students in nearby Buffalo revealed 82–92 per cent double-head kin-related black households. Though not a cliometrician himself he applied quantifiable methods to test how far the black family had survived slavery. His answer, in a book of over a thousand pages, was that, overwhelmingly and remarkably, it had. Quantifying plantation records, kin names, applications for the formalisation of marriages to the Freedmen's Bureau after 1865 and investigations into the testimony offered in court following the outrages of the Klan, he provided substantial evidence to confirm the moving frontispiece – an old group photograph of five generations of a slave family on the Smiths' plantation in Beaufort, South Carolina. Critics accused Gutman of painting too benign, too positive a picture: one, Dan Carter, called the book 'An exercise in wishful thinking and a romanticised portrait'.[40] Genovese criticised it for ignoring the complex interplay between master and slave, and for exaggerating the separate autonomy of a black culture transmitted through the nuclear family.

Since Stampp's pioneering work, and less publicised than the controversial books so far discussed, there has been a slow accretion of historical understanding of the peculiar institution. In his *Slave Community* (1972) John Blassingame, himself a black historian, was the first to make full use of the neglected WPA interviews and was to concentrate more fully on the slave family and depict a rich black culture surviving under adversity. The year 1977 saw the publication of Lawrence Levine's *Black Culture and Black Consciousness*, 1978 Albert Raboteau's *Slave Religion* and Sterling Stuckey's *Black Culture*, subtitled *Nationalist Theories and the Foundation of Black America* (1987), which insisted that 'the humanity of people can be asserted through means other than open and widespread rebellion' and that blacks 'had found a way both to endure and preserve their humanity in the face of insuperable odds'.[41]

It is in the field of black cultural survival that most progress has been made since Stampp. Du Bois had been among the first to look at black spirituals and folklore, and others took up this promising line of investigation. Revealed behind the mask were the Brer Rabbit stories, which repeatedly retold the parable of the weak but crafty outwitting the strong and powerful. It revealed folk songs which ironically undermined and sabotaged the paternalist myth. Another rich area of investigation is in comparative studies: the strategy whereby exploring another slave culture, in time or place, assists self-definition. The early hemispheric comparisons of Richard Klein, Carl Degler and David Brion Davis have grown to embrace illuminating comparisons with South Africa (George Frederickson, *White Supremacy: A Comparative Study in American and South African History*, 1981) and Russian serfdom (Peter Kolchin, *Unfree Labour: American Slavery and*

Russian Serfdom, 1987) and Prussian Junkers (Shearer Bowman, *Masters and Lords: Mid Nineteenth Century US Planters and Prussian Junkers*, 1993). What these comparisons tend to reveal is variability rather than US exceptionalism: the American slaves had the least autonomy along with the highest material standards; sex and race ratios were crucial in shaping different slave societies. The predominance of male slaves, for example, in Central America and South Africa led to higher rates of miscegenation, which blurred racial lines. The documentation of the most silent of all American minorities goes on. In 1972 George Rawick edited the WPA interviews and Ira Berlin is supervising a vast mass of primary material on black emancipation.

Attitudes and the availability of material have both changed dramatically since Phillips wrote. We know far more about the peculiar institution than was the case in 1918 and this says much for the industry of the American historical profession. The subject will always remain immensely contentious; to enter the field is to to enter a minefield. The whole topic is deeply controversial; questions remain unanswered. Did the slave personality survive? Is the topic still approached in a mood of romanticism? Have the historians of black bondage too avidly sought a usable past? Genovese, when dealing with the slaves' response under adversity, does not presume to settle questions once and for all but wisely quotes instead from T.S. Eliot's '*Naming of cats*':

> But above and beyond there is still one name left over,
> And that is the name that you never will guess,
> The name that no human research can discover –
> BUT THE CAT HIMSELF KNOWS and will never confess.

Notes

1 Phillips quoted in Wendell Holmes Stevenson, *The South Lives in History* (New York, 1955), pp. 92, 58, 87.
2 U.B. Phillips, *American Negro Slavery* (New York, 1918), pp. vii, 291. Phillips, *The Slave Economy of the Old South* (Baton Rouge, 1968), p. 274. Phillips, *Life and Labor in the Old South* (Boston, Mass., 1929), p. 161.
3 Peter Novick, *That Noble Dream* (Cambridge, 1988) p. 73.
4 Phillips, *American Negro Slavery*, p. viii.
5 Phillips quoted in Robert Fogel and Stanley Engerman, *Time on the Cross*, II (London, 1974), p. 172; and in Charles Crowe (ed.), *The Age of Civil War and Reconstruction, 1830–1900* (Homewood, Ill., 1975), p. 35.

6 Phillips, *Life and Labor in the Old South*, pp. 196, 198, 199, 201, 202, 203, 204.

7 'The plantation as a civilizing factor' is reprinted in *The Slave Economy of the Old South*.

8 Phillips, *Life and Labor in the Old South*, p. 162.

9 *Ibid.*, p. 205.

10 Channing quoted in Stanley Elkins, *Slavery: A Problem in American Institutional and Intellectual Life* (Chicago, 1959), p. 7 n. 7. Hofstadter quoted in Elkins, *Slavery*, p. 18 n. 23. Snyder quoted in Phillips, *Life and Labor in the Old South*, p. 201.

11 Phillips, *American Negro Slavery*, p. 327.

12 Du Bois quoted in Robert Fogel, *Without Consent or Contract* (New York, 1989), p. 155. Woodson quoted in Fogel and Engerman, *Time on the Cross*, II, p. 195.

13 Kenneth Stampp, *The Peculiar Institution* (New York, 1956), p. vii.

14 *Ibid.*, pp. 4, 6, 14, 103, 399.

15 Phillips, *Life and Labor in the Old South*, p. 215.

16 Weld reprinted in Richard Hofstadter, *Great Issues in American History*, II, *1864–1957* (New York, 1958), pp. 328–9.

17 Stampp quoted in August Meier and Elliott Rudwick, *Black History and the Historical Profession, 1915–1980* (Urbana, 1986), p. 109.

18 Stampp, *The Peculiar Institution*, p. 85.

19 *Ibid.*, p. 303. Fogel and Engerman, *Time on the Cross*, II, p. 225.

20 Elkins, *Slavery*, p. 93.

21 *Ibid.*, p. 132.

22 *Ibid.*, p. 317.

23 The word 'proposal' appears on p. 224; the section on 'Analogy as evidence' on p. 250.

24 A.H. Conrad and J.R. Meyer, 'The economics of slavery in the antebellum South', reprinted in Peter Temin (ed.), *New Economic History* (Harmondsworth, 1973), p. 357.

25 Fogel and Engerman, *Time on the Cross*, I, p. 6.

26 *Ibid.*, II, p. 5.

27 R.H. Campbell and A.S. Skinner (eds), Adam Smith, *An Inquiry into the Nature and Causes of the Wealth of Nations*, I (Oxford, 1976), pp. 98–9.

28 Fogel and Engerman quoted in *The New York Review of* Books, Vol. 21, No. 5, p. 4.

29 Barrow's Journal quoted in Paul David *et al.* (eds), *Reckoning with Slavery* (Oxford, 1976), pp. 68, 91, 92.

30 Peter Parish, *Slavery: History and Historians* (New York, 1989), p. 35.

31 *Ibid.*, p. 40. David, *Reckoning with Slavery*, p. 30.

32 Genovese quoted in Michael Kraus and Davis Joyce, *The Writing of American History* (Norman, Okla., 1983), p. 350.

33 Eugene Genovese, *In Red and Black* (New York, 1972), p. 408.

34 Eugene Genovese, *Roll, Jordan, Roll* (New York, 1976), p. xvi. Genovese in Ann Lane (ed.), *The Debate over Slavery* (Urbana, Ill., 1971), p. 294.

35 Genovese in Allen Weinstein and F.O. Gatell (eds), *American Negro Slavery* (London, 1968), p. 284. David Brion Davis quoting Genovese in *The New*

York Review of Books (42:15, 1995), p. 44. Eugene and Elizabeth Fox-Genovese in J. William Harris (ed.), *Society and Culture in the Slave South* (London, 1992), p. 36.

36 Genovese, *Roll, Jordan, Roll*, pp. 28, 35.

37 Karl Marx quoted in Weinstein and Gatell, *American Negro Slavery*, p. 267.

38 David Brion Davis, *From Homicide to Slavery* (New York, 1986), p. 201. Kenneth Lynn, *The Airline to Seattle* (Chicago, 1983), p. 205.

39 Crowe, *The Age of Civil War and Reconstruction*, p. 53. Genovese, *The Southern Tradition: The Achievement and Limitations of an American Conservatism* (Cambridge, Mass., 1996), p. ix. Genovese quoted in Lynn, *The Airline to Seattle*, p. 205. It was Richard Hofstadter who applied the phrase 'Marx of the master class' to Calhoun.

40 Dan Carter, review in *Reviews in American History* (5, 1977), p. 169.

41 Stuckey quoted in Meier and Rudwick, *Black History and the Historical Profession*, p. 158.

Selective bibliography

Blassingame, John, *The Slave Community: Plantation Life in the Antebellum South* (New York, 1972).

Bowman, Shearer, *Masters and Lords: Mid Nineteenth Century U.S. Planters and Prussian Junkers* (New York, 1993).

Carter, Dan, 'Moonlight, magnolias, and Collard Greens: black history and the new romanticism', *Reviews in American History* (5, 1977).

Conrad, A.H. and Meyer, J.R., 'The economics of slavery in the ante-bellum South' reprinted in Peter Temin (ed.), *New Economic History* (Harmondsworth, 1973).

David, Paul, Gutman, Herbert, Sutch, Richard, Temin, Peter, and Wright, Gavin (eds), *Reckoning with Slavery* (Oxford, 1976).

Davis, David Brion, 'Slavery and the post World War Two historians' in his *From Homicide to Slavery* (New York, 1986).

Davis, David Brion, 'Southern comfort', *The New York Review of Books* (42:15, 1995).

Degler, Carl, *Neither Black nor White: Slavery and Race Relations in Brazil and the United States* (New York, 1971).

Elkins, Stanley, *Slavery: A Problem in American Institutional and Intellectual Life* (Chicago, 1959).

Fogel, Robert, *Without Consent or Contract* (New York, 1989).

Fogel, Robert, and Engerman, Stanley, *Time on the Cross* (2 vols, London, 1974).

Frederickson, George, 'From exceptionalism to variability: recent development in cross-national comparative history', *Journal of American History* (82:4, 1995).

Frederickson, George, *The Arrogance of Race* (Middletown, Conn., 1988).

Frederickson, George, *White Supremacy: A Comparative Study in American and South African History* (New York, 1981).

Genovese, Eugene, *In Red and Black* (New York, 1972).

Genovese, Eugene, *Roll, Jordan, Roll* (New York, 1976).

Genovese, Eugene, *The Political Economy of Slavery* (New York, 1967).

Genovese, Eugene, *The Slaveholder's Dilemma* (Columbia, S.Ca., 1992).

Genovese, Eugene, *The Southern Tradition: The Achievement and Limitations of an American Conservatism* (Cambridge, Mass., 1996).

Genovese, Eugene, *The World the Slaveowner Made* (London, 1970).

Gutman, Herbert, *The Black Family in Slavery and Freedom, 1750–1925* (Oxford, 1976).

Harris, J. William (ed.), *Society and Culture in the Slave South* (London, 1992).

Klein, Herbert, *Slavery in the Americas: A Comparative Study of Virginia and Cuba* (Chicago, 1967).

Kolchin, Peter, 'American historians and Antebellum Southern slavery, 1959–1984' in William J. Cooper, Michael Holt and John McCardell (eds), *A Master's Due: Essays in Honor of David Donald* (Baton Rouge, 1985).

Kolchin, Peter, 'Comparing American History', *Reviews in American History* (10:4, 1982).

Kolchin, Peter, *American Slavery* (Harmondsworth, 1993).

Kolchin, Peter, *Unfree Labor: American Slavery and Russian Serfdom* (Cambridge, Mass., 1987).

Lane, Ann (ed.), *The Debate over Slavery* (Urbana, Ill., 1971).

Levine, Lawrence, *Black Culture and Black Consciousness* (New York, 1977).

Owens, Leslie, *This Species of Property: Slave Life and Culture in the Old South* (New York, 1976).

Parish, Peter, *Slavery: History and Historians* (New York, 1989).

Phillips, Ulrich Bonner, *American Negro Slavery* (New York, 1918).

Phillips, Ulrich Bonner, *Life and Labour in the old South* (Boston, Mass., 1929).

Phillips, Ulrich Bonner, *The Slave Economy of the old South: Selected Essays in Economic and Social History* (Baton Rouge, 1968).

Raboteau, Albert, *Slave Religion: The 'Invisible Institution' in the Antebellum South* (New York, 1978).

Rawick, George, *From Sundown to Sunup: The Making of the Black Community* (Westport, Conn., 1972).

Stampp, Kenneth, 'The historian and Southern Negro slavery', *American Historical Review* (63, 1958).

Stampp, Kenneth, *The Imperiled Union* (Oxford, 1980).

Stampp, Kenneth, *The Peculiar Institution* (New York, 1956).

Stevenson, Wendell Holmes, *The South Lives in History* (New York, 1955).

Stuckey, Sterling, *Slave Culture* (New York, 1987).

Temin, Peter (ed.), *New Economic History* (Harmondsworth, 1973).

Tipton Jr, Frank, and Walker, Clarence, review of R. Fogel and S. Engerman, *Time on the Cross*, in *History and Theory* (14, 1975).

Weinstein, Allen, and Gatell, F.O. (eds), *American Negro Slavery: A Modern Reader* (London, 1968).

Woodward, C. Vann, review of E. Genovese, *Roll, Jordan, Roll*, in *The New York Review of Books* (21:5, 1974).

3

Abolitionism

The historiography of the abolitionist movement has been one of deification followed by neglect and denigration, then finally vindication. An early providential history depicted the abolitionists rousing a torpid nation to fight the gross evil of slavery, of Lincoln and the North taking up the summons to purge the nation of its guilt, emancipate the slave and remove, once and for all, the stigma of racism from the historical record.

Throughout its history the abolitionist movement had to struggle with a variety of strategies to achieve its end – the emancipation of slaves and the setting up of the freedmen on an equal footing with white citizens. As Howard Temperley, the English historian, has written, it was easier for the abolitionists to agree about ends than about means, which could often seem vague, contradictory and impractical, owing to the seemingly insuperable obstacles the movement faced. It was because slavery was embedded in the fabric of the Constitution and of the Union that Garrison, one of the more extreme abolitionists, advocated the pursuit of a higher law above and beyond the Constitution, and disunion. By the 1830s a militant South had become implacably opposed to emancipation (the state of Georgia, for example, offered a $500 reward for the abduction of Garrison) while the North, with the exception of about 1 per cent of the population, remained indifferent or negrophobe. Tocqueville observed in his *Democracy in America* that racial prejudice was stronger in the North than in the South, and although only 1 per cent of the North's population were blacks, they were discriminated against, disfranchised and segregated. In 1813 Illinois territory passed a law which ordered every incoming free black to leave the territory under penalty of thirty lashes repeated every fifteen days until he or she left, and in its original constitution Oregon, which joined the Union as a free state in 1859, forbade black immigrants from entering it. Added to this was the problem of what was to be done if and when the black was emancipated, for it was widely assumed, both North and South, that the two races could not live amicably together and that race warfare would ensue inevitably. In 1817 the American Colonisation Society was established as a solution to this problem and luminaries such as Jefferson, Madison, Clay and Lincoln supported its aim to transport the black to Africa. But increasingly this policy was rejected as a moral evasion and various strategies of gradual and compensated emancipation were considered till the more radical wing of abolitionists adopted immediatism as its central doctrine. The emancipation of British West Indian slaves in 1833 and the intransigence of Southern slave owners contributed to this change of heart, but it was a central insistence upon the evil of slavery and a refusal to compromise with it, or accommodate to it, which held Garrison and his followers together. On 1 January 1831 Garrison issued the first number of his paper, *The Liberator*, and publicly recanted the pernicious doctrine of gradualism. Yet many abolitionists did not subscribe to Garrison's radical trajectory, which, with its accompanying anticlericalism, feminism and pacifism moved logically and inexorably towards a form of Christian anarchy. Rather the movement was made up of a large spectrum ranging from Garrison's absolutism at one end to those who advocated political means and co-operation within the existing party system on the other. A belief in gradual reform, exerting pressure through party voting, led first to the establishment of the Liberty party (1844) then of the Free Soil party (1848), which ran Martin Van Buren and Charles Francis Adams as their candidates and polled 14.4 per cent of the Northern vote while failing to gain a single electoral college vote, then to the creation of the Republican party in the aftermath of the Kansas–Nebraska controversy, which led finally to the candidacy and election of Lincoln as President on a platform committed to the non-extension of slavery. It was the fundamental division over whether abolitionists should dabble in partisan politics which led to the major split in their ranks in 1840 with the anti-Garrisonians forming the American and Foreign Anti-slavery society. But it would be wrong to see the Garrisonian wing as bearing the torch of emancipation alone. The history of the movement was a history of sectarian splinterings with many whose awareness of the evil of slavery was heightened by the rhetoric of its leaders swelling the ranks of political reformism, voting for the Free Soil party, engaging in postal campaigns, rallies, assisting the underground railroad, helping runaways to escape, flouting the fugitive slave laws which were tightened in 1850 and fighting the gag rule in Congress. All these were practical activities outside the private pursuit of Garrisonian perfectionism. The historians' response to the abolitionist movement was to be shaped, then, not primarily by judging the movement's ends, but rather by assessing the legitimacy of the various means employed to achieve those ends. Radical historians would approve of radical strategies: conservative historians would, in turn, condemn them and judge them harshly.

The earliest writings on the movement, by Richard Hildreth, Charles Ticknor, Horace Greeley, Henry Wilson, Joshua Giddings and George Julian, many of them personally involved as abolitionists and radical Republicans, were largely uncritical and moulded in their views by teleological considerations. But increasingly, in the aftermath of the failure of Southern Reconstruction, doubts and criticisms grew.

Henry Wilson, senator for Massachusetts and later Grant's Vice-president, was a Republican party politician puzzled by the 'practical solecism' of Garrison's rejection of political reformism.[1] His *History of the Rise and Fall of the Slave Power in America* (1873) interpreted the era in essentially partisan terms. The Missouri compromise of 1820 was a victory for the slave power, opening up the south-west with the extension of the black Cotton Belt, and Jackson's election in 1828 over the New Englander, John Quincy Adams, established the domination of the Democratic party and the slave interest until 1860. How did the abolitionists react to this power struggle? Under the predominant influence of Garrison, abolitionists fought the political evil of slavery by rejecting politics; sought change yet rejected co-operation with the Republican party; promoted the efficacy of 'moral suasion' yet rejected the authority of the Church. Thus, for all his boldness and dedication, Garrison went against the common patriotism, partisanship and religious sentiments of the majority of his countrymen in the North, and marginalised his cause.

James Schouler, the epitome of Gilded Age complacency, was sharper in his critique. Abolitionists, in their questioning of the rights to property in the form of slave ownership, of the Union and of the Constitution, were anarchists who threatened the very foundations of the state. In the fourth volume of his *History of the United States under the Constitution* (1889), which was published three years after the Haymarket riots in Chicago, when bombs were thrown, eleven people died and 'anarchists' were put on trial for the outrage, Garrison, despite his pacifism, was referred to as a 'bomb thrower'. The anti-abolitionist mobs who threatened Garrison's life were ignorant and vicious but, Schouler insisted, also sterling patriots combating wild nihilism. Those mobs, not the abolitionists, were the true embodiment of American values. 'Antipathy to weaker men and races, and a dogged attachment to property as something with which none others are to interfere, save as their own property may be injured by it, are two strong traits of the Anglo-Saxon.'[2] James Ford Rhodes, writing in 1892, while more measured, saw fit to play down abolitionist radicalism while praising its impact in rousing the Northern conscience and laying the foundations of a triumphant Republican party.

By the turn of the century not only the influence of the radical abolitionists was downplayed but also the Constitution's fatal compromise with slavery. The early historians of abolitionism had interpreted the Constitution as a counter-revolutionary document undermining the claims of the Declaration of Independence to universal equality, and arguing that this tension remained unresolved until the Civil War. In 1903, however, Max Farrand published his highly influential *Framing of the Constitution*, which, though based on Madison's famous notes on the Constitutional Convention of 1787, played down Madison's assertion that free Northern and Southern slave sectionalism was the fundamental split at the convention. Thus around 1900, just as the black was rendered invisible, so the sacred Constitution's accommodation with slavery was rendered equally invisible.

In 1845 Garrison had burnt a copy of the Constitution on the grounds that it represented 'a covenant with death and an agreement with hell'. Max Farrand notwithstanding, the Constitution did recognise the South's peculiar institution: in the cynical three-fifths rule which distributed representation and taxation in the South ('Representatives and direct taxes shall be apportioned among the several States which may be included within this Union, according to their respective numbers, which shall be determined by adding to the whole number of free persons ... three-fifths of all other persons'), in its acceptance that the slave trade could continue until at least 1808, and in the constitutional edict that slaves, as property, had, if they escaped, to be returned to their masters.

It may be thought that progressive historians, wedded to the theme of fundamental conflict and reformism, would have shed new light on a group who were, perhaps, the greatest reformers in American history. But Frederick Jackson Turner, who identified the impulse to radical change as emanating from a western frontier, had little to say about a movement centred in Boston and New York. Charles Beard, who sought the dynamics of change in economic motives, was mystified, admitting that 'the sources of this remarkable movement are difficult to discover'.[3] The abolitionists were activated by deeply held religious beliefs, but then, their enemy, the Southern slave owner, was equally religious. The abolitionists appealed to the secular authority of Jefferson, and the Declaration of Independence which declared all men equal, yet Jefferson was himself a Southern slave owner and his party, the Democratic party, identified increasingly with the slave power. Because Beard was convinced that slavery was not the cause of the Civil War, the abolitionists were assigned a minor and ignominious role. 'Nobody but agitators, beneath the contempt of the towering statesmen of the age, ever dared to advocate Abolitionism.'[4]

Vernon Parrington, in the second volume of his *Main Currents in American Thought*, admired the abolitionists precisely because of their idealism and because they put individual conscience before economic self-interest. Together, he insisted, these reformers attacked the moral indifference and the crass Yankee commercialism which had joined the lords of the loom to the lords of the lash in a demeaning, unholy and materialistic alliance, for, 'as a matter of sober historical fact, they were the kindliest of men, with generous sympathies and disinterested motives'. Parrington wrote positively of the poet John Greenleaf Whittier, Harriet Beecher Stowe, the author of *Uncle Tom's Cabin*, and Garrison, of whom he declared: 'His like has too rarely appeared in America. Arrogant, dictatorial, intolerant, he might be, as his warmest friends admitted, but it is a foolish judgement that will dismiss him thus. Unyielding as granite, sheer Yankee will driven by a passionate energy, he was born for hazardous leadership.' Nor was Garrison ineffectual: rather he was, in particular, the vital link between rhetoric and action responsible for the emancipation of the slave, it being a 'short step from prophet to soldier and from conscience to the Emancipation Proclamation'.[5] But, at the same time, Parrington was not entirely free of Beardian assumptions. His homespun rural radicalism, with its aversion to Northern plutocrats and corrupt trusts, led him into a sympathetic portrayal of those plucky Southern states' rights advocates – Calhoun, Fitzhugh, and Hammond – whose theorising served to strengthen the hand of those lords of the loom whom Parrington ostensibly condemned. This blunted his insights considerably.

In the immediate aftermath of the abortive raid on Harper's Ferry, John Brown was transfigured by Emerson and Thoreau into a Christlike figure. Union soldiers marched to the words 'John Brown's body lies a-mouldering in the grave but his soul goes marching on', and Louisa May Alcott wrote of him that:

> Living, he made life beautiful,
> Dying, made death divine.

The earliest biography, by James Redpath (1860), denied Brown's involvement in the savage killing of five pro-slavery settlers at Pottawatomie Creek in 'Bleeding Kansas', the bloody civil war in Kansas. Other biographers justified the killings on the grounds of self-defence. With the failure of Reconstruction and the general neglect of the black racial problem in America, Brown's reputation, along with that of other abolitionists, slumped. One notable exception was a biography written by Oswald Garrison Villard, the grandson of Garrison, a newspaper editor and, rather surprisingly, a militant pacifist. Villard was a staunch liberal and a dedicated supporter of black rights, helping to establish the National Association for the Advancement of Colored People in 1909. His biography of Brown was to be his contribution to the black cause, celebrating the fiftieth anniversary of Harper's Ferry and the outbreak of civil war. Villard did hold Brown responsible for the bloody crime of Pottawatomie Creek, which was unjustified, despite 'the wealth of self-sacrifice and the nobility of [Brown's] aims', but Harper's Ferry atoned for it. Brown was not a lunatic, as many held, for no madman could have written letters of such singular nobility or met his end so bravely. Throughout Brown was motivated by pure anti-slavery sentiment: imperfect and flawed, perhaps, but immortal. 'His own country, while admitting his mistakes without undue palliation or excuse, will forever acknowledge the divine within him by the side of what was human and faulty and blind and wrong.' In his desire to depict Brown in heroic proportions, Villard sometimes doctored the evidence. In citing a letter from Thomas Wentworth Higginson, one of the Secret Six who funded the raid of 1859, Villard took the phrase 'sly old veteran' but omitted the word 'sly'. This was done in order to avoid the charge, frequently levelled against Brown, that he manipulated the Secret Six, and played one off against another, in order to extract the maximum amount of money for his quixotic venture. Three years later a Kansas politician, Hill Peebles Wilson, was paid by the wife of an ex-governor of Kansas to attack Villard's 'fulsome panygyrics' and destroy the Brown legend.[6] In his *John Brown: Soldier of Fortune* (1913) Brown was depicted as a crook, a horse stealer and an inept businessman who was perpetually in debt and took up the anti-slavery cause merely to mend his fortunes.

The first scholarly and comprehensive historical survey of abolitionism, William Barnes's *The Anti-slavery Impulse* (1933), had little time for either John Brown or for Garrison or for their radicalism. Barnes and his assistant Dwight Dumond were both Mid Westerners and both taught at Michigan, where they studied under Ulrich Bonner Phillips. (Barnes dedicated his book to Phillips.) Together they discovered a large cache of letters in a barn in Allton, Massachusetts, between Theodore Weld and the two Grimké sisters, Angelina and Sarah, which they published in 1934.

Later Dumond went on to discover and publish the James Birney papers too. Their decisive joint influence was to swing the bias of attention on abolitionism away from Boston and New England to the Mid West, and away from Garrison, hitherto considered the leading abolitionist, to the evangelical proselytising of Weld and Charles Grandison Finney, at the Lane and Oberlin seminaries and the 'burnt over' district of western New York State.

Garrison's self-proclaimed leadership of the cause was nothing short of disastrous as far as Barnes was concerned, for he was a man 'of distinctly narrow limitations among the giants of the anti-slavery movement'. Garrison's extremist rhetoric was a liability, for 'the reputation of *The Liberator* was made by its enemies and not by its subscribers'. Personally Garrison was vain and meretricious: 'The head of his offending was his promiscuous vilification of all individuals, institutions and beliefs with which at the moment he did not agree.' His theory of Christian anarchy was reflected in his own anarchic behaviour and his total inability to organise and co-ordinate: 'Once he had tasted the heady wine of anarchism, Garrison drank deep.'[7] His packing of the 1840 Anti-slavery Society Convention had been another total disaster for the cause of emancipation. A separate American and Foreign Anti-slavery Society was established and subscriptions to Garrison's branch fell precipitously. Garrison's anticlericalism had alienated the major wellspring of abolitionist activism and his generalised calls for immediate emancipation did not address the problem of how the freedmen or the white community were supposed to cope with its consequences. His rejection of all political and party activity had earned the censure of ex-President John Quincy Adams, who was nobly fighting against the so-called 'gag rule' which automatically rejected all abolitionist petitions to Congress, between 1836 and 1844. In short, Garrison's contribution was almost wholly destructive and retarded progress towards emancipation.

Barnes and Dumond located the real source of the movement's strength in the evangelical revivalism of the west, and found a new hero in the shape of Theodore Weld. The impulse to reform derived predominantly from a profound religious spirit and the primacy of individual conversion as a preliminary to purging society of sin and of evil. Weld had written that 'Great moral reforms are all born of soul-travail. The starting point and power of every great reform must be the reformer's self. He must first set himself apart, its sacred devotee, baptised into its spirit, consecrated to its service, feeling its profound necessity, its constraining motives, impelling causes, and all reasons why.'[8] Immediate conversion would awaken consciences, which would, in turn, lead to the gradual eradication of the sin of slavery: this, Barnes suggested, was a far more sensible interpretation of imme-diatism than Garrison's. In place of Garrison's counterproductive rhetoric, Weld urged missionaries to go forth and preach the gospel and wrote solid, detailed, highly influential tracts such as *Slavery As It Is* to spread the message abroad.

The new gospel had moved away from the harsh Calvinistic doctrine of predestination and located a degree of freewill within each individual. The necessity of self-control, and a recognition of moral autonomy, operated for Weld both in his courtship and marriage of Angelina Grimké in 1839, and in his insistence upon the fundamental evil of one individual attempting to control and own another. 'The fact that a person intensely desires power over others, without restraint, shows the absolute necessity of restraint.' Both Barnes and Dumond stressed the example of British immediatism – 'In moral even more than in literary affairs, this country was still a British province' – and depicted the move-ment as eminently practical and pragmatic and effective.[9]

It co-ordinated the flooding of Congress with anti-slavery petitions and immeasurably widened the campaign by exposing and publicising the Southern politicians' infringement of civil liberties when it enforced the 'gag rule' in Congress. It also organ-ised the campaign against the fugitive slave laws as reinforced after 1850. Despite Garrison's apolitical stance many abolition-ists, as part of the electorate, voted for the Liberty and Free Soil parties which in turn swelled the ranks of the Republican party in 1856 and 1860. Party politicians like Ben Wade, Henry Wilson and Charles Sumner became advocates who, inspired by the aboli-tionists, turned to argue the case against slavery in the halls of Congress. The ideology of abolitionism began to permeate the speeches of Republican leaders, as illustrated in 1858 by Seward's 'Irrepressible conflict' speech and Lincoln's 'House divided' speech.

Dumond's *Anti-slavery Origins of the Civil War* appeared in 1939 and his vast *Anti-slavery* in 1961. In 1949 he became president of the Mississippi Valley Historical Association and in his presidential address drew attention to the parallels between the slave power's threat to civil liberties in the mid 1840s and 1850s and current Cold War McCarthyism. The Barnes–Dumond approach had the singular advantage of being straightforward and simple. The stress fell on Weld's moral evangelism, not on Garrison's militancy or Brown's resort to violence. Conscientious reformers highlighted the evils of slavery, converted a majority of Northerners, and emancipation came in a violent struggle with the slave power. The stress throughout was on morality and on morality vindicated. Quite simply 'The anti-slavery movement was an intellectual and religious crusade for moral reform.' But to David Potter Dumond's writing was simply a vast abolitionist tract : it was erudite but lacked subtlety and perspective, while to Vann Woodward, Dumond was 'a modern primitive, à Henri Rousseau of historiography'.[10]

Perhaps Barnes and Dumond were too simpleminded and too singleminded, but Potter's and Van Woodward's milder reservations reflected the revisionist historians' general contempt for the abolitionists. If the Civil War had been wholly repressible, then who needlessly brought it about? If the Civil War, rather than slavery, was an unmitigated evil (the revisionists held that slavery was dying out naturally) the abolitionists, who raised sectional antagonism to an unparalleled height of venom, were largely to blame for the disaster. Self-serving politicians contributed to the conflict by exploiting sectional prejudice and buying votes, but abolitionists were primarily to blame for creating paranoid antagonism in the first place. The revisionists appeared to blame the movement for overmoralising or overpersonalising the issue: once the question of right arose, the question of wrong was also raised, and their central charge against the abolitionists was one of moral absolutism: their insistence upon immediatism and their refusal to compromise or to accommodate. Avery Craven believed the trouble all began when slavery started to be looked upon not as a social evil, which he admitted it was, but as a personal sin perpetrated by each slave owner, for which he had earnestly and instantly to be purged. Ends, he maintained, did not justify means, and the militant strategies employed by the abolitionists were inadmissible and unacceptable. 'Mere desire to do "right",' Craven wrote, 'is no defence at the bar of history.' Fletcher Green – like Craven, a Southerner – appeared to believe that the question of right or wrong, of morality, was illicit and had no place in history in the first place. Reviewing one of Allan Nevins's Civil War volumes, he wrote that 'Like the Abolitionists of the period of which he writes, Nevins seems to be blinded by his sense of moral values.' The abolitionists were primarily to blame for the war because it was they, not the Southerners, who had initiated the sectional divide. Here the chronology is vital: first the initial abolitionist crusade; only secondly the fire-eaters' vehement defence of the peculiar institution. The economic viability of slavery was being questioned in the South, the revisionists insisted. The Virginia state legislature was debating the possibility of emancipation when in 1831 *The Liberator* struck like lightning and humiliated, hurt and wounded Southern pride and forced it to retaliate by tightening up the slave codes and suppressing abolitionist literature and free speech. Craven spoke of Southern intellectual life after 1830 as 'almost frozen, not so much to justify a questionable labour system, as to repel a fanatical attack'. And again abolitionists 'threatened to produce a race problem which had in large part been solved by the institution of slavery'. Craven took the opportunity of drawing the revisionist moral when he reviewed Barnes's book:

> When war broke out between the sections in 1861 Northern men were called out to shoot Southerners. They could do this only for the glory of God and the well-being of mankind. The abolitionist contention that slavery was a crime and slaveholders criminal supplied the moral force needed. The despised or ignored fanatic suddenly became 'respectable' and his distorted attitudes the justification for a holy war. His reward was a place in history so mythical as to justify the charge of 'lies agreed to'.[11]

Mutual misunderstanding, growing estrangement and unreasoning paranoia between North and South were fuelled by the brutal fanaticism of abolitionist language and literature. Frank Owsley in 1940 compared abolitionist propaganda with Nazi propaganda: 'neither Dr Goebbels nor Virginio Gayda nor

Stalin's propaganda agents have as yet been able to plumb the depths of vulgarity and obscenity reached and maintained' by the abolitionists.[12] Coyly he insisted that their language was too indecent to quote from, nor does he quote from the fiery counter-rhetoric of Southern fire-eaters, though he does insist that their language was invariably urbane and restrained, while that of the Northern abolitionists was coarse and obscene. Craven conceded that Southern fire-eaters such as Yancey and Rhett did contribute to the secession fever but, essentially, they were reacting, not initiating the sectional divide. It was the abolitionists who had to take the lion's share of the blame. So successful were the revisionists in getting their point of view into the historical mainstream that, as Fawn Brodie pointed out, Senator Sumner's brief, indelicate reference to a fellow senator, Andrew Butler of South Carolina (which led to his brutal beating by Butler's nephew soon afterwards) was invariably quoted in textbooks, while Butler's thirty-six-odd vituperative speeches, pro-slavery and full of contemptuous references to Sumner, were invariably ignored. The revisionists were imposing an insidious double standard.

Then again, what was all the fuss about, the revisionists asked? Why were the abolitionists poisoning and charging the political discourse of the age when slavery was plainly a dying institution? The abolitionists made a great to-do about the extension of slavery westward, yet the number of slaves in the western territories was negligible. And what of the abolitionists' indictment of the fugitive slave laws which required all citizens to assist in the kidnapping and return of runaway slaves? After 1850 only 803 runaways were forcibly returned to their owners, one-fiftieth of one per cent of the total slave population, as J.G. Randall pointed out.

The revisionist strategy of shifting criticism away from those who owned slaves to those who attacked slave owners applied to causes and motives as well as to consequences. Craven hinted, without providing any evidence, at economic self-interest. The abolitionists 'substituted the southern planter for all aristocracies and all sinners and waged a bitter conflict for [their] own material ends in the name of morality and democracy'.[13] Many revisionists discerned a thread of duplicity running through the abolitionist ranks, culminating in the radical Republicans during

Reconstruction, whose primary aim was to economically invade, divide and conquer the South and turn it into a satellite of Northern commercial interests. More effective still was to accuse the abolitionists of being neurotic, mad and unhinged. If their campaign was essentially irrational, which it was, then surely they must have been activated by irrational impulses? Bastard Freudianism and psychotherapy were popular in America at the time, and the revisionists hunted through the textbook jargon of psychopathology to specify various abolitionist mental disorders: repressed desires, erotic sublimation, psychic maladies and distortions, inferiority complexes and identity crises. The general assumption was that the private and the public were not entirely separable: that various interior tensions could be resolved and relieved only by acting them out in the public sphere of politics and the religion of agitation. Removing the mote from one's brother's eye, Craven wrote, was an ancient practice, and illustrates the abolitionists' pharisaical triumph of emotion over reason. Today, he continued, people like Garrison would be handed straight over to a psychiatrist for extensive treatment, for his hatred of the South was far deeper and more compelling than his love of the black, and was indicative of a deep psychological malaise. David Donald in the first volume of his biography of Charles Sumner, which appeared in 1960, located sexual impotence, latent homosexuality and a sick escapism as the basic motives in his reform politics. Perversely Sumner fed off martyrdom, opposition, masochism, suffering and pain. 'This holy blissful martyr thrived upon his torment.' Social maladjustment was a wider variation on individual psychological maladjustment. Craven, seeking to explain abolitionism 'not entirely in terms of the reactions of a few sensitive souls to well understood evil', sought an explanation in reformers having terrible trouble adjusting in a period of rapid social and economic change.[14]

David Donald argued for this thesis in a highly influential article, 'Toward a reconsideration of abolitionism' of 1956. While conceding the impact of religious revivalism and the British example, Donald was disturbed by the ferocity of abolitionist rhetoric and suggested that when a patient reacted so excessively to so mild a stimulus an enlightened doctor would diagnose a deep-seated trauma. Taking 250 leading abolitionists and analysing 106 of them in detail, he found that in 1831 their median age was twenty-nine – here was a revolt of the young – predominantly New Englanders (85 per cent) and predominantly Whigs. Their fathers tended, on the whole, to be respectable and distinguished leaders of society but that leadership had been swept away by levelling Jacksonian democracy, and their joining the abolitionist ranks was the bitter protest of a class which had been politically, economically and socially displaced. This agitation was, then, less a disinterested crusade for moral enlightenment than a form of personal and social self-fulfilment, apsychological adjustment against both the Southern planter and the new moneyed aristocracy of the Northern textile manufacturers who had peremptorily replaced them. 'They were,' Donald concluded, 'an elite without function, a dispossessed class in American society ... Basically, abolitionism should be considered the anguished protest of an aggrieved class against a world they never made.'[15] Although this article was replete with sweeping assertions based on limited empirical evidence (Donald honestly admitted that his statistics were based on impressionistic evidence and his judgements were subjective) the article held enormous sway and represented the crest of the wave of revisionist thinking on abolitionism. Donald, though settling finally at Harvard, hailed from Mississippi, and was responsible, along with J.G. Randall, for revising later editions of the standard American textbook on the Civil War and the Reconstruction era which did much to reflect revisionist leanings. The first volume of his Sumner biography located that reformer's motivation in disturbing and deep-seated neuroses. The second volume, which appeared in 1970, was to modify this picture considerably and adapt to the more positive interpretation of the abolitionists which began to appear in the late 1960s. But Donald's central assumption that the agitation was prompted by psychological maladjustment, and that the malady was located in the individual agitator and not in society as a whole, was a hallmark of the revisionist school.

Revisionists had been influenced by the writings of the political scientist Harold Lasswell, whose *Psychopathology and Politics* (1930) had argued that interior frustration and aggression frequently led to exterior, public agitation. Another source of influence derived from a body of social scientists such as Seymour

Martin Lipset and Daniel Bell, who attempted to explain the radical right's support for McCarthyism in the late 1940s and early 1950s. Status insecurity and dislocation in a theoretically egalitarian society had been noted as early as the 1830s by the French visitor Alexis de Tocqueville. Richard Hofstadter explored this historical tradition of status anxiety, populism and anti-intellectualism in America. Hofstadter's chosen area of research was post-Reconstruction, and in his *Age of Reform* (1955) he made much use of status anxiety to explain the origins of such reform movements as mugwumpery, populism and progressivism. But just as Hofstadter was the first to challenge the racist mytholologies of Phillips, so Hofstadter, in a chapter devoted to the abolitionist Wendell Phillips, in his *American Political Tradition* (1948) was among the first to challenge the revisionist critique of abolitionism. Beginning with the sentence 'The historical reputation of Wendell Phillips stands very low', he went on to suggest that Wendell Phillips was the most impressive abolitionist: that he was right to challenge Garrison's doctrine of non-resistance, right to work for the improved conditions in Northern wage labour and right to press for the granting of the franchise to the freedmen. Critics had stressed the pornographic, salacious exaggeration of Phillips's rhetoric, but selectively, and to blacken his reputation. 'The South,' they quoted him as saying, 'is one great brothel, where half a million are flogged to prostitution,' while omitting the rest of the sentence, 'or, worse still, are degraded to believe it honourable'. Here Wendell Phillips was stressing the psychological as well as physical harm slavery inflicted on the female slave. Having noted how the historian Ulrich Bonner Phillips had played down miscegenation, Hofstadter knew, too, that Wendell Phillips's abolitionist rhetoric was not entirely false either. Under the subtitle 'The patrician as agitator' Hofstadter concluded that 'The agitator is necessary to a republican commonwealth; he is the counterweight to sloth and indifference.'[16] What is remarkable – and I suspect Hofstadter was prompted, in part, by the current climate of complacency and unthinking support from McCarthyism – is that Hofstadter was returning to an earlier, more radical tradition which identified the militant as honourable and an apathetic North and pro-slave South as dishonourable. Hofstadter's essay was prescient and was to be the prelude to a radical reappraisal of abolitionism in the 1960s.

Stanley Elkins's controversial book on slavery caused, as we have already seen, an immense stir among the historical profession, but he offered an equally controversial, some might say perverse, interpretation of the abolitionists. The abolitionists themselves could not have been more damning of the peculiar institution than Elkins was, yet he was highly critical of the abolitionists because they had palpably failed to match the right means to the ends they desired. He accused them of being anti-institutional and excessively individualistic, abstract, unworldly and guilt-ridden. In a chapter entitled 'Institutional breakdown in an Age of Expansion' he argued that post-Jacksonian America lacked a strong institutional structure of Church, party or aristocracy and that, quoting Tocqueville, the average American had little reverence for institutions, unlike France, whose institutions shaped its citizens. Just as he compared slavery in the United States with Latin American slavery, so Elkins hoped to shed light on the particularity of American emancipation by comparing it with Britain, where abolition had been achieved relatively painlessly and without conflict. Why, he asked (and here the revisionist writers exerted their influence), did the United States have uniquely to resort to war to end slavery? In Britain it had come about by simple Act of Parliament. But America's loose federation, he argued, lacked the institutional means of peaceful reform. There was, after the decline of the Federalist party, no deferential class, no recognisable aristocracy or elite held together by shared establishment assumptions. In Britain – and here he quotes Henry James the novelist – there was a powerful establishment – the Crown, the law courts, Oxford, Eton, the annual aristocratic rituals of Ascot and Epsom – whose members acted together, tacitly understood one another and got things done. Not only was the US political and social system fluid, plastic and structureless, its intelligentsia, the Transcendentalists, centred on the small town of Concord in Massachusetts, reinforced this endemic looseness and decentralisation by a philosophy of extreme individualism. Collectively Emerson, Thoreau, Margaret Fuller, Bronson Alcott, Theodore Parker, William Henry Channing and others preached opposition to all institutions and to the state. Thoreau had famously argued the case for civil disobedience during the war with Mexico. (It took the form of refusal to pay his local poll tax: he went temporarily to prison instead.) Emerson wrote of 'The infinitude of the private man ... To educate the wise man, the state exists; and with the appearance of the wise man, the state expires.' Intellectuals without responsibility, they irresponsibly insisted that slavery was a moral question concerning guilt, moral aggression and atonement: rather than fight against the anarchic spirit of the age, they verified and reinforced it, thereby rendering reasoned discourse impossible. Garrison, of course, comes in for particular condemnation from Elkins.

> Garrisonianism was in the last analysis deeply subversive of anti-slavery's efforts to develop and consolidate organised power. The man himself, with his egocentric singleness of mind, antagonised most of those who tried to combine with him in any action requiring concerted effort ... [The] direction was from complexity of doctrine to simplicity, from organisation to fragmentation, from consolidated effort to effort dispersed, diffuse and pervasive.[17]

Tocqueville had spoken of the spirit of association which, in America, overcame the intense 'individualism' of the age (a neologism Tocqueville had had to invent to describe this new phenomenon), but the greatest of all American associations, the political party, had abandoned its stabilising function of political reconciliation and had broken down into bickering sectionalism. Both politician and intellectual had failed the United States, for, Elkins insisted, the South was not monolithic and could be modified. The slave owner, for example, could have done more to extend the dignity of Christian morality over the brutal institution and sanctified slave marriages.

Now this, even by Elkins's standards, is obtuse, for no one had depicted a more absolutist, 'closed' South than Elkins in the very same book. Slave owners did attempt to impose a quietistic, resigned religion on the slave which the slave stoutly resisted, and the sanctification of slave marriages was directly contrary to a mobile, rapidly expanding system of slave labour. Elkins accused the Transcendentalists of infusing anarchism and an anti-institutional bias into abolitionism, but most Transcendentalists were not formal abolitionists and Thoreau in particular loathed Garrison and others like him who 'wrap you about with their bowels ... Men's bowels are far more slimy than their brain.'[18] And did the majority of Americans adopt radical anarchism any more than the abolitionists did? Elkins managed to accuse the Transcendentalists of holding pernicious doctrines and failing to transcend contemporary culture, yet he specifically quotes Emerson damning the essential selfishness of all trade and the gross materialistic American worship of the almighty dollar. This statement can hardly be said to reflect and confirm the spirit of the age. Did the Yankee, notorious for his cunning entrepreneurial spirit, abandon commerce after reading Emerson? Did he ever read him?

Elkins is on firmer ground when he suggests that abolitionist individualism was a limitation when it came to the consequences of emancipation. Too many, Garrison among them, believed that in 1865 their mission had been accomplished and that the freedman, an individual just like his white brother and sister, could cast off his chains, fend for himself, and require no special favours from government. Here most abolitionists (Wendell Phillips was an exception) can be said to have reflected rather than transcended the limitations of their age, and to have failed to realise that in the matrix of Southern society the freedman might well require political, social and economic aid. But in so far as many in their ranks conceived of a future American society devoid of racial prejudice – that the problem was a problem for whites and not for blacks – they can be seen as forward-looking if over-optimistic. Elkins constantly makes the common mistake of assuming Garrison was the archetypal abolitionist. Garrison, along with Phillips and Foster, may have been anti-institutionalist but Weld, Birney, the Tappan brothers and the majority were not, and were willing to use political and economic pressure to bring about change. The vast majority of their number wished not to repudiate or to destroy institutions but to purify them – Church, State and Union – and supported the Union wholeheartedly during the testing years of war.

Elkins accused the abolitionists of turning an essentially soluble political problem into an insoluble moral issue. But, as Aileen Kraditor argued in her *Means and Ends in American*

Abolitionism (1969), were the abolitionists not right to feel guilty living in a slave-holding Union? 'The unrealism,' she wrote, 'was not the abolitionists'' for feeling guilty, but their neighbours' for *not* feeling guilty.' Morality she regarded as of the essence: 'That is, the charge of abstractionism could be levelled at a movement that did *not* make the moral aspect central.'[19]

David Brion Davis, William Freehling and Howard Temperley have turned their attention to the practical implications of abolitionist strategy and to more pragmatic explanations of abolitionist failure. Temperley found it odd that American historians wrote so negatively about their abolitionists while their British counterparts praised the immediatism of Wilberforce, Clarkson and Buxton while condemning the political caution of Pitt the Younger. But American abolitionists were faced with an insuperable practical task symbolised by the egalitarian doctrine of the Declaration of Independence, and by a Constitution and Union which recognised and protected slavery. The federal government had limited powers, states' rights were deified, autonomy was ferociously held on to and reinforced by Calhoun's doctrine of concurrent majorities and nullification. The slave power was extending into the territories. Cotton was highly profitable and the Southern economy buoyant. Reformers were faced not only by systemic racism but by a large section of the Union utterly determined to maintain slavery as an institution. The extraordinary concentration of power in Britain, symbolised and practically enshrined in the absolute sovereignty of Parliament, enabled it, both for moral and economic reasons, to abolish slavery when it saw fit to do so against a small body of West Indian planters, without having to worry about the racial consequences of a new class of freedman in the far-off Caribbean. It was the ability and the means of the British political elite to act decisively – not the rich social rituals of the Eton wall game or the Derby – that marked the strongest contrast with America. Britain, despite all the praise it received from the conservative Elkins, has so far proved incapable of solving the Irish problem because one sector of that community, Ulster, refuses to be separated from Westminster. Similarly the slave-holding South had the means of controlling majoritarian democracy. As long as slavery was entrenched in fifteen states, slavery could not be abolished by amendment, for amendment required the consent of three-quarters of all the states. Likewise the three-fifths rule gave the white population of the South, only 30 per cent of the total white population, 36 per cent of Congressmen and 36 per cent of the electoral college votes which ensured, for example, the election of Jefferson over John Adams in 1800 and of Andrew Jackson over John Quincy Adams in 1828. Thus after 1828, and through the Democratic party, the South consolidated its power and became an entrenched fortress holding an impregnable constitutional position. Abolitionism, Temperley argued, could plausibly come about only through the acquiescence of the South or presidential decree in time of war – both of them highly improbable scenarios. It was not the abolitionists who failed, for 'Wherever they turned American abolitionists were faced by the fact that there was no effective machinery for coming to grips with the essential problem of slavery as it existed within the individual States.' Meanwhile the reformers could only agitate or vote to change the party political balance of power in their favour. This they did in 1860 with Lincoln's election. Elkins accused the party system of failing to grasp the nettle of slavery and settling instead, as he put it rather contemptuously, for the lowest common denominator of forbidding slavery's extension. It could be argued, on the contrary, that the party system, responding to the shifting wishes of a volatile electorate, functioned perfectly. If Tocqueville coined the word 'individualism' which Elkins makes so much of, Tocqueville also appreciated that individualism and personal isolation in America were offset by the greatest of all groups of associations, the party system. 'In the United States,' he explained, 'associations are established to promote the public safety, commerce, industry, morality and religion. There is no end which the human will despairs of attaining through the combined powers of individuals united into a society.'[20] It was the coming of the Republican Lincoln to power in 1860 which triggered off secession and a civil war which led, in turn, to Temperley's second improbable scenario, abolition by presidential decree in time of war in 1863.

It was in the light of recognition of these well nigh insuperable obstacles that the abolitionists were rehabilitated in the 1960s. Many of the fresh assessments were to come from historians of the left who had actually experienced similar intractable problems of strategy during the civil rights campaign and took part in often dangerous and hazardous freedom marches in the South. Martin Duberman, editor of the *Anti-slavery Vanguard – New Essays on the Abolitionists* (1965), admitted a direct link between the nineteenth and twentieth-century campaigns. 'The scholarship of this generation is no more immune to contemporary pressures than scholarship has ever been.' But he insisted that this relevance did not distort the past so much as shed new light on it. If the past of the 1850s was being repeated in the 1960s it was precisely because the public had not learned from its past and it was the historian's vocation to instruct it. As a civil rights marcher, and later a gay rights activist, he began to appreciate the dedication, courage and determination of the first abolitionists and the stiff opposition they had to face. Just as the South had refused emancipation in the 1830s, so the South in the 1960s would not voluntarily desegregate. 'Contemporary pressures, if recognised and contained, can prove fruitful in stimulating the historical imagination. They may lead us to uncover (not invent) aspects of the past to which we were previously blind.'[21] Kenneth Stampp, who came from a family of Milwaukee socialists, wrote more trenchantly in a letter to his teacher William Hesseltine, 'James G. Randall is a damned Negro-hating Abolitionist-baiting doughface ... I'm sick of the Randalls, Cravens and other doughfaces who crucify the Abolitionists for attacking slavery. If I had lived in the 1850s, I would have been a rabid Abolitionist.' His one criticism of the abolitionists was that they were not radical enough. For Stampp slavery was a moral anachronism. In a country whose independence began with a ringing declaration of equality, the disparity, ideal and practical, was immense and inexcusable and this moral question was central and not peripheral. For as David Brion Davis wrote in his contribution to *The Anti-slavery Vanguard*, 'The inherent contradiction of slavery lies not in its cruelty or economic exploitation, but in the underlying conception of a man as a conveyable possession with no more autonomy of will and consciousness than a domestic animal.' Hitherto revisionist historians had obtusely attempted to play down the personal and the moral, but the new abolitionists were right to concentrate on the individual questions of guilt and of sin. Taking their cue from Hofstadter, these historians argued that minority agitation against majoritarian oppression and indifference was a healthy element in a thriving democracy. To denounce radicalism was to assume complacently that there was nothing wrong with the *status quo*. They concurred with Wendell Phillips's assertion that 'The anti-slavery agitation is an important, nay, an essential part of the machinery of the state. It is not a disease nor a medicine. No, it is the normal state – the normal state of the nation.' Likewise they agreed with Phillips's frontal assault on deadening conformity and majoritarian tyranny – 'More than any other people we are afraid of each other' – as they in turn challenged the smug consensus historians.[22]

Two major biographies of Garrison appeared in 1963. The first, by Walter Merrill, *Against Wind and Tide*, stressed Garrison's outstanding role as a publicist, heightening Northern awareness of the evil of slavery. John Thomas's biography, *The Liberator*, was more ambivalent. While finding Garrison single-minded and determined he also discerned an irascible, irresponsible and vindictive character. Everywhere he found contradictions. Garrison promised political change but urged moral reform instead; he preached immediatism but was incapable of defining it; most important, he urged pacifism but appealed to passion. 'More than any other American of his time he was responsible for the atmosphere of moral absolutism which caused a Civil War and freed the slave.' Following the example of Elkins, Thomas also found Garrison responsible for failing to grasp the institutional character of slavery. 'For the failure of his generation to achieve the racial democracy which a Civil War made possible he must be held accountable.'[23]

Aileen Kraditor, a radical historian who had read these two biographies, began her own study of Garrison with negative opinions. But on reading Garrison herself she increasingly came to admire him, even discovering a vein of humour in him, and found his strategy logically consistent throughout. Denied the choice of reform, because change itself was denied by the South, Garrison was consistent in pursuing militant methods to achieve his aims. On the surface, for example, Garrison's pacifism sat uneasily with his support for blacks entering the Union army. But Kraditor argued that Garrison's conceding free will to blacks who wished to further the cause of freedom was entirely consistent with his overall abolitionism. That is, Garrison tolerated a variety of different means if they contributed to the common end of emancipation. Essentially Kraditor placed Garrison's moralism back at the very centre of her reappraisal. She concluded:

> The point then, is not that Garrison created an atmosphere of moral absolutism, but that the choice that the nation faced was objectively between absolutely antagonistic moral systems. And Garrison's real choice was not between democracy and undemocracy, or fanatical and reasonable agitation, it was between anti-slavery agitation and silence.[24]

The New Left's strategy was to turn the revisionist historians upside down. Borrowing from the psychological writings of Eric Fromm and the polemics of Herbert Marcuse, they asked whether dedicated opposition might not be a measure of sanity in an insane and unjust society. Were the July plotters who planned the assassination of Hitler motivated by personal neuroses? As Tilden Edelstein wrote in his biography of Thomas Wentworth Higginson, one of the Secret Six, 'in times of social injustice it might be the inactive individual, not the reformer, who is mentally disturbed.' The abolitionist leadership had been subjected to intense psychoanalysis on the couch by historians and been found to be mad, bad and dangerous. What historian, Duberman asked, would survive such an onslaught, such relentless detailed prying into his or her subconscious life: what history faculty would emerge unscathed and with a clean bill of health? Howard Zinn went even further: 'It is tempting to join the psychological game and try to understand what it is about the lives of academic scholars which keeps them at arm's length from the moral fervour of one of history's most magnificent crusades.'[25] And why such selective psychological analysis? Why no equivalent psychological investigation of, say, Stonewall Jackson, who took water cures, lived on raw lemons and never leaned back in his chair or crossed his legs for fear of twisting his alimentary canal? And why, moreover, should advocates of change be psychotics when conservatives, insecure, paranoid and morbidly afraid of change and adjustment, might display similar neurotic symptoms? And what if long-term commitment to an abstract goal was not a sign of unresolved conflict, a discharge of psychological frustration, but indicative of unusual sanity, mental stability and disinterested service? Even Emerson, a deeply private man, with many personal problems, appreciated this. Delivering his little known Fugitive Slave Law address of 1854, he put it thus: 'I do not often speak to public questions; they are odious and hurtful, and it seems like meddling or leaving your work. I have my own spirits in prison; spirits in deeper prisons, whom no man visits if I do not.' Garrison might indeed have come from an unstable background and be scatty and obsessive, but what of Birney, Weld or Quincy, who were pre-eminently sensible and solid citizens? Martin Duberman came to the aboli-tionists by way of his excellent biographies of John Quincy Adams and James Russell Lowell. These two were eminently sane, and Duberman went on to observe that it was only with the death of his wife in 1853 and the deep bereavement that followed it that Lowell, distraught, deserted the abolitionists' ranks. Long-term dedication to public causes required maturity, stability and health: 'the very definition of maturity may be the ability to commit oneself to abstract ideals, to get beyond the selfish, egocentric world of children'. Sustained and disinterested agita-tion against moral wrongs was an indication not of psychological sickness but of psychological health, and that personal commit-ment had to be long-term. James MacPherson's *Struggle for Equality* (1964) traced the abolitionist campaign from 1830 to 1870 and beyond, and refuted the common assumption that the black was deserted and left to fend for himself following his emancipation. The high-pitched, emphatic language the aboli-tionists habitually used was not untypical of an age drenched in religious fervour and strong evangelical impulses. Was Garrison not justified in declaring in his famous *Liberator* editorial of 1831:

> I am aware that many object to the severity of my language; but is there not cause for severity? I *will* be as harsh as truth and as uncompromising as justice. On this subject, I do not wish to think, or speak, or write, with moderation ... urge me not to use modera-tion in a cause like the present. I am in earnest – I will not equivocate – I will not excuse – I will not retreat a single inch – AND I WILL BE HEARD. The apathy of the people is enough to make every

statue leap from its pedestal, and hasten the resurrection of the dead. It is pretended that I am retarding the cause of emancipation by the coarseness of my invective, and the precipitancy of my measures. *The charge is not true* ... and posterity will bear testimony that I was right. I desire to thank God that he enables me to disregard 'the fear of man which bringeth a snare' and to speak his truth in its simplicity and power.[26]

This, the neo-abolitionists insisted, was not the deranged ramblings of a psychotic but the authentic voice of justified American protest against injustice. As Howard Zinn wrote, 'the abolitionists quite consciously measured their words to the enormity of the evil'. Were the demands they made, especially immediatism, too impractical and impossible? Donald Mathews argues that they deliberately pitched their demands high as a bargaining counter, with various fallback positions, knowing full well that they would receive less. As Garrison himself, supposedly the most impractical and unworldliest abolitionist, wrote:

> In demanding equality and exact justice we may get partial redress; in asking for the whole that is due to us, we may get a part; in advocating the immediate, we may succeed in procuring the speedy abolition of slavery. But, if we demand anything short of justice, we shall recover no damages; if we ask for a part we shall get nothing.[27]

David Donald's variation on the revisionist theme – that abolitionists were activated by class and status displacement – was also subjected to withering criticism. In 1971 Gerald Sorin published his *New York Abolitionists: A Test Case of Political Radicalism*, which undermined each and every one of Donald's conclusions:

> Abolitionism tended to draw its leadership from urban areas and from the highly educated, moderately prosperous segments of society. The abolitionists' leaders pursued the most influential occupations in their communities and were actively engaged in public service. They generally seem to have had higher status in their respective communities than their fathers had had in theirs. It was impossible to find more than three or four men whose economic, social, or personal dislocation might reasonably be said to have left them discernably insecure and frustrated ... They were motivated by a reawakened religious impulse, a strong sense of social justice, and the sincere belief that they were not only insuring their own

freedom from guilt, but that they would affect society in such a way as to assure social justice for everyone.[28]

The crucial role of the black in his own emancipation was also beginning to receive attention from black historians. Benjamin Quarles's 1948 biography of Frederick Douglass was a pioneering work. Nathan Huggins also wrote a fine life of *Douglass* (1980), as did Philip Foner, and the collected papers are now being published by Yale University Press under the editorship of John Blassingame. Frederick Douglass emerges as a powerful, intelligent militant who founded his own newspaper, *The Northern Star,* staffing it with as many fellow blacks as he could, and broke with Garrison on disunion, party politics and non-resistance. Douglass resolutely refused to be condescended to or turned into a performing ex-slave lecturer, a role many white abolitionists assigned to him. Like other black abolitionists he stressed the practical need for gaining the franchise and for economic assistance for the freedman in order to secure his future in a generally antagonistic white society. Also, while expressing doubts, he became one of the secret supporters of John Brown's raid.

Quarles's 1972 study of John Brown revealed a great deal of black sympathy for the objectives of the Harper's ferry raid. For, as Quarles put it, 'with a perception born of an oppressed minority ... they viewed the incident from a wider perspective of aberrant behaviour in their country, from a greater familiarity with the climate of violence ... in the land of their birth'.[29]

Brown himself was also partially rehabilitated. Using the evidence of affidavits presented at his trial, historians as various as David Potter, Allan Nevins and Coner Vann Woodward had depicted Brown as murderously insane and deranged. In the radical 1960s and early 1970s, Brown was refurbished and depicted as a righteous revolutionary fighting a guerrilla war against an evil society indifferent to the cause of black freedom. Thomas Nelson, in a series of articles in *The Nation*, spoke of Brown with 'love and awe' for his actions, which were 'ethically compatible with actions and tactics familiar to revolutionary guerrilla warfare and liberating resistance movements'.[30] Stephen Oates, in his *To Purge this Land with Blood* (1970), portrayed a genuine believer in racial equality who was motivated throughout by a deep Calvinistic conviction that he was personally enacting the will of God and redeeming his country from the sin of slavery.

Douglass was also an early supporter of women's rights and the only male to play a prominent role at the Seneca Falls conference of July 1848 which called for female emancipation. The contribution of women to abolitionism had hitherto been neglected. The theme of the abuse of power and the sin of possessing other humans as property held direct relevance to women of the time and is a theme which runs through abolitionist thinking, stretching from the physical violation of female slaves to the question of the right of women to own property and secure divorce. Mary Wollstonecraft and Frances Wright had emphasised the obvious links between marriage and slavery, and Sarah Grimké in 1838 published her *Letters on the Equality of the Sexes*. Her sister, Angelina, in marrying Theodore Weld, put some of these advanced ideas into practice: while he renounced his claims on her property she, in turn, avoided the pledge of obedience at their wedding ceremony. Some abolitionists, such as James Birney and the Tappan brothers, rejected feminism, while to many other Americans this *ideé fixe* was yet another infernal New England 'ism', but when Lucretia Mott met Elizabeth Cady Stanton after their credentials had been refused at the world Anti-slavery Convention in London the feminist crusade was born. Sex, no more than colour, should disqualify individuals from equal rights.

Recent historical writing has not been all rehabilitation and uncritical praise. Research has revealed, for example, a good deal of condescension and even racism among the abolitionist ranks. Larry Gara's *The Liberty Line* exposed the myth of widespread white participation in the underground escape routes slaves took northwards beyond the Mason and Dixon line and into Canada, and Leon Litwack's *North of Slavery* sensitively explored the ambivalence of Northerners on the question of race. Vann Woodward has rightly pointed to a degree of Yankee humbug for on the one hand launching an onslaught against slavery while harbouring strong racial prejudices. The stark dichotomy of 'Yankee saints' and 'Southern sinners' is too stark. In an influential 1944 study of West Indian slavery Eric Williams had argued that slavery was abolished in the islands becaue it was no longer profitable. That is, slavery and capitalism were inherently incompatible, and abolitionism was rooted in hard economic realities rather than moral altruism. But the trouble with this thesis, as fresh research revealed, was that slavery was profitable at the time it was abolished.

Howard Temperley has argued in a number of persuasive and brilliant articles that abolitionist ideology was rooted in economic as well as moral concerns. Rejecting what he calls the 'intellectual diffusionist' theory of pure altruism employed by the abolitionists themselves and by neo-abolitionist historians such as Barnes and Dumond after them, he suggests that the Anglo-American drive for emancipation derived from classical economic theory as well as from moral concern: that, in nineteenth-century terms, economics and benevolence, freedom and prosperity, were inextricably linked. Slave labour was an outrage to a capitalist middle-class world emerging from an industrial revolution and assured of its material and moral superiority. Britain's global empire made universal emancipation a practical possibility: the pre-eminent Christian nations were economically prosperous, and abolitionism, a semi-secular form of religion, and triumphant nationalism, concentrating political power, made it possible to act decisively, through Parliament or Congress, to abolish the evil. The emergence of immediatism signalled the triumph of a new bourgeois order dedicated to moral and economic progress, in which slavery was an economic as well as a moral anachronism.

Eric Foner has also located a new capitalist ideology within the abolitionist ranks. Increasingly in the North, as industry expanded, workers were slipping from the promise of self-employment into the growing ranks of wage labour. Wealthy abolitionists, like the Tappan brothers, wished to discipline their work force, forbid Sunday mail and force them to observe the Sabbath. Garrison himself believed that social inequalities were inevitable and denied that wage labour constituted a form of industrial slavery. Believing the freedom of contract between employer and employee to be equal, he preached underlying harmony between capital and labour. But artisans themselves were becoming aware that social and economic mobility was being stifled under a more stringent capitalistic system and Foner suggests that the abolitionist crusade deflected criticism away from the problem of emerging wage labour in the North to that of slave labour in the South. As Edward Bellamy, the late nineteenth-century reformer, wrote of Horace Greeley, the newspaper editor, had he not become an abolitionist first he would have become a socialist.

In *Slavery, Capitalism and Politics in the Anti-bellum Republic* (1995) John Ashworth has taken this analysis of economic ideology a step further in a Marxist interpretation of the causes of the Civil War. In one sense his thesis that the American Civil War constituted a bourgeois revolution takes us back to Charles Beard and Karl Marx. But Ashworth's analysis is far subtler. Like Foner, he sees the immediate ante-bellum period as an awkward time of transition from free to wage labour. But because most Americans were uncomfortable about the implications of dependence and civility which wage labour implied, the North evolved a dual system of morality which separated the harsh operations of the labour market from the domestic sanctification of home and family which constituted 'a haven in a heartless world'.

He argues, dubiously I think, that the abolitionists contributed to severing any links between slavery and wage labour and concentrated their attacks on a Southern system that denied family life and the free will of the individual conscience to the slave. This is an intriguing thesis, but it seems to me to overemphasise the role of the abolitionists in this transformation which was taking place in the North. The thesis seems also to be propelled by personal, subjective concerns. Like Genovese, Ashworth appears to profoundly dislike modern capitalism. One of his contentions, in what is intended to be a two-volume work, is: 'Slavery is, in certain crucial respects, a weaker form of exploitation than wage labour.' Similarly, in a footnote, he states, that while he has a high regard for the abolitionists, he does not share their confidence in capitalist 'progress'. We are not told why and the issue is not developed in his first volume.[31]

The scholarship of the last thirty years has rescued the abolitionists and the abolitionist movement from oblivion and detraction. It has not returned to the early deification of its leaders or the extravagant worship which followed the martyrdom of John Brown. Scholarship has also located a specifically American movement in a more universal development which, in the middle years of the nineteenth century, was forming a wholly new moral and economic order. The abolitionists' limitations and excesses are clearer, as are their remarkable dedication and self-less commitment. Motives were mixed and strategies contradictory. But, as E.M. Forster wrote in his biography of Marianne Thornton, a member of the Clapham sect which was one of the prime sources of the English abolitionist movement: 'Really bad people ... are those who do no good anywhere and ... slip through their lives unnoticed and so escape the censure of historians.'[32] The abolitionists have not escaped the censure of historians, but it cannot be denied that they did much good. At times their tactics were hopelessly impractical. They argued among themselves and fractured into countless bickering groups. It was the politician, Lincoln, who freed the slaves, not Garrison, Weld or John Brown. But through relentless publicity and the practical act of voting they raised the question of slavery and the Slave Power, and forced a generally indifferent public to think about a subject they would much rather not have had to think about. This was an invaluable service. The abolitionists may have been heroes with feet of clay, but heroes they were.

Notes

1 Wilson quoted in George Frederickson (ed.), *William Lloyd Garrison: A Profile* (Englewood Cliffs, N.J., 1968), p. 126.

2 *Ibid.*, pp. 126, 124.

3 Charles and Mary Beard, *The Rise of American Civilisation* (New York, 1930), pp. 698–9.

4 Beard quoted in Howard Temperley, 'Capitalism, slavery and ideology', *Past and Present* (74–7, 1977), p. 100.

5 Vernon Parrington, *Main Currents in American Thought*, II (New York, 1927), pp. 343, 347.

6 Villard quoted in Robert Swierenga (ed.), *Beyond the Civil War Synthesis* (Westport, Conn., 1975), p. 59; and in Hugh Hawkins, *The Abolitionists* (Boston, Mass., 1964), 57. Peebles Wilson quoted in Swierenga, *Beyond the Civil War Synthesis*, p. 64.

7 Dumond quoted in C. Vann Woodward, *American Counterpoint* (New York, 1971), p. 141. Dwight Dumond (ed.), *The Letters of Theodore Weld*, I (New York, 1970), p. viii. Gilbert Barnes, *The Anti-slavery Impulse* (New York, 1933), pp. 91, 93.

8 Weld quoted in Alfred Young (ed.), *Dissent* (De Kalb, Ill., 1968), p. 95.

9 Weld quoted in Dwight Dumond, *Anti-slavery Origins of the Civil War in the United States* (Ann Arbor, rpt, 1960), p. 142. Dumond, *Letters of Theodore Weld*, p. vi.

10 Dumond, *Anti-slavery Origins of the Civil War*, p. 2. Vann Woodward quoted in Merton Dillon, 'Gilbert Barnes and Dwight Dumond', *Reviews in American History* (21, 1993), p. 550.

11 Craven in Hawkins, *The Abolitionists*, p. 80. Fletcher Green in Arthur Link and Rembert Patrick (eds), *Writing Southern History* (Baton Rouge, 1965), p. 241. Craven quoted in Martin Duberman (ed.), *The Anti-slavery Vanguard* (Princeton, 1965), p. 59. Thomas Pressly, *Americans Interpret their Civil War* (New York, 1962), p. 316. Craven quoted in William McLoughlin's introduction to Barnes, *The Anti-slavery Impulse* (New York, 1964), pp. xii–xiii.

12 Owsley quoted in George Tindall (ed.), *The Pursuit of Southern History* (Baton Rouge, 1964), p. 87.

13 Avery Craven, quoted at the sixth annual meeting of the Southern Historical Association by Albert Moore.

14 Donald quoted in Duberman, *The Anti-slavery Vanguard*, p. 66. Craven, *Journal of Southern History* (7, 1941), p. 57.

15 Donald's essay was reprinted in *Lincoln Reconsidered* (New York, 1969), pp. 33, 36.

16 Richard Hofstadter, *The American Political Tradition* (London, 1962), pp. 135–6 and n. 1.

17 Stanley Elkins, *Slavery* (Chicago, 1959), pp. 142, 147, 183, 184.

18 Thoreau quoted in Bertram Wyatt-Brown, *Yankee Saints and Southern Sinners* (Baton Rouge, 1985), p. 24.

19 Aileen Kraditor, *Means and Ends in American Abolitionism* (New York, 1969), pp. 21, 22.

20 Temperley in Duberman, *The Anti-slavery Vanguard*, p. 355. Tocqueville quoted in Ann Lane (ed.), *The Debate over Slavery* (Urbana, Ill., 1971), pp. 367–8.

21 Duberman, *The Anti-slavery Vanguard*, p. ix; and in 'The abolitionists and psychology', *Journal of Negro History* (47, 1962), p. 84.

22 Stampp quoted in Peter Novick, *That Noble Dream* (Cambridge, 1988), p. 349. Duberman, *The Anti-slavery Vanguard*, p. 3. Phillips quoted in Duberman, pp. 102, 115.

23 John Thomas, *The Liberator: William Lloyd Garrison* (Boston, Mass., 1963), pp. 4, 5.

24 Kraditor, *Means and Ends in American Abolitionism*, p. 276.

25 Edelstein in Charles Crowe (ed.), *The Age of Civil War and Reconstruction, 1830–1900* (Homewood, Ill., 1975), pp. 170–1. Duberman, *The Anti-slavery Vanguard*, p. 417.

26 Duberman, *The Anti-slavery Vanguard*, p. 411. Garrison quoted in Richard Hofstadter, *Great Issues in American History*, II, *1864–1957* (New York, 1958), p. 327.

27 Zinn in Duberman, *The Anti-slavery Vanguard*, p. 172. Garrison quoted in Donald Mathews, 'The abolitionists on slavery: the critique behind the social movement', *Journal of Southern History* (33, 1967), p. 167.

28 Gerald Sorin, *The New York Abolitionists* (Westport, Conn., 1971), pp. 119–20.
29 Benjamin Quarles, *Black Mosaic* (Amherst, Mass., 1988), pp. 13–14.
30 Nelson quoted in Stephen Oates, *Our Fiery Trial* (Amherst, Mass., 1979), p. 45.
31 John Ashworth, *Slavery, Capitalism and Politics in the Ante-bellum Republic*, I (Cambridge, 1995), pp. ix, 125 n. 1.
32 Forster quoted in Hawkins, *The Abolitionists*, p. 171.

Selective bibliography

Ashworth, John, *Slavery, Capitalism and Politics in the Antebellum Republic*, I (Cambridge, 1995).
Barnes, Gilbert, *The Anti-slavery Impulse* (New York, 1933; reprinted 1964).
Carwardine, Richard, *Evangelicals and Politics in Antebellum America* (New Haven, 1993).
Curry, Richard (ed.), *Abolitionists* (New York, 1965).
Davis, David Brion, 'Antebellum reform', reprinted in Frank Gatell and Allen Weinstein (eds), *American Themes: Essays in Historiography* (London, 1968).
Davis, David Brion, 'The emergence of immediatism in British and American anti-slavery thought', *Mississippi Valley Historical Review* (48, 1962).
Dillon, Merton, 'The abolitionists: a decade of historiography, 1955–1969', *Journal of Southern History* (35, 1969).
Dillon, Merton, 'The failure of the American abolitionists', *Journal of Southern History* (25, 1959).
Dillon, Merton, 'Gilbert H. Barnes and Dwight L. Dumond: an appraisal', *Reviews in American History* (21, 1993).
Dillon, Merton, *The Abolitionists: The Growth of a Dissenting Minority* (New York, 1974).
Donald, David, 'Towards a reconsideration of abolitionists', reprinted in David Donald (ed.), *Lincoln Reconsidered* (New York, 1969).
Duberman, Martin, 'The abolitionists and psychology', *Journal of Negro History* (47, 1962).
Duberman, Martin (ed.), *The Anti-slavery Vanguard* (Princeton, 1965).
Dumond, Dwight, *Anti-slavery Origins of the Civil War in the United States* (Ann Arbor, 1939; reprinted 1960).
Dumond, Dwight, *Antislavery: The Crusade for Freedom in America* (Ann Arbor, 1961).
Foner, Eric, 'Ambiguities of anti-slavery' in Eric Foner (ed.), *Politics and Ideology in the Age of the Civil War* (Oxford, 1980).
Frederickson, George (ed.), *William Lloyd Garrison: A Profile* (Englewood Cliffs, N.J., 1968).
Hawkins, Hugh, *The Abolitionists* (Boston, Mass., 1964; Lexington, Mass., 1972).
Hofstadter, Richard, 'Wendell Phillips's in Richard Hofstadter, *The American Political Tradition* (London, 1962).
Kraditor, Aileen, *Means and Ends in American Abolitionism* (New York, 1969).
Lane, Ann (ed.), *The Debate over Slavery* (Urbana, Ill., 1971).

Mathews, Donald, 'The abolitionists on slavery: the critique behind the social movement', *Journal of Southern History* (33, 1967).

Merrill, Walter, *Against Wind and Tide* (Cambridge, Mass., 1963).

Oates, Stephen, 'John Brown and his judges' in Robert Swierenga (ed.), *Beyond the Civil War Synthesis* (Westport, Conn., 1975).

Oates, Stephen, *Our Fiery Trial* (Amherst, Mass., 1979).

Oates, Stephen, *To Purge this Land with Blood* (New York, 1970).

Quarles, Benjamin, *Black Abolitionists* (New York, 1969).

Rose, Willie Lee, 'Killing for freedom' in Willie Lee Rose (ed.), *Slavery and Freedom* (Oxford, 1982).

Skotheim, Robert, 'A note on historical method', *Journal of Southern History* (25, 1959).

Sorin, Gerald, *The New York Abolitionists* (Westport, Conn., 1971).

Temperley, Howard, 'Anti-slavery as a form of cultural imperialism' in Christine Bolt and Seymour Drescher (eds), *Antislavery, Religion and Reform* (Folkestone, 1980).

Temperley, Howard, 'Capitalism, slavery and ideology', *Past and Present* (74–7, 1977).

Temperley, Howard, 'Competing scenarios: Antebellum images of American society and emancipation' in Brian Holden Reid and John White (eds), *American Studies: Essays in Honor of Marcus Cunliffe* (London, 1991).

Temperley, Howard, in David Ellis and James Walvin (eds), *The Abolition of the Atlantic Slave Trade* (Madison, Wis., 1981).

Thomas, John, *The Liberator: William Lloyd Garrison* (Boston, Mass., 1963).

Woodward, C. Vann, 'John Brown's private war' in C. Vann Woodward (ed.), *The Burden of Southern History* (Baton Rouge, 1974).

Woodward, C. Vann, 'The Northern crusade against slavery' in C. Vann Woodward (ed.), *American Counterpoint* (New York, 1971).

Wyatt-Brown, Bertram, *Yankee Saints and Southern Sinners* (Baton Rouge, 1985).

4

The causes of the Civil War

Given the peculiar, fratricidal nature of civil wars, the debates surrounding the causes of the American Civil War, which raised such thorny questions as war guilt and conspiracy theory, has been especially bitter and acrimonious, with as much ink being spilt as blood. Partisanship has been so intense that historians have not even been able to agree on what to call the conflict in which over 620,000 soldiers died – more than all the casualties of all wars fought by American soldiers put together. To many Northerners at the time it was 'The War of the Great Rebellion', for Lincoln never recognised the constitutionality of secession, while to the South it became the 'War for Southern Independence', or the 'War between the States', or the 'War of Northern Aggression'. Yet one historian, James MacPherson, has recently referred to 'the War of Southern Aggression'. What are we to make of all this when the debate has, from the first, been hopelessly mired in bitter sectional wrangling?

Lincoln, at least, was clear concerning the causes, and exonerated himself and the North for initiating the conflict. In his second inaugural address of 4 March 1865 he evoked the providential workings of the will of God, but at the same time securely fastened responsibility on the human agencies of the Confederacy, when he recalled his first presidential address of 1861.

> While the inaugural address was being delivered from this place, devoted altogether to *saving* the Union without war, insurgent agents were in the city seeking to *destroy* it without war and seeking to dissolve the Union and divide effects by negotiations. Both parties

deprecated war, but one of them would *make* war rather than let the nation survive, and the other would *accept* war rather than let it perish, and the war came.[1]

Henry Wilson, senator and historian, essentially endorsed the martyred President's interpretation of causes. Publishing his *History of the Rise and Fall of the Slave Power in America* (three volumes, 1872-77) during the period of Reconstruction and the passing of the three Civil War amendments, he firmly identified the peculiar institution as a primary cause of the war.

> American slavery reduced man, created in the divine image, to property ... It made him a beast of burden in the field of toil, an outcast in social life, a cipher in the courts of law, and a pariah in the house of God. This complete subversion of the natural rights of millions ... constituted a system antagonistic to the doctrines of reason and the monitions of conscience.

Like Lincoln, Wilson discerned conspiracy and concerted collaboration in the events of the 1850s: in the election of pro-Southern Presidents, Pierce and Buchanan, the passing of the Kansas–Nebraska Bill of 1854 which nullified the Missouri compromise of 1820, the Dred Scott decision which confirmed the status of slavery as property (to confiscate which was contrary to the Fifth Amendment of the Constitution) and left the territories open to the extension of slavery, and Buchanan's adoption of the fraudulent pro-slavery Lecompton Constitution for Kansas. Lincoln's election was merely the culmination of decades of growing sectional enmity:

> After aggressive warfare of more than two generations upon the vital and animating spirit of republican institutions, upon the cherished and hallowed sentiments of the Christian people, upon the enduring interest and lasting renown of the Republic, organised treasonable conspiracies raised the standard of revolution, and plunged the nation into a bloody contest for the preservation of its threatened life.[2]

In his history Wilson was keen to refute the Southern argument that the sacred principle of state rights, and not the protection of slavery, triggered off secession. Out of deference to the existing states, and in order to mollify anti-federalist opposition, the founding fathers at the Philadelphia constitutional convention of 1787 distributed powers between the states and the new federal government. Furthermore the first ten amendments of that constitution, known collectively as the Bill of Rights, and ratified in 1791, included a Tenth Amendment which left all powers not specifically delegated to the new federal government in the hands of the thirteen separate states. It was John Calhoun (1782–1850), Vice-president, senator for South Carolina and political theorist, who developed most systematically the Southern doctrine of states' rights in the defence of slavery. While ostensibly a struggle by South Carolina against President Jackson's 'Tariff of Abomination' of 1828, which fell more heavily on the Southern cotton-exporting states, Calhoun's threat to nullify the tariff was also, as William Freehling argued, a rehearsal for secession. Too ill to deliver his final speech personally in the senate on 4 March 1850 in the debate on the Great Compromise of that year, Calhoun reasserted his conviction that the federal government had ignored the wishes of the founding fathers and developed an autocratic centralised government against which Calhoun demanded cast-iron guarantees in order to protect the South's peculiar institution.

The first pro-Southern tract on the war's causes was written by the hapless Pennsylvanian ex-President James Buchanan, who had witnessed the drift towards war. In his *Mr Buchanan's Administration on the Eve of Rebellion* (1866) he raised two points which were long to serve the Confederate cause. The first was that irresponsible politicians, Southern as well as Northern, but predominantly Northern, and William Henry Seward in particular, with their appeals to a 'higher law' above the Constitution and their doctrine of the irrepressibility of sectional conflict, had heightened the crisis in the secession winter of 1860–61. Base political opportunism had replaced enlightened statesmanship. The second point, re-emphasising the needlessness of the conflict, was that slavery would have died quite naturally if not interfered with and left to itself, 'through the wise ordinances of superintending providence.'[3]

The defeated President of the Confederacy, Jefferson Davis, added his two-volume vindication in 1881 with *The Rise and Fall of the Confederate Government*. Slavery had long since been abolished, but Davis continued to emphasise the paternalistic aspects of slavery which elevated blacks 'from brutal savages into docile, intelligent and civilised agricultural labourers, and supplied [them] not only with bodily comforts, but with careful religious instruction, under the supervision of a superior race'. But slavery, as such, was not the real cause of the war. Davis's big guns were not aimed at the abolitionists: they were foolish and misguided philanthropists, but their motives and opinions were manifestly open and clear. It was the Free Soil and Republican party politicians who, under the guise of humanitarian concern, had engineered the war to further Northern political and economic aggrandisement against the South. 'That the agitation was political in its character, and was clearly developed as early as 1803, it is believed has been established in these pages. To preserve a sectional equilibrium and to maintain the equality of the States was the effort on one side, to acquire empire was a manifest purpose on the other.' The South, in turn, had no alternative but to secede, owing to a 'persistent and organised system of hostile measures ... devised and prosecuted for the purpose of rendering insecure the tenure of property in slaves'. The South had gone down to defeat in the defence not of slave property but of principle.

> The object of this work [he stated at the outset] has been from historical data to show that the Southern States had rightfully the power to withdraw from a Union into which they had, as sovereign communities, voluntarily entered; that the denial of that right was a violation of the letter and the spirit of the compact between the states; and that the war waged by the Federal Government against the seceding states was in disregard of the limitations of the Constitution, and destructive of the principles of the Declaration of Independence.

Evoking the sacred name of Jefferson and states' rights, of a loose confederation of states against a tyrannical majoritarian public opinion and a centralised and authoritarian government, he asserted that 'the war was one in which fundamental principles were involved; and ... force decides no truth'.[4] In this apologia Jefferson Davis remained unrepentant; the lost cause was the just cause.

The Lost Cause was the resonant title given to Edward Pollard's rationale (1866). A prolific Richmond journalist, Pollard contributed to the general Southern strategy of moving the moral question of slavery from centre stage. Slavery was not fundamental to the conflict but an excuse for sectional animosity, despite the insistence of the abolitionists – 'a few thousand disordered consciences', as he referred to them. The real distinction between North and South was essentially one of character and of civilisation. Here the lost cause became the nobler, superior cause. Colonial New England had been settled by cheerless puritans, while the cavaliers who 'drank in their baronial halls in Virginia confusion to roundheads and regicides' had settled in the South. The grubby plutocrats of the North, who dabbled in trade, were jealous of the truly aristocratic pride and manners of the South; 'the civilisation of the North was coarse and materialistic. That of the South was scant of shows, but highly refined and sentimental.'[5] Vulgar *nouveaux riches* had trampled down a superior civilisation out of spite and greed.

Alexander Stephens's *A Constitutional View of the Late War between the States* (two volumes, 1868–70) is a classic exposition of states' rights principles by the one-time Vice-president of the Confederacy and senator from Georgia. In 1860 he had been a reluctant secessionist arguing presciently that slavery would not be directly threatened under the Constitution so long as the South remained in the Union. But in an exchange of letters with Lincoln before the final breach he made it abundantly clear that slavery was the main point at issue. To the Confederacy he said: 'The cornerstone of our new government rests upon the great truth that the negro is not equal to the white man; that slavery, subordination to the superior race, is his natural and normal condition. Our new government is the first in the history of the world based upon this great physical, philosophical and moral truth.' With Southern defeat and the abolition of slavery Stevens changed tack and resorted to constitutional arguments in palliation of the Southern cause. Only superficially, he now argued, was battle engaged between slavery and anti-slavery: the deeper reason was a struggle between federal and national interpretations of government in which the South bravely fought against 'the banner of Consolidation'.[6]

Arthur Schlesinger Sr questioned this constitutional argument as early as 1922 in an article entitled 'The state rights fetish' reprinted in *New Viewpoints in American History*. In the early days of the republic the founding fathers had considered parties factious and hoped the republic would be held together by consensual unity. But in the absence of formal adversarial parties Jefferson and Madison had evoked states' rights to counter the Federalist John Adams's Alien and Sedition Acts of 1798, which were aimed at the Republican party opposition. The Virginia and Kentucky Resolutions which Jefferson and Madison wrote to nullify the Sedition Acts were essentially oppositional weapons employed against the Federalist party which controlled the administration. When Jefferson and the Republicans were elected to office in 1800 little more was heard of states' rights in the Republican ranks. Rather, in 1803, without reference either to Congress or to the separate states, Jefferson negotiated the Louisiana Purchase, which doubled the size of the United States at a stroke and ensured the continued western advance of the nation so dear to his heart.

The Hartford Convention of 1814 was to show that states' right theories were not limited to the South alone. In 1807 Jefferson had imposed an Embargo Act, an isolationist, non-importation, non-exportation piece of legislation intended to spare the United States involvement in the Napoleonic conflict in Europe. Its consequences hit New England manufacture and trade especially hard, and the rump of the remaining Federalists, concentrated in New England, met in Hartford in Connecticut and threatened to nullify this pernicious Republican party measure.

With the South Carolina Ordinances of Nullification of 1832 states' rights became increasingly identified with the South's strategy of protecting the peculiar institution from any federal interference, and Calhoun attempted to make this yet more watertight by means of the doctrine of concurrent majorities whereby each state and section of the Union had, separately, to concur fully in federal legislation. Even so, this doctrine was not exclusive to the South. In 1844, for example, the state of Massachusetts threatened secession if Texas was annexed and cut up into slave states. But essentially, as Schlesinger argued, it was the protection states' rights offered the South to retain slavery, not the doctrine itself, which motivated the Confederacy: a constitutional tactic, not an end in itself. And for all its much vaunted principled stand on this issue, the South could decisively attack states' rights when it was in its interest to do so. The South for example entirely disregarded Northern states' rights when it reinforced the fugitive slave laws in 1850 which compelled Northern state authorities to assist in the apprehension of runaway slaves. With the constitutional election of the 'black Republican' Lincoln in 1860, the South followed through the logic of its tactics and seceded from the Union altogether.

The American Civil War was to have worldwide repercussions. With the Emancipation Proclamation of 1863 the war could be interpreted in Europe as a crusade against the anachronism of slavery. But in his Gettysburg address of 19 November 1863 Lincoln went further, widening the struggle, and endowed the Unionist cause with the universal application of democratic government everywhere. It began: 'Four score and seven years ago our fathers brought forth on this continent a new nation, conceived in liberty, and dedicated to the proposition that all men are created equal. Now we are engaged in a great civil war, testing whether that nation, or any nation so conceived and so dedicated, can long endure.' Lincoln concluded: 'We here highly resolve that these dead shall not have died in vain; that this nation, under God, shall have a new birth of freedom; and that government of the people, by the people, for the people, shall not perish from the earth.'[7] Throughout the war, James MacPherson notes, Lincoln tended to refer increasingly to the 'nation', rather than just to the 'Union', and to the future of that nation as one of democratic and representative government. In Germany, meanwhile, and contemporaneously, Bismarck was constructing a quite different model of the nation state and national identity based on blood and iron.

In Britain opinion was deeply engaged and deeply divided. Conservatives such as Robert Cecil (the future Lord Salisbury) and Lord Acton, the Catholic historian, were convinced that the democratic experiment was, by its very nature, doomed to failure and threw their considerable polemical skills behind the Confederate cause. In 1861 and again in 1866 Acton turned his fire on the abolitionists and politicians such as William Henry Seward, Lincoln's Secretary of State, who questioned the

Constitution which recognised slavery. 'To appeal from the Constitution to a higher law, to denounce as sinful and contrary to natural right an institution expressly recognised by it, is manifestly an assault upon the Union itself,' Acton wrote. On slavery Acton was more ambivalent. He rehearsed the usual biblical arguments culled from St Paul: suggested that the institution had good points as well as bad, citing the virtues of sacrifice from the slave and charity from the master. But if, as in 1866, he argued that slavery had been wickedly defended he insisted that it was more wickedly removed. Borrowing from Calhoun and Alexander Stephens, he interpreted the struggle in terms of Jeffersonianism versus Hamiltonianism, of the necessary countervailing force of states' rights against Northern democratic despotism. Acton, at this stage, was profoundly averse to the twin levelling doctrines of equality and majoritarian rule and the omnipotent nation state. His admiration for the Confederacy and for its heroes, especially Robert E. Lee, stemmed from what he took to be the ordered, hierarchical nature of Southern society. Slavery was an essential and necessary part of this God-given order. Hence 'the decomposition of Democracy was arrested in the South by the indirect influence of slavery ... The North has used the doctrines of Democracy to destroy self-government. The South applied the principle of conditional federalism to cure the evils and to correct the errors of a false interpretation of Democracy.' In 1866, after the defeat of the Confederacy, Lord Acton wrote directly to Lee.

> I saw in State Rights the only availing check upon the absolutism of sovereign will, and secession filled me with hope, not as the destruction but as the redemption of Democracy ... I deemed that you were fighting the battles of our liberty, our progress, and our civilisation; and I mourn the State that was lost at Richmond more deeply than I rejoice over that which was saved at Waterloo.[8]

John Stuart Mill countered this thesis from the liberal wing in Great Britain. But Mill was in something of a quandary, for the liberals had traditionally identified with the emerging European force of national self-determination and self-government, with Mazzini's Italy and Kossuth's Hungary, for example, against the multi-national despotisms of Austria-Hungary and of Turkey. But now it was conservatives like Acton who were upholding the sacred right to insurrection, and liberals who were opposing minority nationalist aspirations. Mill overcame this difficulty, firstly, by identifying Northern republican opinion and the Unionist cause with the progressive English middle class, such as himself, who were pressing for parliamentary reform against a reactionary British caste which displayed all 'the fanaticism of a class for its class privileges'. Secondly, and most successfully, Mill played the moral card of anti-slavery.

> The South are in rebellion not for simple slavery; they are in rebellion for the right of burning human creatures alive ... Secession may be laudable, and so may any other kind of insurrection; but it may also be an enormous crime. It is the one or the other, according to the object and the provocation ... War, in a good cause, is not the greatest evil which a nation can suffer. War is an ugly thing, but not the ugliest of things: the decayed and degraded state of moral and patriotic feeling which thinks nothing worth a war is worse ... As long as justice and injustice have not terminated their ever-renewing fight for ascendancy in the affairs of mankind, human beings must be willing, when need is, to do battle for the one against the other.[9]

Karl Marx was another keen observer of the conflict and, along with Engels, wrote thirty-seven articles on the Civil War for *Die Presse* of Vienna. Marx had no wish to preserve Acton's semi-feudal state or to usher in Mill's bourgeois reformism, but looked to the long-term consequences of his material dialectic realising itself in an unfolding history. Marx rejected as superficial the imposition of Northern tariffs as a cause of secession but looked rather to the deeper clash of labour systems – free and slave, North and South – which were in conflict one with the other. Borrowing from John Cairnes, he believed expansion and conquest were essential to slavery's survival and he squarely accused the South – 'it is not a country at all but a battle-cry' – of an aggressive programme of conquest which, if successful, would end in the enslavement of the Northern working class. Free labour could never flourish until slavery was abolished, and Marx viewed the Civil War as a necessary bourgeois revolution which would usher in, in time, an emergent proletarian dictatorship.

As in the eighteenth century the American War of Independence

sounded the tocsin for the European middle class, so in the nineteenth century, the American Civil War sounded it for the working
class ... from the commencement of the titanic American strife the
working men of Europe felt instinctively that the star-spangled
banner carried the destiny of their class.[10]

The crusading spirit which transformed the war for Unionism
into a war which began the slow progress towards racial equality
was sustained during the early years of Southern Reconstruction.
But bitter Southern white opposition and the growing indifference of the North to the black cause led to the last Union troops
evacuating the South in 1877. In return for white 'redemption,'
and Southern 'home rule', there was tacit acceptance that the
South could deal with its race problem in whatever way it saw fit.
Southern politicians in Washington acquiesced in confirming the
nomination of the Republican Rutherford Hayes as President in
the disputed presidential election with the Democratic candidate,
Samuel Tilden. Northern public opinion had grown bored with
the eternal black question and its attention was focused instead
on happenings closer to home: the flood of new immigrants
surging into Northern urban centres and the attendant social and
political problems they brought with them; the rash of corruption
at every level, from the city ward boss up to Grant's Cabinet, that
seemed to typify the crass materialism of the Gilded Age; the
growing strife between workers and employers and the growing
class stratification in which hitherto self-employed artisans fell
increasingly into the growing pool of factory wage labour. In
1876 the centennial exhibition, held in Philadelphia, celebrated
the new industrial might of America by displaying the vastly
impressive Corliss dynamo. The exhibition was a gigantic manifestation of the Union's material might and prosperity: people
wanted to put the animosities of the Civil War behind them and
turn to the more mundane but satisfying activity of making
money. Increasingly the business of America was business, and the
business interest became closely identified with the Republican
party. Republicans were less prone to 'wave the bloody flag'
against the Democratic party tradition of 'rum, romanism and
rebellion'; Union and Confederate veterans began to hold joint
grey and blue reunions, from which, of course, black veterans
were excluded. The general disposition was to look to the future

rather than brood on past wrongs, and the new South itself began to industrialise with the aid of predominantly Northern capital.

The centennial year was also the year in which America's first Center for Graduate Historical Studies opened at Johns Hopkins University in Baltimore under the leadership of Herbert Baxter Adams. Adams, like most of his academic contemporaries, had been German-trained and it was in the attempt to achieve a comparable level of historical research that the institute was established. Frederick Jackson Turner and Woodrow Wilson, the future President, were among its first recruits. The high prestige of German scholarship helped to bolster the reputation of Hermann von Holst, who came to America soon after the Civil War and who espoused the cause of the Republican party. Von Holst was also an admirer of Bismarck and German nationalism. His eight-volume *Constitutional and Political History of the United States* (1877–92) was predominantly Hamiltonian and Unionist in its sentiments. The emergence of a powerful nation state was as inevitable in the United States as it was in Germany, but America had first to destroy the last vestiges of slavery and states' rights theory, which hampered this centripetal trend. Calhoun had audaciously raised the issue of nullification in South Carolina in 1832; the election of Polk had led to a war with Mexico and had resulted in the extension of the slave empire. Douglas's solution of popular sovereignty, allowing each state the right to choose between slavery or freedom, was typical of the 'moral hollowness' of that appeasing politician. The pro-Southern majority of the Supreme Court which handed down the Dred Scott decision was 'the greatest political atrocity of which a court has ever been guilty', while John Brown's raid on Harper's Ferry exemplified his 'great, ideal loftiness of soul'. Von Holst believed in the racial superiority of the German-Americans to the Irish-Americans, and he attacked the Know Nothing party for its attempt to divert attention away from the South and from slavery. The slave holders' expansionist and decentralising policies had to be met decisively by a manifest nationalist destiny which dictated the necessity of conflict and war for reunification. Lincoln met that challenge after 1860 and the ensuing righteous conflict destroyed the pernicious institution of slavery and the divisive doctrine of states' rights once and for all. Quoting

Bismarck with approval, he wrote that 'Sovereignty can only be a unit and must remain a unit – the sovereignty of law.' Von Holst depicted Lincoln as the American Bismarck who preserved the Union and the Constitution in their full integrity. Reviewing the first volume in 1876, Henry Adams and Henry Cabot Lodge, both trained in Germany, summarised the moral of the book as one which depicted 'all the steps by which the federal power slowly converted the national government into an instrument of its own will'.[11]

Von Holst's volumes were read, but their obvious partisanship and their depiction of a Southern conspiracy were too intemperate for the conciliatory mood of the time. A new professional class of historians were growing up – John Bach MacMasters, born 1852, Edward Channing (1856) and Albert Bushnell Hart (1854) – with no direct memories of the war. All of them wanted, in a general way, to emphasise that the national government emerged triumphant, tempered and purified, from the ordeal of war. This need was met by the pre-eminent nationalist historian of the period, James Ford Rhodes. Rhodes was born in Cleveland, Ohio, in 1848 and his father, who was a friend and relative of Senator Douglas, was a Democratic 'Copperhead' and a wealthy industrialist. Rhodes, the historian, changed his party affiliation a number of times during his life (his brother-in-law was Mark Hanna, who became the powerful kingmaker of the Republican party) and he always insisted upon his strict impartiality in his *History of the United States from the Compromise of 1850* (1893). Wishing to write, he retired early from the family firm and settled in Beacon Hill, in genteel Boston, in 1883. Rhodes sincerely believed that the time had come when the Civil War could be studied, as Michelet put it, with all the disinterestedness of the dead, much as one might approach the Peloponnesian wars of ancient Greece. 'All the right is never on one side,' he wrote, 'and all the wrong on the other.' His writings were the historical equivalent of the political compromise of 1877: differences were to be sunk and the approach was to be scrupulously evenhanded. This did not mean absence of moral judgement. Rhodes stated quite unequivocally that slavery was the single cause of the war: that with no slavery there would have been no secession and no Civil War. Southern secession in defence of slavery was equally wrong: 'the judgement of posterity is made up: it was an unrighteous cause which the South defended by arms; and at the tribunal of modern civilisation, Calhoun and Davis must be held accountable for the misery which resulted from this appeal to the sword.' Like von Holst, Rhodes condemned Douglas, whom he had met in his father's house as a young boy. Douglas 'sinned as a politician' because he did not consider slavery a grave moral evil, and because his Kansas–Nebraska Bill erased the stabilising Missouri compromise of 1820 and raised the vexed question of slavery in the territories. As a nationalist Rhodes praised Webster for his role in the great compromise of 1850 and condemned Garrison for pursuing the extremes of disunionism. But if the right side had won the war, the wrong side, the South, gained his sympathy for the miseries it suffered during Reconstruction. His own father had been contemptuous of blacks and he himself opposed black enfranchisement, carried by the Fifteenth Amendment. Rhodes's writings served to even the scales between North and South. Slavery was an evil, but had flourished for essentially economic reasons following the invention of the cotton gin by Eli Whitney. Britain and the North, the manufacturers of raw cotton, collaborated in this system of exploitation and were partially culpable and could not cast the first stone. Without evoking the deity, as Lincoln did in his second inaugural, Rhodes similarly depicted the battle as preordained and predetermined. The South was wrong to maintain slavery and secede: the North was wrong to impose radical Reconstruction on the South. No section was wholly to blame, neither section was wholly absolved. Rhodes received universal praise and approval for his volumes from all sections: from Charles Francis Adams in New England, John Reed and Walter Fleming from the South; Frederick Jackson Turner from the West, and George Julian, previously a radical Republican, from Indiana. Julian, writing to Rhodes after reading his history, said that it showed 'fairness in dealing with sectional and party issues and happily voices the general feeling of reconciliation and peace'. William Dodd, the Southerner, who taught at the University of Chicago, wrote that 'It is a sign that our country ... is really getting past the time when the differences of 1861–1865 served as a red rag.'[12]

That each section sought historical reconciliation can be illustrated by the writings of Woodrow Wilson, the future President. Born in 1856 in Virginia, he recalled in later life asking his father about the significance of Lincoln's election in 1860. Before becoming a politician he made his reputation as a historian (he contributed to Lord Acton's *Cambridge Modern History*), political scientist and university administrator, becoming president of Princeton in 1902. His highly influential *Congressional Government* (1885) argued against the excessive checks and balances of committee government in Congress and for a strengthened and active executive to offset the political torpor of the Gilded Age. The book was, in many ways, a blueprint for Progressive reformism in government and when Wilson was elected President in 1912 he was only the second Democrat (Grover Cleveland had been the first) to break the Republican hold on the presidency since the Civil War, and the first President since the Civil War to hail from the South. A strong nationalist and Unionist theme was also present in his historical writings such as *Division and Reunion* of 1893. It was, he wrote, because he loved the South so much that he rejoiced in the failure of the Confederacy, otherwise two weaker, separate states might have emerged and the evils of slavery might have been extended. He went on to praise the bravery and noble sacrifices of the Confederate army but concluded that 'Even the damnable cruelty and folly of reconstruction was to be preferred to helpless independence.' He also made much of the territorial theme, moving the conflict away from a simplistic North *v.* South conflict: 'Kansas showed us what the problem was, not South Carolina.'[13]

Wilson's election as President was a clear indication that the South had re-entered the mainstream of American life and was willing to relinquish the lost cause. Frederick Jackson Turner's seminal *The Frontier in American History* appeared in the same year as Wilson's *Division and Reunion*, 1893, and professionally symbolised the emergence of a western historian to challenge the long dominance of New England. Politically, towards the end of the century, conflict between North and South was in abeyance: instead the line of friction was between western populism and eastern capitalism. Turner was an embodiment of this new radical agrarianism and displayed many of its characteristics such as an anti-east coast bias, a more general and xenophobic anti-Europeanism and an anti-intellectual celebration of intuitive natural living over a cloying eastern culture.

> The wilderness masters the colonist. It finds him a European in dress, industries, tools, modes of travel and thought. It takes him from the railroad car and puts him in the birch canoe. It strips off the garments of civilisation and arrays him in the hunting shirt and the moccasin.

Turner's greatest achievement was to turn the axis of historical debate latitudinally from North and South to a new dynamic longitudinal western frontier. His writing was imbued both with wistful nostalgia, for the passing of the frontier announced by the 1890 census, and with the celebration of a unique and vibrant American character whose source was the perennial spring of the west. Turner was born in Portage, Wisconsin, in 1861, where he spent an idyllic youth, studied under Ulrich Bonner Phillips at Wisconsin and under Gilman and Adams at Johns Hopkins, returned to teach for a long and fruitful period at Wisconsin before settling, rather uncomfortably and ill at ease, at Harvard. Turner was repelled by the dry Germanic history that was inculcated at Johns Hopkins and countered the genetic institutional school of history, which sought the origins of the American character in a European past, with a historical and environmental transformation brought about by life on the physical frontier. It was this environmental impact, and not the European inheritance, which decisively shaped and moulded Americans and made them entirely new. 'This perennial rebirth, this fluidity of American life, this expansion westward with its new opportunities, its continuous touch with the simplicity of primitive society, furnish the forces dominating American character. The true point of view in the history of this nation is not the Atlantic coast, it is the Great West.' 'Because,' Turner continued, 'behind institutions, behind constitutional forms and modifications, lie the vital forces that call these organisations into life and shape them to meet changing conditions.' Turner chided von Holst for his superficial concentration on states' rights, Unionism and slavery. For 'When American history comes to be rightly viewed it will be seen that the slavery question is an accident' and relevant only in so far as it involved the territories and western expansion. After 1850 slavery held 'primary but far from exclusive importance' in American history. 'Such a struggle as the slavery contest can only be understood by bearing in mind that it was not merely a contest of North versus South, but that its form and its causes were fundamentally shaped by the dynamic factor of expanding sections, of wests to be won.' Turner was later to give greater emphasis to sectionalism over both class and frontier, but his earlier, more influential writings did little to distinguish north-west from south-west. Turner not only downplayed slavery, he conjured up a division in the South between slaveless democratic Piedmont farmers and a slave-owning tidewater aristocracy. This enabled him to treat the Southern frontiersman as having all those characteristics of his Northern counterpart: idealism, individualism and a spontaneous democratic spirit. Andrew Jackson, one of his heroes, was 'not so much a cotton planter and slave-owner as a personification of western wishes and western will.' On the matter of slavery Turner followed the benign view of his teacher, Phillips. If the northern abolitionists were convinced the slave must be unhappy, it must be because they imagined how they would feel if they were in the slave's place. But in truth most slaves were well looked after and generally contented with their humble lot. If Phillips's solution to the race problem was to return the black to the plantation, Turner's was, in contrast, to remove the black from the American heartland altogether: 'The negro is still the problem of the South and, while he remains, there will be a Southern sectionalism. If the negro were removed, it seems not unlikely that the unity of the Mississippi Valley would once more have free play.' Furthermore Turner did not reject the Teutonic germ theory entirely or the implicit racial bias which underlay it. He showed as little concern for the destruction of the Indian as he did for those in permanent chattel bondage. Though he had rejected the myth of the Teutonic forest as a seedbed of Aryan destiny, he transferred this vital, inexorable source of white conquest and advance to the Mississippi valley. There, Turner believed, the Mississippi frontier exerted a nationalising impact on diverse peoples, dissolving superficial sectional differences: from that frontier in Kentucky Lincoln, the supreme nationalist of his day, was raised before moving north to

Springfield, Illinois: Lincoln was 'a magnificent example of the melting pot typical of frontier life'.[14] What Turner carefully avoids, as Staughton Lynd has pointed out, is the fact that the evil and sadistic Simon Legree of *Uncle Tom's Cabin* was himself a frontiersman. Slavery on the ever-extending Black Belt frontier was notoriously more brutal and the percentage of slaves working on that frontier was never less than 10 per cent of the total slave population and, in the case of Mississippi and Louisiana, over 40 per cent of slave labour in these respective states.

Charles Beard was, if anything, even more influential than Turner, and his writings and theories dominated the profession until the emergence of a group of post-Second World War consensus writers. Born in 1874 in Indiana, he joined the history faculty of Columbia University in 1907 and made New York City his home until his death in 1948. One formative influence on him was that of America's home-grown philosophy called Pragmatism. Rejecting the absolute idealism that derived from Hegel and dominated American philosophy previously, Pragmatism dealt with working hypotheses which had to be empirically tested by experience rather than vainly searching for hidden, absolute philosophical truths. Truth was not something 'out there' which philosophers were trained to discover but, rather, a creative engagement with a multiplicity of circumstances in which the thinker, instead of being a detached observer, was actively engaged in making true, shaping and reshaping truth as he went along. As a philosophy which was infinitely fluid and flexible it was highly suspicious of formal rules and definitive logic. 'Damn the Absolute,' as William James, one of its leading publicists, wrote. This fresh, innovative, experimental method permeated all areas of American thought and served as an impulse to progressive political reform in America at the turn of the century. The accepted order of Social Darwinism – inflexible, predetermined, unchangeable and unalterable by human agency – gave way to a greater faith in the capacity of human beings to change and reorder things, actively to bring about much needed reforms, rather than accepting inevitable natural laws.

Pragmatism was a liberating philosophy to Beard, which emboldened him to embark upon radical historical reappraisals. Politically he was influenced by Marx and English socialist writings, studying for a time at Ruskin College, Oxford, set up by the British trade union movement. This infused his writings with a good deal of crude economic determinism, a determinism far cruder than Marx's own. He was deeply suspicious of *laissez-faire* capitalism and conceived American history in terms of a perpetual conflict between capital and labour, wealth and poverty, the democratic, agrarian spirit of Jefferson against the concentration of political and economic power advocated by Hamilton and his followers. At the turn of the century this eternal conflict took the form of western populist revolt against eastern finance, and progressive reform against political and economic corruption in the cities. Beard was always on the side of the small man against the powerful, especially the farmer, who represented for him the persistent, lasting radical element in American history. His first major study, *The Economic Interpretation of the Constitution* (1913), almost got him sacked from Columbia University for depicting the founding fathers at the Philadelphia Convention of 1787 not as demigods but as all too fallible human beings making a personal profit out of funding the new federal government debt. Quite simply the anti-federalist farmers were good Jeffersonian Democrats opposing a counter-revolutionary constitution formulated essentially for the benefit of the wealthy plutocrats of the north-east and the slave holders of the South.

This Manichean formula stalks all Beard's writings. Because the farmer was the embodiment of all that was best in American values, he was never able to explain satisfactorily why the overwhelmingly agrarian republic of 1787 was to ratify an ostensibly anti-democratic constitution. Similar problems were to arise when he dealt with the Civil War era, most fully in *The Rise of American Civilization* (1927), written in collaboration with his wife, Mary. In Beard's rewriting the North was driven essentially by economic motives to serve the interests of business, banking and finance – the Carnegies, Rockefellers and Morgans of the day – to gain Republican party control at Washington, and reduce the South to an economic satellite of Northern capitalism. Because the South was overwhelmingly rural (here he blurred the distinction between subsistence and commercial farmers, independent yeoman farmers and slave-owning planters), and because it opposed Northern capitalist demands for tariffs, subsidies, banks and a stable currency, his interpretation was perilously close to being pro-Southern and echoed the earlier indictment against Northern economic aggression put forward by Jefferson Davis. It served, too, not only to downplay the significance of the Civil War itself, which was dismissed as a 'fleeting incident', but also the moral significance of slavery.[15] The war was irrepressible because of the inevitable clash of an agrarian society on the one hand and an emerging industrial, urban society on the other, but it was fought for economic, not idealistic, reasons. This had to be so because Beard believed that the reason you gave for doing something was never the real reason, which remained always economic, material and unspoken. Thus if the North insisted that it went to war to save the Union, or the South that it seceded in order to preserve the institution of slavery, neither, by definition, could be the real motive. Behind the formalities of the Constitution, behind the grandiose rhetoric of Jefferson Davis and Abraham Lincoln, were the realities for which words were mere camouflage and shadows. The reality, which it was a historian's prime task to unmask, was the economic motive, which, in turn, reflected long-term economic change. Because of this Beard's writing is full of conspiracy theories – on the Constitution, the causes of the Civil War and later when he became obsessively convinced that Roosevelt was deliberately leading America into war for economic motives.

There was growing sectional strife in the early years of the nineteenth century because, in Marxist terms, 'the necessities of the productive system were generating portentous results'. It was no coincidence that the Democrats managed to reduce protection in 1857 and in 1859 to stop government subsidies to transatlantic steamship companies. The old Whigs were utterly unconcerned about the slavery agitation but were desperate to sustain the Hamilton–Webster tradition of government support for business, a sound currency and protection of industry. The Democratic party 'offered nothing to capitalism but capitulation' and the Whigs were concerned that the radical Seward would lead the newly emergent Republican party. Instead Lincoln came to their rescue and won the Republican party nomination in Chicago in 1860. Lincoln was sound on tariffs, banks, currency and homesteads and, 'a local railway attorney, he was trusted among businessmen.[16]

Parties and politicians had to shift to reflect the seismic economic and social changes of the time, and Seward, though a radical with regard to slavery, did recognise that parties were the instruments by which the changes came about. Parties were not abstract, platonic entities. 'A party,' Seward wrote, 'is in one sense a joint stock association in which those who contribute most direct the action of management of the concern.' Seward also appreciated that the sectional struggle was also a class struggle of bourgeois values against Southern aristocratic principles, and that the South would not abdicate its class privileges without a struggle. Hence the 'irrepressible conflict'. The southward pressure of the 'capitalist glacier' was the really revolutionary change, not the war itself. The South was fighting not an army but inexorable census returns which weighed increasingly against it. In place of Lincoln's providential will Beard puts an almost equally nebulous underlying economic transformation. 'The root of the controversy lay elsewhere – in social groupings founded on differences in climate, soils, industries, and labour systems, in divergent social forces, rather than in varying degrees of righteousness and wisdom, and what romantic historians call the "magnetism of great personalities".' And again:

> the core of the vortex lay elsewhere. It was in the flowing substances of things, limned by statistical reports on finance, commerce, capital, industry, railroads and agriculture by provisions of constitutional law, and by the pages of statute books – prosaic muniments which show that the so-called civil war was in reality a second American Revolution and in a strict sense, the first.[17]

Revolutionary, that is, in the sense that the war ended tangibly with the mass expropriation of property in the form of slaves, and America's transition from a rural to a predominantly capitalist industrial state.

Beside such mighty material forces the moral issue of slavery could not be important, and the so-called Civil War and the acts of individual politicians were, as the French *Annales* school would put it, mere superficial *évènements*. Yet the revered James Ford Rhodes had insisted that slavery was the political cause of the war. Not so, Beard retorted. Abolitionism, as such, was never a major issue in the North. 'Nobody but agitators, beneath the contempt of the towering statesmen of the age, ever dared to advocate it.' Lincoln, though he won a plurality of electoral college votes in 1860, was a minority candidate and even he was willing to guarantee slavery where it existed for all time in his first inaugural and simply opposed its extension. States' rights as an issue were also dismissed out of hand as a mere front. The struggle took on a sectional nature only because of the accidents of climate, soil and geography. These factors and the 'silent shift of social and material power' were the real cause of the war.[18]

The Republican party was the chosen vehicle by which Northern capital was to conquer Washington and subdue the South. Beard maintained that the Fourteenth Amendment, ratified in 1868, which held, 'nor shall any state deprive any person of life, liberty or property without due process of law', while ostensibly aimed at civil equality for blacks, was really intended to protect the personalised business classes and corporations, which mushroomed after the Civil War, from state and federal regulation. This amendment was indeed used to protect trusts in the late nineteenth century and was only rarely used to protect the rights of black people, but here Beard was anachronistically reading the concern of his own day with trust regulation and trust busting (which was one of the major aims of progressive reform) back into the Civil War era. His depiction of the yeoman farmer was also anachronistic. Most farmers by the mid nineteenth century, whether they grew cotton or wheat, were capitalists providing primary goods for a growing international market. Similarly Beard's stark division between industrial North and agrarian South was misleading. America, North and South, was still predominantly rural and engaged in agriculture. Even as late as 1850, 80 per cent of the North was engaged in farming as against 92 per cent of the South. Then again it was the Northern urban dwellers – Bostonians, New Yorkers – who voted for moderate candidates because of the textile industries' links with the South. And businessmen, as Stanley Coben has indicated, were as a rule conservative, anti-abolitionist and pro-Southern, afraid of vital cotton supplies being cut off and Southern debts remaining unpaid. Business also feared an uncertain future: Lincoln's election in 1860 caused a plunge in New York stock market values. The North, moreover, was not collectively in favour of high tariffs, as Beard suggests. Pennsylvania ironworks were; New York and New England, dependent upon the export of cotton fabrics, were not. Nor was the North agreed upon a sound currency. Conservative businessmen desired a stable, inflation-proof paper currency pegged to the gold standard, much as they wished for a stable economic future, but, as Irwin Unger has shown, indebted Pennsylvania businessmen demanded free banking and an inflationary, 'soft money' policy.

Beard wrote in the preface to his *Economic Interpretation of the Constitution* that he hoped that 'a few of this generation of historical scholars may be encouraged to turn away from barren "political history" to a study of the real economic forces which condition great movements in politics'. Beard certainly achieved this himself, with the consequence that, despite his lively style, there is an all-pervading sense of disembodied vagueness in his writing: politicians, individuals, seem never to have a life of their own, but are pulled like marionettes by strings, fulfilling, however unconsciously, the economic *Zeitgeist* of their time. Any ideology not strictly economic in origin is dismissed as superficial and misleading. Lincoln is significant not so much for emancipating the slaves as for promising government aid for a transcontinental railroad. Yet the plutocrats, those who purportedly pull the vital strings, are remarkably faceless and bear no names. It was this aspect of Beard's writing which led Peter Geyl to refer to its quality of 'despiritualisation: one-dimensional economic man leaves no room for complexity or idealism'. Du Bois was also dismissive of Beard's 'sweeping mechanistic' interpretation. For Du Bois the Prince of Denmark was entirely missing from *Hamlet*: the black and white struggle for freedom was entirely absent, as was 'the triumph of sheer moral courage and sacrifice' which, Du Bois believed, gave the era real significance.[19]

Algie Simons, a colleague of Beard's at Columbia, was even more crudely Marxist in interpretation. Having been a social worker in Chicago for a number of years, he was fully aware of the human casualties of the capitalist juggernaut. As with Beard, there was no choice, chance or contingency in history, just the implacable working out of material evolution. He concluded in *Class Struggle in America* (1906) that the Civil War, therefore, was simply a contest to secure possession of the 'big stick' of the national government. The northern capitalists wanted it to collect tariffs, build railroads, shoot down workers, protect trusts, and in short, to further the interests of plutocracy. The Southern chattel slave owner wanted it to secure free trade, to run down fugitive slaves, to conquer new territory for cotton fields, and to maintain the supremacy of King Cotton.[20]

Marxism was to revive partially following the great crash of 1929 and the Depression of the 1930s, and again during America's difficult years, both at home and abroad, during the 1960s. But, as Turner suggested, Marxism did not find a congenial welcome among most Americans. Rather than the statist, centralised Marxist–Leninist model of Soviet Russia, America's radical tradition tended to be anti-statist, anti-big business and anti-big government, and to arise spontaneously from grass-roots rural communities such as the populist movement at the end of the nineteenth century. That movement included some genuinely radical and communitarian reforms till it fused with the Democratic party, nominated William Jennings Bryan as its standard bearer in 1896 and ran on the single issue of bimetallism. The radical rural tradition in the South was intensely ambivalent: radical and racist, progressive and nostalgic, at the same time. Coner Vann Woodward's biography of the Georgian senator and populist, Tom Watson, followed him through the early years advocating a class alliance of poor, both black and white, in the South, against the lily-white Democratic establishment, but ended up preaching racial segregation and antisemitism. But it was not Beard and the Marxists who were to dominate the historical profession in the middle years of the twentieth century, but a very powerful Southern school of 'revisionists' who were to argue persuasively and successfully, on the whole, that the conflict had been needless and repressible.

In 1930 the Nashville Agrarians published their manifesto, *I'll Take my Stand.* In 1934 the Southern Historical Association was established. William Dodd was the dean of historians at the University of Chicago, William Dunning, though a Northerner from New Jersey, was profoundly pro-Southern and held sway at Columbia along with John W. Burgess, and Ulrich Bonner Phillips had moved to Yale. All were united, as Frank Owsley put it, in questioning the 'holiness of the northern legend'. Owsley, himself a pupil of Dodd, wrote revealingly to the Southern poet Allen Tate:

> My books will not interest the general reader. Only the historians will read them, but it is the historians who teach history classes and write textbooks and they will gradually, and without their own knowledge, be forced into our position. There are numerous southerners sapping and mining the northern position by objective, detached books and Dodd is certainly one of the leaders.[21]

In the 1930s the Civil War was re-engaged. Southern historians were determined to reverse the defeat of Appomattox and win the historiographical battle.

This Southern school deployed the progressivist interpretation to its own advantage. Avery Craven in his essay, 'The Turner theories and the South', argued that the south-west was the source of American democratic leadership, the area where Jefferson, Madison, Monroe and Jackson had emerged. In their initiative in extending the cotton Black Belt even farther west, and in extirpating the Indian, the Southerners displayed the same enterprising, pioneering resolve as their Northern counterparts. Craven considered it one of the major tragedies of American history that the western states had joined the Union against the South, instead of the Mississippi valley frontiersmen, North and South, combining together to stop the north-east's economic aggression in 1861, and concluded that 'A more democratic story does not appear in American history than that offered by the rise of the planter and his large-scale efforts in the south-west.'[22] Beard also played into the hands of Southern apologists. Borrowing heavily from his writings, the South was depicted in terms of the embattled Jeffersonian farmer, and the North as hypocritical, using the mask of idealism to hide nefarious schemes of economic expansion.

The revisionist school was deeply influenced by America's entry into the First World War, the general disenchantment with the results of the Paris Peace Conference, where Wilsonian idealism seemed to founder in the face of European duplicity and guile, and the general collapse of internationalism following America's failure to join the League of Nations. The United States did not, as is generally supposed, retreat into complete isolation between the two World Wars, but it did remain deeply distrustful of foreign commitments, and this latent suspicion was reinforced by the congressional hearings under Senator Nye of 1935 which held armament manufacturers and war profiteers responsible for taking America into the European conflict in 1917. J.R. Randall, a north-westerner from Indianapolis, had served in Woodrow Wilson's administration and was one of the chief proponents of the 'needless war' school. Avery Craven, from North Carolina, was another, and a lifelong Quaker and pacifist. Randall was determined to strip away the romance surrounding the Civil War and 'the splendour of battle flags'. War, as Sherman rightly said, was hell, and Randall graphically depicted the 'organised murder', the 'human slaughterhouse', 'the stench and hideousness' of battle; the slow death from gangrene which infected wounds, and the piles of amputated arms and legs crudely cut off by army surgeons without anaesthetic and piled up in heaps. Randall in his essay 'A blundering generation' rejected Beard's economic argument and its logical corollary of inevitabilism. Rather, Randall insisted, there was no major cause: it was false to assume, as historians did, that major wars must have major causes. 'One of the most colossal of misconceptions is the theory that fundamental motives produce war. The glaring and obvious fact is the artificiality of warmongering agitation.'[23] War was a profoundly unnatural state of affairs which led men to resort to arms; it represented a breakdown in rational discourse and submission to the forces of unreason, and Randall rightly pointed out that in 1860 most Americans sought and voted for compromise. Yet war came just the same. Randall believed that when conflicts did occur historians, endowed with hindsight, naturally sifted selectively through material all of which pointed irrevocably to conflict which the historian knew was going to occur. But this was to mistakenly read back from consequences to cause, to ignore choice, chance and contingency, and a multiplicity of possible alternatives at each and every juncture. It also imposed a false, predeterminist straitjacket on to events. What of those disputes and disagreements which did not result in war between Britain and the United States? In Oregon in 1840, for example, or the Anglo-American disagreement over Venezuela in 1895, or, indeed, the great compromise between North and South in 1850? Had these disputes led to conflict, in 1840, 1895 or 1850, Randall was convinced, historians would emerge from researching the events insisting upon their inevitability. Randall quoted with approval Norman Angell, who argued, from a pacifist viewpoint, that the belief that wars ever solved anything was a grand illusion, and Randall lambasted Emerson for spouting highsounding nonsense about the purifying impact of war. No, the war was the result of an aberrant 'psychopathology'.

> In contrast to the normal and basically valid demand for peace, the demand for war, or the whipping up of hostile feeling by those who begin a war, is artificial, unnatural and abnormal. When nations stumble into war, there is at some point a psychopathic case. Omit the element of abnormality, of bogus leadership, of inordinate ambition for conquest, and diagnosis fails.

Craven agreed with this verdict and in doing so deftly moved the moral issue away from centre stage. 'Those who force the settlement of human problems by war can expect only an unsympathetic hearing from the future. Mere desire to do "right" is no defense at the bar of history.' Implicit in these judgements was the recognition that the Civil War had been disastrous for the South and the cost, the death of one white soldier for every six freed slaves, too high. Frank Owsley listed the consequences of the war for the South to his friend, the writer Robert Penn Warren. The war had destroyed the South's economic and social institutions, had killed a whole generation of Southern manhood, sterilised Southern intellectual life for thirty years, led the North to impose a protective tariff which hampered Southern agriculture, led to Reconstruction and the souring of race relations in the South, alienated North from South, and encouraged what he called 'those intellectual scalawags' who misrepresented the South in order to curry favour with the North.[24]

Most crucially, slavery was not a real issue. The tightening of the fugitive slave laws in 1850 was a minor irritant only: the South had no real desire to extend slavery into the territories, the Kansas–Nebraska Act over which Lincoln and Douglas argued in their debates – non-extension versus popular sovereignty – was essentially a non-issue, for, in practice, the Bill ensured that those territories would enter the Union as free states; and the North in 1860 had no desire to abolish slavery. To Craven the slave question was 'an artificial creation of inflamed minds'. It assumed a psychological and abstract importance in the opinion of the North far beyond its concrete economic significance. 'What owning and being owned added to the usual relationship between employer and employee,' he wrote, 'it is difficult to say.' To Randall slavery was merely an incubus, for 'in a real sense the whites were more enslaved by the institution than the blacks'.[25] Superficially the crises of the 1850s – the Kansas–Nebraska Bill, the Dred Scott decision, 'bleeding Kansas' and the imposition of the pro-slave Lecompton Constitution – would seem to argue the significance of territorial extension as a major cause of war. But this, too, was a wholly artificial issue. James G. Blaine, the Gilded Age politician, had already pointed out the absurdity of a war resulting from 'an imaginary Negro in an impossible place'. And in 1929 Charles Ramsdell, a Southerner from Texas, wrote an essay, 'The natural limits of slavery expansion', which argued persuasively that climate and soil made any further extension of the Cotton Belt impossible. There was a mere handful of slaves in Kansas and, in spite of being formally admitted as slave states, the number of slaves in Utah and New Mexico was again only a handful. Ramsdell's conclusion was obvious: 'Even those who wished it destroyed had only to wait a little while – perhaps a generation, probably less.' Or, as E. Merton Coulter, another Southerner, put it, 'What good the war produced would have come with time in an orderly way; the bad would not have come at all.' These contributions fitted into Randall's 'needless war' thesis perfectly. 'It will not do to say that a comprehensive principle was bound up in the superficial territorial issue,' he concluded.[26]

But war did come for all that and so, therefore, scapegoats had to be found to explain how a non-existent problem led to a very real conflict. The abolitionists were the obvious candidates. Both Craven and Randall accused them of triggering off a rhetoric of attack and counter-attack which heightened tension and intensified unreason with all 'the avenging force of puritanism in politics'. Frank Owsley went further and accused the abolitionists of being the dupes and vanguard of Northern capitalism: 'industrialists, carefully coached by their lawyers and statesmen and "intellectual" aides, realised the bad strategy of waging a frank struggle for sectional power; they must pitch the struggle upon a moral plain, else many of the intelligentsia and the good people generally might become squeamish and refuse to fight'.[27] But to accuse the abolitionists alone was insufficient, for it was central to the revisionist thesis that the abolitionists were a numerically insignificant and despised minority. The politicians, that blundering generation of the 1850s, had irresponsibly allowed the nation to slip into war – indeed, had positively encouraged conflict for personal political ends. The revisionists were aware that the collapse of the Union had been preceded by a collapse in the second party system: the Whigs had disappeared only to re-emerge as a new Republican party in 1854 supported by nativist Know Nothing voters: the Democratic party had split into northern and southern wings, with two candidates, Douglas and Breckinridge, standing as separate candidates for their respective sections. But these coalescences and splinterings were not the result of conflicting principles: the politicians of that decade stood accused of deliberately whipping up artificial tension to win votes and advance their political careers. Here Douglas, the hero of the revisionist school, was the first revisionist when he turned on Lincoln and the Republican party. 'Why,' he asked, 'should the slavery agitation be kept up? Who does it benefit except the Republican politicians, who use it as their hobby [horse] to ride into office?' Traditionally the role of parties and politicians was to mediate between the disparate sections and opinions, and reach consensus and compromise: palpably this process of conciliation collapsed in the 1850s and party politicians must be mainly held responsible for the breakdown. Craven, in his biography of the Southern fire-eater Edmund Ruffin, accused Lincoln of deliberately engineering war during the Fort Sumter crisis. Many Republicans sought conciliation with the Douglas Democrats but Seward's resort to 'higher laws' and Lincoln's 'House divided' speech deliberately sought to widen the party gulf and make orderly government impossible. Charles Ramsdell likewise held Lincoln responsible for the war. In reply to the point that Lincoln had only wished to provision the fort and that the Confederates fired the first shot, he retorted that 'The Confederate government could not, without yielding the principle of independence, abate its claims to the fort.'[28]

Ramsdell maintained that the publication in 1890 of John Nicolay and John Hays's ten-volume biography of Lincoln had served to deify the martyred President and give a nationalist and anti-Southern slant to Civil War studies. David Donald in *An Excess of Democracy: The American Civil War and the Social Process* (1960) partly explained the conflict in terms of a volatile democratic electorate, but also accused party leaders of responding without policies or principles: 'Never was there a field so fertile before the propagandist, the agitator, the extremist.' Randall went along with this general analysis. 'Minds that should have kept serene were swept into excesses of propaganda, intolerance and hate ... If one word or phrase was selected to account for the war, that word would not be slavery, or economic grievance, or states' rights, or diverse civilisations. It would have to be such a word as fanaticism (on both sides), misunderstanding, misrepresentation, or perhaps politics.'[29] It seems odd that Randall should have hung his entire thesis on the word 'perhaps', and, if the war resulted from a general failure of political leadership, then Randall's hero, Lincoln, must stand principally accused. Randall was the Lincoln scholar *par excellence* of his generation and the author of a definitive four-volume biography completed after his death by Richard Current. Randall overcame this dilemma by emphasising Lincoln's Kentucky origins, his moderation, his opposition to the abolitionists and to John Brown's raid on Harper's Ferry and, despite the Lincoln–Douglas debates, the proximity of Lincoln's moderate views to those of the Democratic leader. He dismissed Ramsdell's suggestion that Lincoln had deliberately engineered the war – 'to say that Lincoln meant that the first shot would be fired by the other side, if a first shot was fired, is by no means the equivalent of saying that he had deliberately manoeuvred to have the first shot fired' – and stressed Lincoln's extreme caution on the question of emancipation during the war and his repeated efforts to keep his radical Republicans on a short leash. Randall so underplayed the role of Lincoln as liberator that Carter Woodson, the black historian, felt compelled to make reference to Randall's 'unconcealed antipathy' to black emancipation.[30] If Lincoln's stock partially fell,

Douglas's rose. James T. Moore Jr, the general editor of the highly popular American Statesmen series, had omitted Douglas from his list of volumes. But whereas before Douglas had been blamed for his moral indifference to slavery and for having split the Democratic party over his 'squatter sovereignty' doctrine, the revisionists exempted the 'giant from Peoria' from their general condemnation of blundering politicians, and praised him for his attempts to avoid conflict and hold the Union together. The argument ran that 'popular sovereignty' could have served as a temporary respite, allowing tempers to cool while slavery ran its natural course towards extinction.

Because the revisionists agreed that there was no real or rational cause for war, they had to scour the Civil War era for irrational manifestations: for mad abolitionists and madder politicians. Avery Craven tended to move away from individual responsibility and believed that slavery became 'a symbol and carrier of all sectional differences'. But he continued to believe slavery remained a symbol and that the sectional differences of free and slave were an exaggerated psychological manifestation rather than an actual, concrete cause of dissension. Roy Nichols, of the University of Pennsylvania, emphasised the 'hyperemotionalism' which characterised the epoch in his detailed political history *The Disruption of American Democracy*. He gave graphic details of the disorderly and unhealthy life of Washington politicians. Carousing all night and rarely eating between 9.00 a.m. and 4.00 p.m., they would have to resort to the Hole in the Wall, where strong alcoholic highballs would be mixed and consumed on empty stomachs. The resort to lurid speeches, Bowie knives and guns was often the result of intoxication, and inebriation was so common that senators and congressmen would often visit the offices of the *Congressional Globe* (the American equivalent of Hansard) the following day to read with horror what they had actually said in their speeches and heavily edit them before publication. President Pierce was one of those politicians who could not hold his liquor. This hapless 'doughface' Democrat from New Hampshire was, along with his wife, a horrified witness to one of his sons being run over and killed by a railway engine. Devastated, Mrs Pierce extracted a promise from her husband that he would renounce all further political ambitions and devote himself to family life. Instead Franklin Pierce became a 'dark horse' candidate for the Democratic nomination and was elected President in 1852. Mrs Pierce remained unforgiving, and when the couple moved into the White House the following year Mrs Pierce pointedly occupied a separate bedroom which she kept locked against her husband. 'Thereafter,' Roy Nichols concludes, 'nothing went right.' This is an amusing variation on the theme of chance, of the 'Cleopatra's nose' theory of history, but part of Nichols's wider explanation of a dysfunctional political system. 'In the last analysis the war was a product of the chaotic lack of system in ascertaining the public will, a chaos exploited by irresponsible and blind operators of local political machinery without adequate central organisation.'[31]

The revisionist mentality was at its most pronounced and unbalanced in the writings of Frank Owsley. Owsley was born in Alabama and studied for his doctorate on states' rights in the Confederacy under Dodd at Chicago. Arguing on the theme of an excess of democracy, Owsley maintained that overscrupulous regard for states' rights and the recalcitrance of such uncooperative governors as Zebulon Vance of North Carolina and Joseph Brown of Georgia hampered the Confederate war effort and contributed to its final defeat. This book was followed in 1931 by *King Cotton Diplomacy*, which drew parallels between the Civil War and the First World War, depicting Great Britain as a mercenary power exploiting the Civil War to make profits. While Phillips idolised the planter and the plantation, Owsley celebrated and romanticised the folk ways of the Southern yeoman farmer class. In private he made no secret of his intense partisanship. Reviewing a book by a certain McElroy on Jefferson Davis which he considered insufficiently respectful of the Confederate President, he wrote insisting that historians should not pass ethical judgements. When his friend and fellow Southern agrarian, Robert Penn Warren, pointed out that he, Owsley, was always making value judgements, Owsley replied, 'Mr McElroy obviously does not have the proper ethical values, and therefore he should not be permitted to express an opinion.'[32]

Owsley managed to convince himself that there had been three determined major crusades aimed at the heart of Southern civilisation. The first was that of the abolitionists. He wrote to a fellow historian, Herbert Agar, 'For years I have personally, and through my students, been digging at the abolitionist roots of American history and its writing. Until recently, I have got mightily far under some of these roots without being distrusted or accused of bias on motive.' The second crusade was radical Reconstruction. The third, the Scottsboro trial after 1931, when a number of blacks were put on trial for raping two white women and the American Communist party exploited the trial, advocating the setting up of separate black states in the South. Owsley set about organising a counter-network of university groups called the Phalanx to counter this obnoxious interference and come to the defence of Southern values. One member of the Phalanx wrote to Owsley apologising for the emotionalism of his letter, to which Owsley replied that there was no need to apologise: 'The angels must weep at the arrogance, complacency, conceit and success of the Northern Industrialist. I am bitter to the marrow, clear through to the marrow. So bitter that I feel that I am losing my poise as a historian.' In this advanced stage of paranoia abolitionists, radical Republicans and communist infiltrators were as one.[33]

In 1930 Owsley contributed a historical essay, 'The irrepressible conflict', to the Southern manifesto *I'll Take my Stand*. As its title suggests, Owsley did not subscribe to the revisionist 'needless war' argument but exploited, instead, Beard's Northern expansionist thesis as a long-term conspiracy aimed at Southern agrarian values. Rhapsodically he wrote of a South which 'reeked of the soil, of the plow and the spade', where 'history and literature, profane and sacred, twined their tendrils about the cottage and the villa, not the factory'. He held that to the South 'the philosophy of the North is the religion of an alien God'.[34] But Owsley emphasised that a clash of values, rather than economic differences, was the central battleground, and he insisted that the moral issue of slavery, as such, was a red herring in historical writing. Slavery was one element, but not an essential element, of the South's vital agrarian tradition: the economic and social life of the South would not have been radically different if slavery had never existed. Many Southerners deplored the institution of bondage, and held fast to the system only to avoid the consequent chaos and destruction of race war which would inevitably follow should the slave be freed. Jefferson had favoured abolition and

Calhoun had propounded states' rights, not in response to the abolitionist crusade but because he was a traditional Southern grass-roots democrat. Owsley selectively quoted from Jefferson's first inaugural of 1801, 'The support of the State governments in all their rights, as the most competent administrations for our domestic concerns and the surest bulwark against anti-republican tendencies,' but omitted the lines immediately following: 'The preservation of the General Government in its whole constitutional vigor, as the sheet anchor of our peace at home and safety abroad.' The North, he insisted, spoke hypocritically of a struggle for freedom, but the real struggle was for the balance of power both in Washington and in the territories, with the North aggressively upsetting the balance in its favour after 1830. Like Calhoun before him, Owsley seemed to assume that, despite the shift of population in favour of the North, which was naturally reflected in the growing disparity of sectional representation in Congress, Southern representation should be frozen and unchanged after 1830. When the North finally declared war on the South it was armed with 'the doctrine of intolerance, crusading, standardising alike in industry and in life. The South had to be crushed out; it was in the way; it impeded the progress of the machine. So Juggernaut drove his car across the South.'[35]

In 1940 Owsley was elected president of the Southern Historical Association and delivered his presidential address on 'The fundamental causes of the Civil War: egocentric sectionalism'. Here he extended his thesis by arguing that the north-west, much like the south-west, had a wide distribution of land ownership and independent, self-sufficient yeoman farmers, which made these two sections spontaneously egalitarian and democratic. Though there was a 'so-called' slave-holding oligarchy it exerted little control over Southern life outside a concentrated Black Belt and even there the large plantation owners represented only 25 per cent of the white male population. Owsley repeated his conspiracy theory that under the rallying cry of 'black freedom' New England was essentially pursuing a policy of hegemony and expansionist capitalism. Behind the fine, nationalist rhetoric of Lincoln's Gettysburg address, the North was intent upon what he called an aggressive, destructive, 'egocentric' sectionalism, unlike the 'constructive', accommodating sectionalism of the South and north-west. The North had deliberately sought to destroy the sectional balance, just as it had sought to destroy the South's three-fifths rule, which, Owsley held, was 'natural inasmuch as the Southerner regarded his slave as a human being and as part of the population'.[36] The anti-slavery campaign was, in reality, a crusade against the entire South, politically, economically, religiously and morally, and, throughout, the North arrogantly and egocentrically refused to respect the dignity, self-respect and distinctiveness of the South.

An all-pervasive air of unreality hangs over many revisionist historical writings because they are invariably trying to explain what did not happen – peace and further compromise – while simultaneously trying to explain away what did – the outbreak of war. It is entirely legitimate to assume that the war was not inevitable; that there were always alternatives, various choices, other roads that could have been taken. As the British historian Denis Brogan wrote (with reference to David Potter on the causes of the Civil War): 'If we think that the way things did turn out was the only way things could turn out, we will not be able to understand why they did turn out the way they did.'[37] What is not legitimate is to attempt to explain away, counterfactually, something which happened because you wish it had not happened. Many revisionists were also locked in their own determinist straitjacket. While validly arguing that war was not inevitable, they argued, simultaneously, that slavery would inevitably have died out. There is no evidence for this at all in 1860 – indeed, it would have been highly irrational for the Confederacy to go to war in defence of a dying institution. The Cotton Belt was flourishing in 1860. The land devoted to cotton doubled between 1860 and 1890 and had more than doubled again by 1925. And Robert Starobin has amply demonstrated that slavery could have been adapted to industry. Then again the revisionists' pro-Southern bias led them into double standards. Southerners adopt a principled stand for honourable reasons: Lee, for example, anti-slavery and anti-secessionist, nobly and tragically puts loyalty to his state of Virginia above loyalty to the United States. Northerners like Lincoln, Seward and Garrison are either fanatical, wrongheaded believers or they adopt high-sounding principles to mask rampant self-interest. Most improbably of all, the revisionists adopt a model whereby unprincipled politicians exploit and manipulate a mass electorate, artificially conjure up issues which, apparently, the electorate, initially at least, are wholly indifferent to. Here, instead of Beard's model of faceless industrialists and robber barons, decisively propelling and controlling events and using politicians as stooges, we have devious politicians manipulating innocent voters. It is true, as Edward Everett said at the time, and as David Donald and Roy Nichols have confirmed, that 'frequent elections keep us in hot water', but is it really feasible to assume that the electorate, with election turn-outs during this period often over 70 per cent of those qualified to vote, were totally duped and imposed upon? Is it not rather that, far from illustrating an 'excess' of democracy, the ante-bellum period witnessed the workings of a highly efficient democracy? Since the Jacksonian period American politics had been the politics of mass, participatory democracy. In an open political market the political entrepreneur responded to, and reflected, the wishes of his constituency. The politician might focus, clarify, even dramatise issues: what he could not do was conjure them up from nowhere. If the American electorate followed the Lincoln–Douglas debates of 1858 with bated breath and acute attention, it was because the American public was profoundly concerned with the issues raised in that senatorial contest in Illinois. As Lincoln himself said: 'In this age, in this country, public sentiment is everything. With it, nothing can fail; against it, nothing can succeed.'[38] Perhaps the collapse of the second party system reflected, only too well, the collapse of consensus in the 1850s and the effective response of party and politician to that collapse.

Owsley proved correct in his assumption that revisionist thinking on the Civil War era would find its way into textbooks, and President Truman, in the midst of the Cold War, hoped he had learned the dire lesson from Pierce and Buchanan that weakness and drift could lead to needless war. But the tide was beginning to turn. When C.E. Cavthen contributed an essay on Civil War historiography to a collection of writings on Southern history in 1965, he let fly with a degree of asperity. 'Presumably to satisfy the new nationalists, I not only cannot consider the Civil War repressible but also must write with righteous indignation against the South.' This change of opinion came about during the critical decades of the Second World War and the Cold War that followed, a period of unparalleled and extended crisis, with America and its military industrial complex on a permanent war footing. In 1951 Samuel Eliot Morison, who had served in the US navy during the Second World War, unequivocally asserted that 'war does accomplish something, that war is better than servitude, that war has been an inescapable aspect of the human story'. Arthur Schlesinger Jr, a young Harvard historian, encapsulated the new mood and interpretation in an article of 1949, the year in which America 'lost' China to communism and Soviet Russia developed the atom bomb, entitled 'The causes of the Civil War: a note on historical sentimentalism'. His father had already exploded the myth of states' rights as a primary cause of the war, and in his early book *The Age of Jackson* (1945) the younger Schlesinger had already insisted that 'the emotion which moved the North finally to battlefield and bloodshed was moral disgust with slavery'.[39]

Many intellectuals, Schlesinger included, were impressed by the writings of the theologian, Reinhold Niebuhr, with their emphasis upon human evil and an implacable original sin at work in history. In an early review of a Civil War history by Columbia University's Allan Nevins, Schlesinger drew direct comparisons between Douglas's appeasement of the South in the 1850s and Henry Wallace's misplaced attempts to appease Soviet Russia in the 1940s. Soviet Russia, like Nazi Germany before it, 'may respond much more to a firmness which wakens them to some sense of actuality than to a forbearance which is never great enough and always to be discounted'. One active Cold War warrior, Winston Churchill, had asserted that the American Civil War was 'the noblest and the least avoidable of all the great mass conflicts'. Schlesinger, whose writings John Higham once referred to as a historical rearming for the Third World War, thought likewise. His generation, as President Kennedy put it in his inaugural address of 1961, was 'born in this century, tempered by war, disciplined by a hard and bitter peace' and saw themselves as cool, pragmatic realists. The sentimentality of the revisionist school revealed itself in a belief that wars could always be avoided and that men ought always to act rationally to resolve major disagreements. This historical sentimentality was born of American innocence and rooted in a national tradition of passive isolationism. Such self-indulgence was no longer an option in the midst of Cold War. The younger Schlesinger made room in his analysis for rational principles and irrational behaviour. He suggested that the politicians of the 1850s, rather than irresponsibly whipping up artificial issues, reflected the very real ideological and sectional splits of the era, nor did he believe that the slavery issue could be resolved amicably without resort to arms. He did not believe that abolitionist fanaticism halted moves toward emancipation in the South, and to condemn the abolitionists for holding strong anti-slavery convictions was tantamount to saying there should have been no anti-fascists in the 1930s or any anti-communists in the late 1940s. Schlesinger believed that the slave economy was buoyant and expanding in the 1850s, and denied that Southerners would have accepted a compromise of compensated emancipation. Lincoln had suggested this as late as 1862 but the border states, the most likely to consider it, had rejected it out of hand. To suggest, as the revisionists did, that the territorial question was unreal was rather like saying the German invasion of Poland in 1939 was 'unreal' and insignificant to Britain and the United States, because they had not themselves been invaded. The revisionists were as one in sentimentally refusing to face up to the moral dilemmas and irreconcilable ideological differences and acting upon them, as Lincoln was finally forced to do in 1861. 'A society closed in the defence of evil institutions thus creates moral differences far too profound to be solved by compromise ... To reject the moral actuality of the Civil War is,' he concluded, 'to foreclose the possibility of an adequate account of its causes.'[40]

Peter Geyl's 'The American Civil War and the problem of inevitability' (reprinted in *Debates with Historians*, 1962) also tackled the revisionists for being over-rational. He conceded that Lincoln, though constitutionally elected in 1860, was a minority President and that the majority of public opinion understandably wanted to avoid extreme solutions to the slavery issue. But majorities, Geyl insisted, never make the rules in history, and events, as Lincoln himself admitted, were frequently beyond the control of human agencies. Passion, emotion, conviction, prejudice and mutual misunderstanding all played their part and Geyl thought Lincoln's appreciation of the inevitably tragic events operating beyond and outside human control showed much greater wisdom than Randall's cold rationalism. Randall's accusation of a blundering political generation 'belittles what had real greatness; it ignores the tragedy of that struggle with an overwhelming moral problem, slavery'.[41]

Allan Nevins, probably the best-selling historian of his day, was born in Illinois in 1890 and became professor at Columbia in 1928. Attempting, like Rhodes before him, to be fair to both sides, his Solomonic judgements on the era frequently provoked criticism on all sides. If he was more charitable to the South than Arthur Schlesinger, the New Englander, and if the South inflexibly refused to modify its peculiar institution, the North was accused of racism and indifference to the black cause. Nevins was an anti-revisionist in that he placed full emphasis upon the moral issue of slavery. 'The main root of the conflict (and there were minor roots) was the problem of slavery with its complementary problem of race-adjustment. It was a war over slavery and the future position of the Negro race in North America.' Douglas's failure to appreciate this made him a lesser politician than Lincoln, but Nevins did not find politicians guilty of artificially whipping up the slavery issue and the question of the territories: 'For, while hysteria was important, we have always to ask what basic reasons made possible the proposals which aroused it ... Obviously ... it is the forces behind these decisions which demand our study; the waters pouring down the gorge, not the rocks which threw their spray into the air.'[42]

This new nationalist school may have swung too far in the opposite direction in its desire to break loose from the revisionist consensus. Perhaps Schlesinger placed too much emphasis on the morality of anti-slavery, and too little on the negrophobe roots of opposition to the slave power, for the North did not resort to arms initially to free slaves. But generally its influence was salutary. Slavery was once more brought back into the foreground, and historians concentrated on a war that actually occurred rather than looking for reasons why it should have been avoided.

Genuine hatred of godless communism and the enforced conformity of the McCarthy era encouraged an atmosphere in which a group of consensus historians emerged. They tended to celebrate the uniqueness and the continuity of American democracy. Daniel Boorstin's three-volume history of the American experience is a vibrant celebration of practical, down-to-earth American values and Yankee can-do. *The Genius of American Politics*, based on a series of lectures he delivered at the University of Chicago in 1952, reflected the soporific triumphalism of the Eisenhower years perfectly. If the American revolution illustrated revolution without a dogma, the Civil War, rather bizarrely, is dealt with under the oxymoronic chapter heading 'The spirit of compromise'. Much like the revisionists, Boorstin has to ingeniously explain away something he wished had not happened in the first place.

> For us who boast that our political system is based on compromise, on the ability to organise varied regions and diverse institutions under a single federal union, it offers considerable embarrassment ... From any point of view it is one of the grimmest, most inexplicable, and most discouraging events of the modern era.[43]

Undeterred, however, Boorstin argued that the sections came to blows on strictly empirical, not metaphysical, grounds, and that this made it a very *American* civil war: that the South pointed to a slave system that was workable and profitable, the North to the superiority of free labour and a dynamic urban industrial economy. Both sides might interpret the Constitution differently, but Alexander Stephens appealed to a restoration of the original principles of 1776, not to a revolution, and went on to head a Confederate constitution remarkably similar to that of 1787. But no one, with the exception of the abolitionists, made revolutionary appeals beyond the Constitution. Instead the conflict revolved around differing sectional interpretations – of labour, of the rights of states – rather than questioning fundamentals, and the clash of arms came within the parameters of pragmatic American experience.

The new age of the computer made itself felt in the field of Civil War causation as in that of the re-evaluation of slavery. The brave new world of sophisticated high-tech machinery ushered in a new language of 'bivariate regression analysis' and 'scalograms'. Before the advent of the computer historians had tended to rely upon formal speeches, newspapers and private correspondence, but the new machines could easily analyse the 500,000 congressional roll calls (votes taken in both Houses) between 1836 and 1877, could quantify election poll books, local voting patterns, county directories and customs reports.

Lee Benson in his book *The Concept of Jacksonian Politics: New York as a Test Case* (1961) was the first to employ this new methodology and come up with some novel findings. Michael Holt in *Forging a Majority* (1969) was to follow it up with a study of the origins of the Republican party in Pittsburgh, Pennsylvania. Both discovered a seething world of local ethno-cultural struggles which determined voting patterns, rather than large sectional fissures over the broader issue of slavery. Intense partisanship, both Northern and Southern, Whig and Democrat, held this diverse electorate together, and helped keep the growing sectional divide at bay by bartering accommodation and deals. This new political history also drew attention to a crucial demographic element that had hitherto been generally ignored. In 1850 nine out of ten Americans were native-born, but in that critical decade some 2.5 million immigrants poured into America, transforming and reshaping its political life. Microscopic quantification revealed that voters were likely to divide on such ethnocultural issues such as prohibition, sabbatarianism, naturalisation, local denominational education, racism, patronage, anti-Catholicism, and nativist Know Nothingism.

Religious affiliation was especially crucial, the Whig party being identified with pietistic denominations (mainly Episcopalian and Congregationalist), the Democrats with ritualistic and liturgical denominations, including Irish Catholics. These local issues, and not the national issues of slavery and sectionism, dominated in 1844, according to Benson, and even up until 1852, Joel Silbey argued, local issues, along with tariffs, finance and homestead policies, dictated voting patterns. Most vitally, up at least to the Kansas–Nebraska Bill and the emergence of the Republican party, the party system, contrary to the revisionists, was fulfilling its traditional function of overcoming and harmonising major intersectional differences. In Washington, for example, voting on the settlement of the Oregon question and the admission of Texas to the Union was strictly partisan and national. In the House of

Representatives 82.3 per cent of the Democrats voted for the admission of Texas and 74.5 per cent of Whigs opposed. In the Senate the figures were 78.1 per cent Democrats for admission and 100 per cent Whigs against. Calhoun, despite all his attempts at forming a solid Southern pro-slavery bloc, was unable to break this national party pattern. Political partisanships surmounted sectional cleavages.

This new political history has yielded interesting material but, as Eric Foner has argued, with its emphasis on structure and the continuity of events, it tends to turn the Civil War into a non-event and replaces Beard's economic man with a new localised ethnocultural man indifferent to moral issues and wider concerns. Such is the school's emphasis on unchanging partisanship that Joel Silbey has referred to the war as 'a pernicious influence' which 'distorted the reality of political behaviour' and the school's depiction of a stable two-party system comes perilously close to the intellectual *cul-de-sac* of revisionism – why could there ever have possibly been a war?[44] And the new religious man presents problems too: the Republican party was grounded on pietistic beliefs, but then, so was the puritan South, with Baptists and Methodists predominating. And what of Lincoln, who, Kentucky-born and a deist, should, according to this model, have emerged as a fully fledged pro-slavery Democrat!

But, having said that, it is possible to synthesise rather than reject these new findings. There is no reason why a sophisticated electorate could not vote on local and national issues simultaneously. An Irish New Yorker, for example, could vote Democrat in order to allow him to continue drinking on the sabbath and confirm his racist attitude to blacks who might offer labour competition and lower his wages. Likewise a pietist Protestant could vote Republican as a nativist who wanted to restrict Irish Catholics and immigrants, and also vote against the slave power which threatened to cut off the safety valve of free labour in the west. For all its emphasis on structural organisation and party continuity the school is unable to explain away the collapse of the second party system in the 1850s: the sectional splintering of the Democratic party and the emergence of a wholly new Republican party, phoenix-like, out of the ashes of Whiggism and Know Nothingism. This new sectional party managed to square the circle: it was prohibitionist, it was nativist and anti-Catholic, it was pietist and anti-slavery, it offered free labour and free soil in the west, and in the 1860s it garnered sufficient votes in the North to capture the presidency. But 1860 marked the culmination of a growing divide. In 1844 Southern Democrats moved to deny the New Yorker, Martin Van Buren, a second term in office, and in 1848 Van Buren stood as a candidate for the new Free Soil party. In that same year Lewis Cass, the Democratic candidate, produced two separate editions of campaign literature, one for the North and one for the South, and Pierce was the last presidential candidate to carry a substantial number of votes in both North and South. Joel Silbey provides figures to illustrate the partisan voting in both houses on the Kansas–Nebraska Bill: 75 per cent of Democrats for it but only 27 per cent of Whigs. But the voting now was also sectional: 89 per cent of Southern congressmen voted for the Bill but only 36 per cent of Northern congressmen. David Potter, in his *Impending Crisis*, also drew attention to the highly sectional nature of the voting under the Wilmot Proviso to exclude slavery from territories acquired from the Mexican War. The constancy and closeness of electoral results, Southern control of the Senate and Northern control of the House of Representatives, the concept of the negative state, and the territorial question, all reinforced this determining trend.

In his *Free Soil, Free Labour, Free Men* (1970) and his *Politics and Ideology in the Age of the Civil War* (1980) Eric Foner has utilised the best of the new political history and synthesised it with his own study of Republican party ideology. That party's ranks consisted of pietists, imbued with the free labour work ethic which typified the North. Rather than, like Donald, depicting the abolitionists as a declining social class, Foner sees them as cultural imperialists along lines similar to Temperley and Ashworth, heralding a new, conscientious, capitalist wage labour system. But, ironically, just as the South brought on emancipation by secession, so the North went to war under Lincoln to protect the institution of self-employed free labour which the war would go far to destroy. Slave labour threatened free labour everywhere in America, the extension of slavery into the territories threatened 'free soil' and the promise that the west would remain open to white labour – hence the non-extension plank in the Republican party platform; hence Lincoln's guarantee to the voters of Illinois that that state would remain a white man's state. And if the Southern planter could enslave the black could he not, as Fitzhugh suggested, also enslave free white men? The average Republican voter could be intensely negrophobe, Unionist and anti-slave power at the same time. As Frederick Douglass rightly observed at the time: 'The cry of the free man was raised, not for the extension of liberty to the black man, but for the protection of the liberty of the white.' But wherever one looked, and however indirectly, every source of conflict was connected by invisible threads with slavery. As Thomas Hart Benton, the old Jacksonian, exclaimed with exasperation in 1848, 'You could not look upon the table but there were frogs, you could not sit down at the banquet but there were frogs, you could not go to the bridal couch and lift the sheets but there were frogs.'[45] The multiplying frogs were the multiplying consequences of slavery and the slave power.

Peculiarities in the federal system contributed to a head-on clash. A deliberately cumbersome amendment procedure (two-thirds of Congress and three-quarters of all the states) gave the South a veto over change as long as it could hold on to fifteen states. Hence the attempt by Southern Democrats to split the newly acquired Texas into five separate states, and their filibustering on Cuba and Nicaragua. The Democratic party was for long the pre-eminent national party, used to controlling the reins of federal power, but its two-thirds majority rule for electing presidential candidates, first used in 1844 to exclude Van Buren and ensure a victory for Polk and the Southern expansionist faction, led to a succession of weak, innocuous Presidents such as Pierce and Buchanan and finally deprived Douglas of the Democratic nomination in 1860, and totally split the party into Northern and Southern wings. As David Potter has shown in his *Impending Crisis*, the popular southern vote for moderation and compromise (Douglas or Bell) was, combined, 46 per cent of the total vote and greater than that for the Southern extensionist candidate, Breckinridge, while that of the Northern was greater for Douglas and Bell than for Lincoln, the 'black Republican'. Yet, given the state-by-state composition of the electoral college and the convention of winner takes all, Lincoln, with his strength concentrated in the North, converted his popular vote of only 39 per cent into an electoral college win of 180 over Douglas, whose 29 per cent popular vote was converted into only twelve electoral college seats. In other words, Lincoln won the election with the same percentage of votes Herbert Hoover got in the 1932 election against Roosevelt! Then again, the lame duck period of 120 days between election and inaugural left Buchanan nominally President yet constitutionally incapable of coping with the growing crisis: such, in contrast, was the speed of secession in the South that Jefferson Davis, the new Confederate President, delivered his inaugural in Montgomery, Alabama, days before the President of the United States delivered his own in Washington, D.C.

Contingency and chance almost certainly played their part, as they do in real life. The 1860 presidential election which followed so closely upon the raid on Harper's Ferry kept public opinion in a state of intense excitement. The choice of venue for the party convention that year may also have influenced events. The Democrats chose Charleston, the epicentre of fire-eaters and secessionists, while the Republicans chose Chicago, giving Lincoln, Illinois's favourite son, an advantage over Seward, a New Yorker and his chief rival for the nomination. Again, if Lincoln had not packed the Chicago 'Wigwam' with his supporters and bought states such as Pennsylvania with promises of office, Seward would probably have secured the Republican nomination and his radicalism would almost certainly have deprived him of the presidency. Then what?

Lincoln's election triggered off secession because the Republican party threatened the extension of slavery and because Lincoln, the 'black Republican', vaguely threatened the honour and survival of the planter class. This, in a sense, was a pre-emptive strike against the Northern enemy before it became overwhelmingly superior. The President was constitutionally required to maintain the Union, and in this he received the overwhelming support of the North.

Lincoln hoped to avoid coercion and disunion but he was also required to hold federal forts in the South. Yet if he insisted upon holding Fort Sumter could he also hold on to the strategically vital middle states which had not yet declared for or against secession? John Tilley, a lawyer from Montgomery, Alabama, had argued that Lincoln deliberately manoeuvred the South into war in *Lincoln Takes Command*, and Ramsdell concurred in the verdict. Lincoln had insisted at the time that Colonel Anderson had sent a message from Fort Sumter to the President requesting supplies. Tilley and Ramsdell insisted that no such message was sent, but in 1954 Potter found the letter, which had been misplaced in the federal archives, and proved that Lincoln had indeed told the truth.

Yet Potter still had qualms about the war and had some sympathy, much as revisionists had, for Douglas as the one politician aware of the abyss that yawned in the winter of 1861 and the only statesman capable of circumventing it. But this, too, is a strange judgement, for Douglas's policy of 'popular sovereignty' exacerbated rather than resolved sectional differences. Opposition to it split the Democratic party and created a new Republican party which galvanised the North. Douglas's solution was eventually rejected by all sides precisely because it was a solution. By the 1850s each section was seeking, not compromise, but a cast-iron guarantee of its own position.

But Potter did absolve Lincoln of the accusation of engineering war. He argued that up to the last Lincoln sought peace. Even Lincoln's rejection of the Crittenden compromise, a scheme which would have re-established the Missouri compromise line of 36° 30' and extended it to the Pacific, was a defensive peace move. That is, Lincoln was convinced that the South had cried wolf once too often and it was time this secessionist bluff was called. The President was also aware of divisions in the South and exaggerated the strength of Unionism in the South. Lincoln thought that by rejecting the Crittenden compromise he could hold on to the vital middle states and compel the deep South to abandon its bid for independence. Potter, in his *Lincoln and his Party in the Secession Crisis* both in the 1942 and in the 1962 introduction, insisted that acceptance of the compromise would have held the border states and avoided war. But, as Denis Brogan pointed out, accepting it would have destroyed the whole Republican party principle of the non-extension of slavery, and was therefore never really feasible. At this stage only seven states had seceded and Virginia had, on 4 February 1861, voted against secession. There is reason to believe that Lincoln might have abandoned Fort Sumter if Virginia had abandoned secession: certainly Seward, working behind Lincoln's back, gave Davis the impression that the fort would be abandoned. When news reached Montgomery that ships had been sent to provision – not arm – the fort, Davis gave orders on 9 April to fire, and on 12 April the first shots of the war were fired.

The debate on the causes of the Civil War continues. Potter continued to ask whether the *per capita* cost of freeing the slaves was not too high. 'All I suggest is that historians who believe so zealously in the virtue of facing up to the issues in the past ought not to believe in the expedients of peace in the present.' To which Kenneth Stampp has replied, how many more generations were to suffer the indignities of slavery before the peaceful winning of emancipation? But in his last book, *The Impending Crisis*, Potter's stance was closer to Stampp than before. 'Slavery,' he concluded, 'presented an inescapable ethical qustion which precipitated a sharp conflict of values ... [it was] a transcendent sectional issue in its own right, and a catalyst of all sectional antagonisms'[46] – a conclusion reaffirmed in 1996 by William Gienapp: 'Without slavery it is impossible to imagine a war between the North and the South (or indeed, the existence of anything we would call "the South" except as a geographical region).' We end, then, where the chapter began, with Lincoln's second inaugural. 'One-eighth of the whole population was colored slaves, not distributed generally over the Union, but localized in the Southern part of it. These slaves constituted a peculiar and powerful interest. All knew that this interest was somehow the cause of the war.'[47]

Notes

1 Lincoln quoted in Richard Hofstadter, *Great Issues in American History*, II, *1865-1957* (New York, 1958), pp. 415–16.
2 Wilson quoted in Richard Leopold *et al.* (eds), *Problems in American History*, I (Englewood Cliffs, N.J., 1966), p. 329; and in Gerald Grob and George Billias (eds), *Interpretations of American History: Patterns and Perspectives*, I (New York, 1972), p. 243.
3 Buchanan quoted in Edwin Rozwenc (ed.), *The Causes of the American Civil War* (Boston, Mass., 1961), p. 65.
4 Davis quoted in Rozwenc, *The Causes of the American Civil War*, p. 32. Jefferson Davis, *The Rise and Fall of the Confederate Government*, I (New

York, 1881), pp. vi–vii. Davis quoted in Kenneth Stampp, *The Imperiled Union* (Oxford, 1980), p. 192. Davis, *Rise and Fall*, I, p. v. Davis quoted in Leopold, *Problems in American History*, I, p. 398.

5 Pollard in Rozwenc, *The Causes of the American Civil War*, pp. 51, 52.

6 Stephens quoted in Lord Acton, *Historical Essays and Studies* (London, 1907), p. 136; and Rozwenc, *The Causes of the American Civil War*, p. 69.

7 Lincoln quoted in Hofstadter, *Great Issues in American History*, II, pp. 414–15.

8 Gertrude Himmelfarb (ed.), *Acton's Essays on Freedom and Power* (London, 1956), p. 215. Acton, *Historical Essays and Studies*, pp. 137, 142. Acton's letter to Lee quoted in Carl Degler, *One among Many: The Civil War in Comparative Perspective* (Gettysburg, 1990), p. 14.

9 J.S. Mill, *Dissertations and Discussions*, III (London, 1875), pp. 195, 204–5.

10 David Fernbach (ed.), *Marx: Surveys from Exile: Political Writings*, II (Harmondsworth, 1973), p. 344; and Marx quoted in James McPherson (ed.), *We Cannot Escape History* (Urbana, Ill., 1995), p. 10.

11 Von Holst quoted in Michael Kraus and Davis Joyce, *The Writing of American History* (Norman, Okla., 1983), pp. 167–70. Adams and Lodge quoted in Thomas Pressly, *Americans Interpret their Civil War* (New York, 1962), p. 75.

12 Rhodes quoted in Pressly, *Americans Interpret their Civil War*, pp. 171–2, 173, 179; Kraus and Joyce, *The Writing of American History*, p. 180.

13 Wilson quoted in Pressly, *Americans Interpret their Civil War*, p. 203.

14 Turner quoted in Staughton Lynd, *Class Conflict, Slavery and the US Constitution* (Indianapolis, 1967), pp. 138, 142, 143. Turner quoted in Pressly, *Americans Interpret their Civil War*, p. 208. Turner's essay is reprinted in Daniel Boorstin (ed.), *An American Primer* (Chicago, 1968), pp. 544–67.

15 Charles and Mary Beard, *The Rise of American Civilisation* (New York, 1930), p. 54.

16 *Ibid.*, pp. 3, 32.

17 *Ibid.*, pp. 7, 51, 54.

18 *Ibid.*, pp. 38, 55.

19 Beard quoted in Marcus Cunliffe and Robin Winks (eds), *Past Masters* (New York, 1969), p. 133. Peter Geyl, *Debates with Historians* (New York, 1962), p. 245. Du Bois quoted in Pressly, *Americans Interpret their Civil War*, p. 261.

20 Simons quoted in Kenneth Stampp (ed.), *The Causes of the Civil War* (Englewood Cliffs, N.J., 1963), p. 65.

21 Owsley quoted in Michael O'Brien, *The Idea of the American South, 1920–1941* (Baltimore, 1979), pp. 162, 169.

22 Avery Craven, *An Historian and the Civil War* (Chicago, 1967), p. 195.

23 Randall quoted in Pressly, *Americans Interpret their Civil War*, p. 306; in Grob and Billias, *Interpretations of American History*, p. 450; and in Geyl, *Debates with Historians*, p. 247.

24 Randall quoted in Pressly, *Americans Interpret their Civil War*, p. 308; Craven quoted in Peter Novick, *That Noble Dream* (Cambridge, 1988), p. 237; and Owsley in O'Brien, *The Idea of the American South*, p. 170.

25 Craven, *An Historian and the Civil War*, p. 46. Craven cited by Grob and Billias, *Interpretations of American History*, p. 461. Randall quoted in Stampp, *The Imperiled Union*, p. 201.

26 Blaine quoted in David Potter, *The South and the Sectional Conflict* (Baton Rouge, 1968), p. 98; Ramsdall in Robert Fogel and Stanley Engerman, *Time on the Cross*, II (London, 1974), p. 185; Coulter in Pressly, *Americans Interpret their Civil War*, p. 286; and Randall, 'The Civil War restudied', *Journal of Southern History* (6, 1940), p. 442.

27 Randall quoted in Grob and Billias, *Interpretations of American History*, p. 463; and Owsley in O'Brien, *The Idea of the American South*, p. 171.

28 Douglas quoted in Stampp, *The Imperiled Union*, p. 204.

29 Donald's essay is reprinted in Stampp, *The Causes of the Civil War*, p. 95. Randall cited in Novick, *That Noble Dream*, p. 237. Randall's 'A blundering generation' is also reprinted in Stampp, *The Causes of the Civil War*, p. 84.

30 Woodson quoted in Merrill Peterson, *Lincoln in American Memory* (Oxford, 1994), p. 309.

31 Craven quoted in Potter, *The South and the Sectional Conflict*, p. 149. Nichols interviewed in John Garraty (ed.), *Interpreting American History*, I (London, 1970), p. 287; and quoted in Arthur Link and Rambert Patrick (eds), *Writing Southern History* (Baton Rouge, 1965), p. 238.

32 Owsley quoted in O'Brien, *The Idea of the American South*, p. 170.

33 *Ibid.*, pp. 179, 173.

34 Louis Rubin Jr (ed.), *I'll Take my Stand* (New York, 1962), pp. 70, 123, 122.

35 Jefferson quoted in Hofstadter, *Great Issues in American History*, II, p. 189; *I'll Take my Stand*, p. 91.

36 Frank Owsley in George Tindall (ed.), *The Pursuit of Southern History* (Baton Rouge, 1964), pp. 85–9.

37 Brogan in Cunliffe and Winks, *Past Masters*, p. 322.

38 Lincoln quoted in T. Harry Williams, *Lincoln and his Generals* (London, 1952), p. 375.

39 Cauthen quoted in Link and Patrick, *Writing Southern History*, p. 240 n. 61. Morison cited in Grob and Billias, *Interpretations of American History*, p. 433; and Schlesinger in David Potter, *The South and the Sectional Conflict*, p. 99.

40 Schlesinger quoted in Pressly, *Americans Interpret their Civil War*, pp. 273–4. Kennedy in Hofstadter, *Great Issues in American History*, III, p. 546. Schlesinger's essay is reprinted in his *The Politics of Hope* (London, 1964), pp. 43, 47.

41 Geyl, *Debates with Historians*, p. 262.

42 Nevins quoted in Pressly, *Americans Interpret their Civil War*, p. 349.

43 Daniel Boorstin, *The Genius of American Politics* (Chicago, 1953), p. 99.

44 Silbey quoted in Don Fehrenbacher, *Lincoln in Text and Context* (Stanford, 1987), p. 78.

45 Douglas quoted in Eric Foner, *Politics and Ideology in the Age of the Civil War* (Oxford, 1980), p. 49. Benson quoted in David Potter, *The Impending Crisis, 1848–1861* (New York, 1976), p. 49.

46 David Potter, *Lincoln and his Party in the Secession Crisis* (New Haven, 1962), pp. xx–xxi; and *The Impending Crisis*, pp. 41, 48.

47 Gienapp quoted in Gabor Boritt (ed.), *Why the Civil War Came* (Oxford, 1996), p. 82. Lincoln quoted in Hofstadter, *Great Issues in American History*, II, p. 416.

Selective bibliography

Beard, Charles and Mary, *The Rise of American Civilization* (New York, 1930).

Benson, Lee, *Towards the Scientific Study of History* (Philadelphia, 1972).

Bonner, Thomas, 'Civil War historians and the "needless war" Doctrine', *Journal of the History of Ideas* (47, 1986).

Boorstin, Daniel, 'The Civil War and the Spirit of Compromise' in his *The Genius of American Politics* (Chicago, 1953).

Boritt, Gabor (ed.), *Why the Civil War Came* (Oxford, 1996).

Craven, Avery, 'Coming of the war between the states: an interpretation', *Journal of Southern History* (2, 1936).

Craven, Avery, *An Historian and the Civil War* (Chicago, 1967).

Craven, Avery, *The Coming of the Civil War* (Chicago, 1957).

Donald, David, 'An excess of democracy: the American Civil War and the social process', reprinted in his *Lincoln Reconsidered* (New York, 1969).

Fehrenbacher, Don, *Lincoln in Text and Context* (Stanford, 1987).

Foner, Eric, 'The causes of the Civil War: recent interpretations and new directions', in Robert Swierenga (ed.), *Beyond the Civil War Synthesis* (Westport, Conn., 1975).

Foner, Eric, 'Politics, ideology and the origins of the American Civil War' in his *Politics and Ideology in the Age of the Civil War* (Oxford, 1980).

Foner, Eric, 'The causes of the American Civil War: recent interpretations and new directions' in his *Politics and Ideology in the Age of the Civil War* (Oxford, 1980).

Geyl, Peter, 'The American Civil War and the problem of inevitability' in his *Debates with Historians* (New York, 1962).

Hofstadter, Richard, *The Progressive Historians* (New York, 1970).

Holt, Michael, *Forging a Majority* (New Haven, 1969).

Holt, Michael, *Political Parties and American Political Development: From the Age of Jackson to the Age of Lincoln* (Baton Rouge, 1992).

Kousser, Morgan, 'The irrepressible, repressible conflict theory', *Reviews in American History* (4, 1975; 21, 1993).

Lynd, Staughton, *Class Conflict, Slavery and the U.S. Constitution* (Indianapolis, 1967).

McPherson, James, 'The War of Southern Aggression' in his *Drawn with the Sword* (Oxford, 1996).

McPherson, James, *Battle Cry of Freedom* (Harmondsworth, 1988).

Nichols, Roy, *The Disruption of American Democracy* (New York, 1948).

Potter, David, *Lincoln and his Party in the Secession Crisis* (New Haven, 1962).

Potter, David, 'The literature on the background of the Civil War' in his *The South and the Sectional Conflict* (Baton Rouge, 1968).

Potter, David, *The Impending Crisis, 1848–1861* (New York, 1976).

Pressly, Thomas, *Americans Interpret their Civil War* (New York, 1962).

Randall, J.R., 'A blundering generation', reprinted in Kenneth Stampp (ed.), *The*

Causes of the Civil War (Englewood Cliffs, N.J., 1963).

Randall, J.R., 'The Civil War restudied', *Journal of Southern History* (6, 1940).

Reid, Brian Holden, *The Origins of the American Civil War* (London, 1996).

Rozwenc, Edwin (ed.), *The Causes of the American Civil War* (Boston, Mass., 1961).

Schlesinger Jr, Arthur, 'The causes of the Civil War: a note on historical sentimentalism' in his *The Politics of Hope* (London, 1964); reprinted in Edwin Rozwenc (ed.), *The Causes of the American Civil War* (Boston, Mass., 1961).

Schlesinger, Arthur, 'The states' rights fetish' in his *New Viewpoints in American History* (New York, 1922).

Silbey, Joel, *The Partisan Imperative: The Dynamics of American Politics before the Civil War* (Oxford, 1985).

Stampp, Kenneth (ed.), *The Causes of the Civil War* (Englewood Cliffs, N.J., 1963).

Stampp, Kenneth, 'The irrepressible conflict' in his *The Imperiled Union* (Oxford, 1980).

Stampp, Kenneth, *And the War Came* (Chicago, 1980).

Swierenga, Robert (ed.), *Beyond the Civil War Synthesis* (Westport, Conn., 1975).

5

The American Civil War

North and South

The historiography of the Civil War began in a smoke of charge and counter-charge, accusation and vindication, especially in the South, where the war had been lost, and someone or something had to be held responsible for the shattering defeat. Just as ante-bellum abolitionists believed that slavery had providentially withered away because of its immoral roots, so the north came to believe that God was not only on the side of the big battal-ions but had also ensured victory for a divine and righteous cause.

The South could have chosen to fall back upon belief in the inevitability of defeat because of its inferior forces, and Robert E. Lee, for one, was convinced that without European aid the Confederate cause was doomed from the start. As he wrote to Jubal Early at the end of the war: 'It will be difficult to get the world to understand the odds against which we fought.'[1] But then to concede the inevitability of defeat from the start was to ques-tion the collective sanity of the Confederacy. No, the South's was a high-risk strategy, but sometimes risks pay off.

In 1861 both the Confederacy and Europe (and possibly some in the North too) believed that the South would succeed in its bid for independence. General Joseph Johnston maintained in his *Memoirs* that the South had not been 'guilty of the high crime of undertaking war without the means of waging it successfully'. General Pierre Beauregard made the same point: 'No people ever warred for independence with more relative advantage than the

Confederates.'[2] But the high-risk strategy failed disastrously and led to the imposition of radical Reconstruction.

David Donald has written that 'a historian is a camp follower of the successful army' and hence views the war from the privileged hindsight of an ineluctable Northern victory. Richard Current, in a collection of essays edited by David Donald, has indeed concluded that God was on the side of the big battalions, but Grant, who led those battalions, was unconvinced by this deterministic theory at the time. It was, in part, to refute the assumption that Northern victory was predetermined by its superior resources that Grant wrote his *Memoirs*. 'The cry,' he wrote, 'was in the air that the north only won by brute force; that the generalship and valor were with the south. This has gone into history with so many other illusions.' The illusion was held especially by Southern commentators as a means of salving their honour in the midst of defeat. As one Virginian insisted, 'They never whipped us, Sir, unless there were four to one.' Or, as Lee put it to his troops at Appomattox, 'the Army of Northern Virginia has been compelled to yield to overwhelming numbers and resources'.[3] Grant insisted that, while he did command vastly greater numbers of men, the South enjoyed a major strategic advantage: it had simply to hold on to its independence and vast territorial expanse, while the North was compelled to invade the South, bring it to heel and force it back into the Union. The Confederacy enjoyed the incomparable advantage of interior lines of communication, and, in the east, riverways running west to east which provided natural lines of defence. In Grant's opinion this, and the fact that the North had to operate throughout in enemy territory, more than made up for the North's superiority in numbers. Furthermore, the North's three-year enlistment ended in the critical year of 1864 and, although 136,000 soldiers re-enlisted, 100,000 did not, causing the Union army to become considerably depleted. Public opinion on both sides demanded set-piece battles and conclusive victories, and the assumption is that the North had a limitless supply of cannon fodder, but such was not the case. When casualty figures began to mount inexorably from Shiloh until the bloody battles of the Wilderness Northern public opinion was appalled and demoralised and, while in 1864 Grant gained a reputation as a 'butcher', in practice he was careful to husband his supply of soliders precisely because those human resources were not unlimited.

Given its problems of early recruitment the North did not possess overwhelmingly superior manpower resources until 1863. The September 1862 invasions of Kentucky and Maryland, and the battles of Antietam and Perryville, were close-run things. In the summer of 1863 Lee was again close to victory. The fall of Vicksburg was a major blow to Confederate morale, but this was partially reversed by the victory at Chickamauga in September. Hattaway and Jones maintain that the South could have won the war before the reversals the South suffered in the capture of Forts Henry and Donelson (1862), while James McPherson has argued that, while the North's superior numbers were a necessary prerequisite of victory, they were not in themselves sufficient to guarantee it. In place of inevitabilism, McPherson has consistently argued for the significance of contingency and chance. What, for example, might have happened if Stonewall Jackson had not been mistakenly shot by one of his own soldiers at Chancellorsville? What if the presidential elections in the North had been held in August rather than November 1864? In August Northern morale was extremely low, the Peace Democrats had fielded a strong candidate in General McClellan, and Lincoln himself was uncertain of being re-elected. But by November Sherman had captured Atlanta and Sheridan was scoring a series of successes in the Shenandoah valley. Sherman's 'Christmas present' for the President arrived just in the nick of time.

Although Richard Current has argued forcibly for the case of inevitabilism, historical precedent tends in the opposite direction. That is, an inferior but determined foe can overcome overwhelming odds and succeed against greater forces. The Netherlands, for example, gained their independence from Habsburg Spain and, more relevantly, the American colonies defeated Britain in the eighteenth century. Charles Roland has argued that this latter parallel is not helpful: that Britain did not mobilise all the forces at its disposal, and that the colonies were aided by France. But the victory of the Viet Cong, against an overwhelmingly superior American army, concentrated the minds of military historians wonderfully and forced them to look afresh at the American Civil War.

Be that as it may, it is generally agreed that the North's superior manpower resources played a more decisive role as the war continued and its strategy of attrition began to bite. In 1860 the sixteen southern slave states made up 39 per cent of the total population of the United States. Without the border states, which remained either loyal to the Union or far from loyal to the Confederacy, that overall figure drops to 27 per cent, and, excluding the black population, the figure is reduced even further, to 15.5 per cent. The Confederacy partly made up for it by rapidly expanding conscription to include all able-bodied men between the ages of seventeen and fifty, and in 1863 the Southern army reached its maximum strength of 260,000 men in active combat. While the Union enlisted approximately half its population of military age, the Confederacy enlisted four-fifths. Excluded from enlistment were slave owners with over twenty slaves, and a substantial number of the military, furthermore, were detailed to guard the hinterland and avoid slave insurrection. But the existence of a 4 million slave labour force kept the Southern economy going and released many whites to join the military front. Lee's plea for 5,000 blacks to be enlisted into the army in 1864 was at first rejected by the Confederate government and the influential slave-owning classes, and Lee got his way only in the last stages of the war when it was too late to affect the outcome.

The Civil War was characterised by appalling casualty figures, and, given its limited resources, the South was increasingly unlikely to win. For casualty figures, military historians have been forced to rely upon the flawed statistics of Thomas Livermore's *Numbers and Losses of the Civil War in America*. But with modern recomputation Southern casualty figures appear approximately 4 per cent greater than the North's (20 per cent as against 16 per cent). Comparable figures put these dry percentages into grim perspective. If the colonies had suffered as many losses as the Confederacy did their casualty figures would have been 94,000, not 12,000: if those losses were extrapolated and extended to the Second World War, losses would have been in the region of 6 million, not the actual 300,000 American losses. The fatalities and wounded at Antietam, 23,000, were four times greater than those experienced by American troops in the D Day landings of 1944. By 1865 the Union had a superior ratio of men in arms of 5:1 and over a quarter of the original Confederate army was dead. Both armies suffered from soldiers taking extended furloughs or deserting. On 1 August 1863 President Davis issued the first of three amnesties in the hope of getting his soldiers back to the front. But to little avail, for by late 1864 50 per cent of the Confederate army, fearful of their families starving or of blacks rising up on the plantations, were absent without leave. By late 1864 there were more slaves working on the cotton plantations than there were white soldiers fighting in the Confederate army. Twice as many men died of wounds as on the battlefield, and primitive medical conditions decimated the troops further, with diarrhoea, dysentery, typhoid, malaria and pneumonia rampant.

Another factor which lends credence to the inevitability thesis is the infinitely superior industrial forces available to the North. As Charles Roland wrote in his *History of the Confederacy*: 'Forge and lathe, plow and reaper, rail and piston: all weighed in the balance against Lee and his associates.' This is undoubtedly true, but possibly not decisive. On paper the disparity appears formidable. The North's industrial base was approximately ten times greater than that of the South. Though the South's main product remained cotton, only 5 per cent of it was manufactured in Southern textile mills, and the industrial base of New York and Pennsylvania alone was greater than all the South's put together. The North had more than twice the rail mileage of the South, and it was of a uniform gauge, unlike the South's. Railways were absolutely vital in moving troops and supplies to the battle front, and strategically the South's railway system was most developed along the Atlantic coast and the border states, and therefore highly vulnerable. Also vulnerable was Southern manufacture, two-fifths of which was concentrated within the four border states, and among the first to succumb to the advance of Union troops. The North was also aided by superior technological innovations. Grant in Virginia and Sherman in Georgia, for example, could keep in daily telegraphic contact.

The rifle completely transformed the strategy of the Civil War, and was chiefly responsible for its huge casualty figures. During the Mexican war the effective range of the rifle was eighty yards. The new Springfield and Enfield rifles were highly effective at 400 yards and could extend to a maximum 1,000 yard range. Likewise their firing capacity increased to up to three times a minute. The rifle became absolutely lethal, but it took time for the strategic consequences of this technological revolution to sink in. Stonewall Jackson was still demanding pikes rather than rifles before he fell at Chancellorsville. General Winfield Scott, aged veteran of the Mexican war and Lincoln's first commander-in-chief, was still urging the efficacy of artillery over muskets. Hitherto military manuals had argued for bayonet charges in massed columns, with the consequence than even as late as 1864 33,292 fatalilies in the eastern theatre were due to bullet wounds and only thirty-seven to bayonet wounds. But the growing recognition that this was to be a war of rifles and trenches rather than set-piece battles was learned by the South as well as the North.

Recent scholarship has argued that the South responded with amazing speed to the outbreak of war and the need to enlist troops and, under the exigencies of conflict, effected an industrial revolution. The greatest advocate of this thesis has been Raimondo Luraghi, who insists that 'never before in history has anything like this been seen. A backward agricultural country, with only small, truly pre-industrial plantations, had created a gigantic industry, investing millions of dollars, arming and supplying one of the largest armies in the world.'[4]

It is in the field of finance, rather, that Charles Ramsdell, E. Merton Coulter, Clement Eaton and James McPherson have discerned seeds of Confederate failure. The South began the conflict with a highly unbalanced economy, skewed towards the production of cotton by slave labour. Although it contributed 30 per cent to the national income, it held only 12 per cent of the currency in circulation and 21 per cent of the banking assets. Its real wealth was locked up in land and slaves. In August 1861 the government imposed a 2 per cent income tax which was hard to raise and widely evaded. The South raised only 5.6 per cent to finance the war from taxes, as against 21 per cent from the North. The Confederacy had consequently either to borrow heavily or to print paper money, which resulted in massive inflation. Many states and cities in the South took to printing their own money, and between 1861 and 1862 the quantity of dollars in circulation rose from 119 million to 400 million, so that by 1865 the value of the Confederate dollar was a mere 2 per cent of its 1860 level. The South increased its money supply by 60 per cent as against the North's 13 per cent. Stanley Lebergott lays the blame for this disastrous monetary policy at the door of the slave-owning classes. Instead of collaborating with the Confederate government in its official policy of 'King Cotton' – of denying supplies of cotton to Europe in order to draw Europe into the war and break the Northern blockade – they continued to pursue profit margins and to supply both Europe and the North. The Confederate congress urged this class to grow food instead of cotton to aid the war effort, but its pleas were ignored and by 1865 a slave army was still growing 7 million bales of cotton per annum. Congress placed a tax on cotton but it was a miniscule eighth of a cent per pound of cotton and this itself was evaded as much as the impressment of cotton, wheat, horses and mules. Indeed, it is hard to have much sympathy for the slave-owning classes: first they led the Southern people into a war, then, for selfish profit motives, helped contribute to defeat. Taxation, inflation and impressment fell more heavily on the poor. As the war progressed, morale declined and the Southern soldier was less inclined to fight for the rich. As Lebergott concludes: 'The South's most unexpected adversary in the Civil War, and most deadly, proved to be the South itself ... the Confederacy's indefatigable pursuit of commercial goals contributed decisively, for it constricted the flow of every major resource required to fight and win.'[5]

The North undoubtedly handled its finances more wisely. Under the capable management of the Secretary of the Treasury, Salmon Chase, it introduced a progressive income tax in 1861 and passed a Legal Tender Act in February 1862 which printed $150 million worth of greenbacks which depreciated against gold reserves but did not lead to the hyperinflation of the South. Because the Union raised money by progressive tax rather than a regressive duty on foreign imports the majority of Northerners were not disgruntled, and the war effort was sustained by loans, many of which took the form of war bonds, of which 1 million – one out of every four families – were bought patriotically. The

North financed two-thirds of its war effort from such loans as against only two-fifths in the South.

The North

The Northern battle of words over the war was less bloody than that of the South: the North, after all, had won, and justice and Unionism were vindicated. We owe the publication of Ulysses S. Grant's *Memoirs* to tragic circumstances. Emerging as a towering general by the end of the war, Grant, unlike Sherman or Lee, was tempted by politics, but, as Henry Adams acidly commented, a giant general could prove a pygmy politican, and Grant left office in 1877 hopelessly mired in scandal and rumours of corruption. In 1881 he put all his savings in a friend's bank but the friend, Ward, proved to be a swindler. The bank failed, and Grant, bankrupt, was forced to sell his Civil War swords and trophies in order to keep financially afloat and provide for his family. Then another tragedy struck: Grant was diagnosed as having throat cancer and, terminally ill, fought against time to complete his manuscript, which he did just two days before dying. The two volumes were a huge financial success: over 300,000 copies were sold, which earned $450,000 for his family.

But the book, with its terse, dry, pragmatic prose, was also a literary success. Mark Twain referred to its 'simplicity, naturalness and purity' and readers as varied as Matthew Arnold, Edmund Wilson and Gertrude Stein have also admired it. What emerges is Grant's great admiration for his commander-in-chief.

> Mr. Lincoln gained influence over men by making them feel it was a pleasure to serve him. He preferred yielding his own wish to gratify others, rather than to insist upon having his own way. It distressed him to disappoint others. In matters of public duty, however, he had what he wished, but in the least offensive way ... Mr. Lincoln was not timid, and he was willing to trust his generals in making and executing their plans.

Davis, on the other hand, did interfere disastrously when, for example, he replaced General Joseph Johnston with the foolhardy Hood. Johnston, whom Grant admired as an adversary even more than Lee, wisely husbanded his army, hoping to lengthen the war and exhaust the North by avoiding direct confrontation. As the book's narrative speeds up, one has a growing sense of an unbeatable Union army, skilfully directed by Lincoln, Grant, Sherman and Halleck working together to bring the South to its knees. As Grant wrote to Sherman on 10 September 1864: 'We want to keep the enemy constantly pressed to the end of the war. If we give him no place while the war lasts, the end cannot be distant.' When the end comes, at Appomattox courthouse, the description is moving in its magnanimity. 'I felt like anything rather than rejoicing,' he recalled, 'at the downfall of a foe who had fought so long and valiantly, and had suffered so much for a cause, though that cause was, I believe, one of the worst for which a people ever fought, and one for which there was the least excuse.' Nor was this mere empty rhetoric, for Grant allowed Lee's 25,000 strong army to retain its side arms and its horses, which could assist in ploughing the much needed spring crops. He also stopped the planned 100 gun salute, for 'The Confederates were now our prisoners, and we did not want to exalt over their downfall.'[6]

General Tucumseh Sherman, though the brother of a power-ful Republican senator, sensibly steered clear of politics and refused to stand as a presidential candidate in 1883, remaining in the army until his retirement in 1884. If anything, Sherman's prose is even crisper and drier than Grant's, with a wry appreciation of the subjectivity and self-serving involved in military reminiscences. If three witnesses to a bar room brawl could give contradictory evidence to a courtroom, what, then, are the retro-spective memories of a vast and confusing battlefield? Nevertheless, 'each of them won the battle. None of them ever lost. That was the fate of the old man who unhappily commanded.'[7] Sherman was also sceptical of soldiers who wrote of their insensibility to danger in the heat of battle. Sherman's own experience led him to believe that real courage consisted of keeping cool while retaining a very lively awareness of danger.

Like Grant, Sherman was unimpressed by Jefferson Davis's military capabilities and criticised a number of inaccuracies in Davis's recollections. Likewise Sherman entertained a high respect for Lincoln: 'Of all the men I ever met, he seemed to possess more of the elements of greatness, combined with goodness, than any other.' This he illustrated by an anecdote of Lincoln visiting Sherman along with Seward, immediately after the disaster of the first battle of Bull Run. Having gone to raise morale, Sherman nevertheless suggested to Lincoln that there should be no cheering. Lincoln immediately grasped Sherman's point. 'Don't cheer, boys. I confess I rather like it myself, but Colonel Sherman here says it is not military and I guess we had better defer to his opinion.' Alongside his wide strategic grasp, Sherman offered small but revealing details: that his men, for example, were willing to forgo even bread for the narcotic stimulus of coffee and sugar; of sassafras, mustard, turnip tops and dandelion leaves, serving as natural antidotes to scurvy for his soldiers. Again there is a growing sense of an implacable Northern war machine brutally perfecting itself. 'We are not only fighting hostile armies, but a hostile people, and must make old and young, rich and poor, feel the hard hand of war, as well as their organised armies.' Most crucially, an army, like an individual, he believed, had a soul, and the commander, the soul of the army, must always lead from the front. 'The directing mind must be at the very front of the army – must be seen there – the effect of his mind and personal energy must be felt by every officer.'[8]

Initially the Northern army was unprepared for a civil war. Previously, armed with the textbook maxims of Jomini, the commanders had fought a classic West Point war in Mexico against an inferior enemy. But West Point and Jomini, as Bruce Catton pointed out, did not prepare soldiers for a real war, for West Point prepared professionals for fighting according to set eighteenth-century rules and within predetermined limits. So the fact that the Union possessed an overwhelming majority of West Pointers such as Halleck, Buell and Meade (754 in all, as against 253 in the Confederacy) was not necessarily an advantage. Jomini had argued for the offensive and for the taking of enemy territory, and the Mexican war had practically confirmed these military axioms. Jomini had also argued for the cavalry charge and bloc formations descending upon the enemy. But in the early days of the war these principles proved disastrous, for the massively improved firing power of the rifle made direct close-order infantry assaults suicidal, while the entrenched enemy usually held his ground.

Winfield Scott, who became commander-in-chief of the Union army at its inception, was indicative of this old school. Seventy-five years of age, incapable of mounting a horse because of his gout, 'old Fuss and Feathers' applied outmoded military dicta to what was to become the first mechanised modern war. Yet, by the same token, he did formulate the overall Northern strategy, the anaconda strategy, that would eventually bring the South to its knees. This plan involved a three-pronged assault upon the South: one to capture the Mississippi, the second to seal off the Atlantic by a naval blockade, and the third to sweep through Tennessee into the Southern heartland, cutting it in half and approaching the Confederate capital, Richmond, from behind. This essentially was the combined achievement of Grant, Sherman and Sheridan in the latter stages of the war. The only drawback of this strategy, however, was that it would take time to yield results, and politicians and public opinion, both North and South, were impatient and demanded swift, decisive results.

The first major engagement of the war, Bull Run (or Manassas, as the South called it), combined elements of the old and the new military orders. Parties and picnics were arranged by civilians to observe the set-piece battle from a distance, hoping to amuse themselves as the epic unfolded before them. Many were to be captured and temporarily imprisoned. Battle uniforms were motley, so a number of soldiers were killed by their own side, and Wade Hampton, a South Carolinian nabob, raised, feudal-like, his own regiment to fight. But Stonewall Jackson's daring charge against Union troops, and the transfer of General Johnston's army from the Shenandoah valley by train in time for the engagement, were both signs of things to come. War was going to be hell, not a jousting tournament, and rails and technology were going to play a crucial role in victory or defeat. Even the impalpable consequences of First Bull Run were ambivalent. Though a shattering initial defeat for the Union, made worse by the English *Times* war correspondent, William Howard Russell's, graphic description of Northern soldiers running away, the shock made the North resolve to improve and regroup, while the South, fed on its own legend of superior martial prowess, suffered a false euphoria which was not helpful to its long-term cause.

The politics of a democratic war compounded the North's

initial problems. The congressional Committee on the Conduct of War tended to distrust professional soldiers and preferred political appointees, while Lincoln had always to keep politics in mind and make military appointments, such as Hooker, Banks, Burnside and Ben Butler, which proved mistaken. But the professionals, too, were over-cautious and slow to adapt to new conditions. Time and again they failed to follow through on victories and finish off the retreating enemy. The North was to pay dearly for the caution of Halleck after Shiloh, of McClellan after Antietam and of Meade after Gettysburg. In this last critical battle Meade, having gained the initiative and harried Lee's troops out of Pennsylvania, called a halt and considered he had done enough by freeing Northern soil of the enemy.

Following the second defeat at Bull Run Lincoln turned to McClellan in desperation. Military historians have varied considerably in their estimate of the 'Young Napoleon'. George Hillard's 1864 biography of McClellan, for example, was pure hagiography, campaign literature published in the year McClellan ran as Democratic candidate for the presidency. Judgement by American historians was less harsh following the First World War. Just as Senator Douglas had attempted to avoid a needless war, so McClellan tried to avoid the butchery of modern warfare. But for a number of prestigious British historians, Basil Liddell Hart and Fuller, and for American historians who had witnessed the totalising impact of the Second World War, such as T. Harry Williams, Allan Nevins and Bruce Catton, McClellan was the epitome of all that was wrong with early Unionist leadership. They condemned his Corsican strutting and his Messiah complex. 'By some strange operation of magic,' McClellan wrote on his appointment, 'I seem to have become the power of the land.' He appeared only to want to play at soldiers. As he wrote to Lincoln in July 1862: 'It should not be at all a war upon a population, but against armed forces and political organisations. Neither confiscation of property, political execution of persons, territorial organisation of states, or forcible abolition of slavery, should be contemplated for a moment.'[9]

Yet it was precisely in all these directions that the war was drifting. McClellan was, at the same time, a highly political animal, distrusted by Lincoln and the radical Republicans as a peace Democrat, disloyally seeking a compromise with the South, and a highly apolitical military man. That is to say, he did not begin to appreciate that in a modern democracy war was politics. Even in his last report to Lincoln he insisted that 'In the arrangement and conduct of campaigns the direction should be left to professional soldiers.' Most damningly, McClellan seldom moved and he rarely engaged the enemy in conclusive battle. Not until *McClellan's Own Story* appeared after his death was it clear, in letters to his wife, how immobilised by fear he was, how he grossly exaggerated enemy numbers, and how insubordinate a commander he was. For example: 'I am here in a terrible place. The enemy have from 3 to 4 times my force – the Presd. is an idiot, the Old General in his dotage – they cannot or will not see the true state of affairs.' Grant in his *Memoirs* could afford to be considerate towards him and allude to the 'terrible test' and 'vast and cruel responsibility' which burdened him in the early disorganised and demoralised days of the war. Even Lincoln, who, when McClellan was in command, sent innumerable urgent telegrams demanding action, recognised in retrospect his invaluable organisation of the army of the Potomac. 'If he can't fight himself, he excels in making others ready to fight.'[10] But, though his soldiers loved him when he led them, they overwhelmingly voted against him in the 1864 elections.

For, while McClellan might spare their lives, he did not win the war for them. But a new leadership, shaped by the bloody combat of the western theatre, was emerging which would. There was a hiatus in command between McClellan's dismissal in 1862 and Grant's appointment in 1864. But, thereafter, Grant advanced the likes of Sheridan and Sherman, and in Washington, with the experienced executive, and with Halleck as the chief of staff and go-between, a new concentrated energy was evident.

In a letter to Grant of March 1863, Halleck indicated this transformation: 'The character of the war has very much changed within the last year. There is now no possible hope of reconciliation with the rebels. The Union party in the South is virtually destroyed. There can be no peace but that which is forced by the sword. We must conquer the rebels or be conquered by them.' At first, Grant, with his band of raw Illinois troops, was afraid of confronting a formidable opposition, but then he realised that the

THE AMERICAN CIVIL WAR

enemy was as afraid of him as he of them, and, thereafter, his fear vanished and he was to harry the enemy mercilessly. His early small command in the western theatre helped him realise the vital importance of grasping the details of ammunition, supplies and transport which served him well later, along with his extraordinary grasp of topographical detail. Lincoln came rapidly to appreciate a commander who fought and fought decisively. Following Shiloh the President insisted, 'I can't spare this man: he fights.' Then, with extraordinary daring, innovative tactics and extended lines of supply, Grant laid siege to Vicksburg, the 'Gibraltar of the west', and on 4 July 1863 finally captured it. This, following so soon upon the battle of Gettysburg, fought between 1 and 3 July, was a decisive turning point in the war. The entire length of the Mississippi was now in the hands of Union troops and 'the Father of Waters', as Lincoln put it, 'again goes unvexed to the sea'. Thereafter Grant assumed command of the army of the Potomac and implemented his very simple, and very ruthless, principles of strategy. 'The art of war,' he wrote, 'is quite simple enough. Find out where your enemy is. Get at him as soon as you can and keep moving on.' As he informed Lincoln during the Wilderness campaign: 'I propose to fight it out on this line if it takes all summer.' Yet, for all his outward simplicity, there was a deep reserve about his character, an inexplicable enigma. As Sherman observed, Grant was 'a strange character ... to me he is a mystery, and I believe he is a mystery to himself'.[11] Following his death in 1885 his reputation declined. Stories emerged of long periods of total withdrawal and inebriation. He remained, in James McPherson's phrase, an unheroic hero, and, to J.F.C. Fuller, uncanonised.

Major-General J.F.C. Fuller, or 'Boney' Fuller as he was known to his friends, was one among a group of influential British military historians who were decisively to influence Civil War studies and reassess the reputations of its commanders. That the American Civil War was studied in British military academies was chiefly owing to Colonel G.F.R. Henderson. After Oxford and a spell in the army, Lord Wolseley, who had himself followed Lee's army closely in the Virginian campaign, appointed Henderson to an instructorship at Sandhurst. In 1886 he published an analysis of *The Campaign of Fredericksburg*, and in

1898 the classic two-volume *Stonewall Jackson and the American Civil War*. The purpose of this book was, in part, to swing military attention away from an obsession with the Franco-Prussian War of 1870–71. Moltke's army was a model of discipline and organisation but that war was the last traditional war and held few lessons for the future. The American Civil War showed the shape of wars to come. Democracies fighting total wars which engulfed the civilian population, and the profound impact of rifle fire which led to the superiority of the defensive position, were aspects of the conflict which held particular relevance for Henderson. Like McClellan, he was concerned about rapidly conscripting and training an army from scratch in Britain. Like Lee and Jackson, Henderson was also determined to learn the lessons of surprise attack and daring leadership. In place of old manuals, Henderson offered the crucial intangible of bold leadership: 'In short,' he wrote, 'the higher art of generalship, that section of military science to which formations, fire and fortifications are subordinate ... has neither manual nor textbook.'[12]

The trauma of the First World War, in which both Fuller and Basil Liddell Hart fought, and the lessons which might be learnt from that conflict, were decisively to shape their writings. Henderson contributed to the British military establishment's greater admiration for Southern generalship, Lee's in particular. To the blimpish mind Lee was a cavalier and a gentleman, almost indeed an Englishman. Fuller and Liddell Hart, in their joint struggle against the orthodoxy of the military establishment, intended to replace romanticism and nostalgia with hard realism, and were to look to the Union command for their heroes.

Fuller (1878–1966) joined the Sandhurst staff in 1913, fought in the First World War and retired, disgruntled, from the army in 1933, having failed to get the War Office to think through the full military consequences of advanced technology. His chosen hero, the leader who he hoped would counter the deadly, unimaginative example of Haig, was Grant. In 1929 he published his *Generalship of Ulysses S. Grant* and in 1933 *Grant and Lee*. Before turning to study the Civil War, Fuller assumed, like everyone else, that Grant was a butcher and Lee vastly superior as a general. Grant was generally underestimated and misunderstood by an establishment of 'elderly gentlemen ...

deeply concerned in discovering peaceful platitudes whereon to found a Sunday School universe'. In particular his reading of J.C. Roper's *The Story of the Civil War* (1894–98) made him realise that the author had failed entirely to grasp the overwhelming reality of rifle warfare. 'His knowledge,' Fuller wrote, 'enables him to place his finger on the pulse of war, yet he cannot count its hard throbs, nor can he diagnose its fever.'[13] Grant's reputation as a butcher was easily disposed of. Of the forty-six major battles of the conflict, Northern losses were on average 12.07 per cent as against the South's 12.25 per cent. In the brutal last days of the war, from May 1864 onwards, when Grant pursued Lee through the Wilderness, Grant's losses, though absolutely greater (55,000 against Lee's 33,000) were proportionately less than those of Lee (20 per cent as against 16 per cent for Grant's). Fuller held that Lee's reputation was entirely undeserved. Instead of striking at the enemy's vital rail links around Chattanooga, he fought a narrow and unwinnable battle in Virginia. Though possessed of technical flair, Lee was entirely lacking in overall strategic intelligence. In a democratic war he remained politically naive and interpreted his command in narrow military terms. He refused, for example, to advise President Davis on the possibility of moving the Confederate capital from strategically vulnerable Richmond to Atlanta, Georgia, on the grounds that it was a purely political matter. But Fuller insisted that it was a military decision, and Lee's failure to grasp this was indicative of his backward thinking. Like Henderson, Fuller believed that over-concentration on the lessons of the Franco-Prussian War had had disastrous consequences for British military thinking. Given his magnificently trained troops, Moltke could co-ordinate and lead from the rear, and Haig and the top brass had followed this example in 1914. But the effectiveness of Grant and Sherman proved that leaders should lead from the front and be in the very thick of battle.

Fighting soldiers repeatedly followed the stilted teaching of the military academies; 'since the advent of the war schools, native genius had been crippled by pedantry' and this pedantry was crystallised in the armchair tactics of arid textbooks: 'It does not probe into the viscera of living war; it merely rattles the skeletons of our military ancestors.' So when Fuller alighted upon

Grant's remark in the *Memoirs* – 'They were always thinking about what Napoleon would do. Unfortunately for their plans, the rebels would be thinking about something else' – he appreciated that here was a man of action after his own heart. If Lee were the last of the old school, fifty-three years old and the typical product of agrarian nostalgia, Grant, aged thirty-nine, was the first representative of the new industrial order. War was total: every aspect of the enemy's strength – physical, morale, social, industrial, financial – had to be relentlessly attacked. Grant had a horror of bloodshed, but throwing his men decisively at the enemy might end the war sooner and save more lives in the long run. After the fighting of Spotsylvania and the Wilderness, Southern ordnance officers collected 120,000 lbs. of lead for recasting. Computing that each spent bullet weighed 2 oz, Fuller concluded that 19 million shots had been fired, and a forest had disappeared in the crossfire. This was the shape of wars to come and Grant grasped the fact. And grasped, too, the fundamental role of decisive leadership. This, wrote Fuller, was the 'man who belongs to the earthquake and the storm, who is as steadfast as a mountain, as indolent as a desert, and as active as a volcano'.[14] There was a strong element of hero worship in Fuller. He admitted that Grant was slow to grasp the strategic impact of firepower and the trench; that Grant should have secured the port of Wilmington and stopped Confederate supplies getting through before launching his final campaign. But here, most decisively, was a hero who offered an escape from the fatalism of Haig and the devastating immobility and slaughter of the western front.

Douglas Freeman and Charles Roland have been highly critical of Fuller, for perversely demoting Lee and exploiting the Civil War for propaganda purposes without much real understanding. Brian Holden Reid, in an excellent appraisal of Fuller, has made some telling points also: that, for example, in praising Grant for his pursuit of Lee following the fall of Richmond, Fuller tends to assume, wrongly, that the two armies were roughly equal in size; again, while Fuller makes much of the social and industrial aspects of the conflict, he ends conventionally by stressing the crucial determinant of leadership.

Basil Liddell Hart (1895–1970) was a companion-in-arms of Fuller, though at times they came to blows over their respective chosen heroes. 'Because my Grant does not coincide with your Sherman, it is not Sherman who is injured but your colossal vanity,' Fuller wrote to Liddell Hart in 1929.[15] But these were minor tiffs, for, in essence, both were fighting on the same side: their aim was to come up with fresh strategic thinking by applying surprise, rear offensive, outflanking movements, alternative objectives and 'baited gambits', as Liddell Hart called them, but, above all, the application of new technology, the armoured tank especially, to break through the stranglehold of immobile warfare.

Liddell Hart had first conceived of the concept of deep strategic penetration when studying the swift advance of the Mongols westward in the thirteenth century. Sherman, in his daring march from Atlanta to the sea, also travelled light, lived off the land, drew the enemy into mistaken attacks, flanking and outflanking them, and keeping them uncertain as to where he would next move. 'Without mobility,' Liddell Hart wrote, 'an army is but a corpse – awaiting burial in a trench.' Sherman realised, too, that war was not just a military affair, but an all-out offensive aimed at the entire population, breaking down its very will to fight. 'War is cruelty,' Sherman affirmed,

> and you cannot refine it, and those who brought war into our country deserve all the curses and maledictions that people can pour out ... Every attempt to make war easy and safe will result in humiliation and disaster. My aim ... was to whip the rebels, to humble their pride, to follow them to their inmost recesses, and make them fear and dread us. 'Fear of the Lord is the beginning of wisdom.'[16]

Fuller wrote to Liddell Hart that it was foolish to argue the toss over who was superior. Sherman or Grant? Or, indeed, Fuller or Liddell Hart? Jointly, their Civil War studies were to have a profound impact on future strategy. Their contribution was to elevate the reputations of Grant and Sherman and, simultaneously, to contribute to Second World War victories, though it was Hitler's commanders who first applied their lessons.

The mystique of the 'lost cause' served to influence the historical profession as much as the popular imagination, and when Philip Paludan came to write his *People's Contest: The Union and the War* for the prestigious New American Nation series in 1988, he was surprised to discover that his was the first book to tackle the subject since 1910. Yet, while the war was fought predominantly on Southern soil, its impact on the 20 million population who lived north of the Mason–Dixon line was obviously immense. No one remained unaffected: every family was touched by news of dead or wounded relatives: every able-bodied Northerner contributed economically to the cause; every woman played her part, however indirectly, in sustaining the Union war effort. Even the reclusive poet of Amherst, Massachusetts, Emily Dickinson, could not escape the war's consequences. In late 1862 she penned the following invocation:

> At least to pray – is left – is left
> Oh Jesus – in the Air –
> I know not which thy chamber is –
> I'm knocking – everywhere –
> Thou settest Earthquake in the South –
> And Maelstrom, in the Sea –
> Say, Jesus Christ of Nazareth –
> Hast thou no Arm for me?

Edmund Wilson's vast and rambling *Patriotic Gore* (1962) vividly captures a variety of individuals, soldiers and statesmen, diarists and poets, both north and south, caught up in these mighty events. George Frederickson's *The Inner Civil War: Northern Intellectuals and the Crisis of the Union* (1965) looks also to the repercussions of the war: the discipline and order of the US Sanitary Commission; the martyrdom of Robert Gould Shaw, who proved that the Northern aristocracy was not emascu-lated, or wedded merely to grubby commercialism. Throughout, the war is an implacably modernising force from which the Union emerges, in Herman Melville's phrase, with 'law on her brow and empire in her eyes'.[17]

Fascination with defeat, coupled with historical determinism, has tended to downplay the question of Northern morale. But it was a problem for the North, as it swung up and down, as it did in the South, in response to the military situation. And these mood swings directly affected parties and politics. The victory at Antietam stopped the Democrats gaining the House of Representatives in mid-term elections, and Sherman's taking of Atlanta ensured Lincoln's re-election in November 1864.

The war commenced in a mood of euphoria. Oliver Wendell Holmes Jr, for example, began as an ardent idealist and abolitionist, volunteered from Harvard in 1861 and later wrote in glowing terms of the transfiguring impact of the war: 'Through our great good fortune, in our youth our hearts were touched by fire. It was given us to learn at the outset that life is a profound and passionate thing.'[18] But letters to his parents at the time revealed a rather different Holmes. He had been wounded three times, and he was mentally and physically exhausted. His disenchantment grew when he discovered, three years into the war, that he was back in the Wilderness, where he had begun fighting three years earlier, and, having served his time, he did not re-enlist. Contemporaries had not the faintest inkling of the psychological consequences of combat, of shellshock and post-traumatic stress syndrome. Only recently have interesting studies of combat stress compared the Civil War soldier with those who fought in Vietnam and the Gulf War. Indeed, only fairly recently has the historian turned his attention from leadership to the common soldier who ultimately wins or loses battles or wars. The pioneering studies by Bell Wiley of *The Life of Johnny Reb* (1943) and *The Life of Billy Yank* (1952) gleaned 30,000 letters from soldiers and 1,000 diaries and discerned no dominant ideology which led soldiers on either side to fight. But James McPherson in his *For Cause and Comrades* (1997) and *What They Fought For* (1994), having read 1,076 letters and diaries, concludes that soldiers were highly motivated on both sides: the North talking predominantly of duty, the South of honour and preserving homes from the invader. But there are problems here. The letters are self-selecting. Deserters, blacks, immigrants and working-class recruits were often illiterate. The surviving letters tend to come from early draftees and professional soldiers, and the mouthing of duty and sacrifice was a cultural convention of the day. McPherson writes also of the narcotic rush of adrenaline which operated on the battlefield; of a battle rage which often left guns with five or six balls locked in their barrels; of a commitment to the Union which led half the Northern army to re-enlist freely in 1864 and Southern forces to fight on, under Lee, to the bitter end.

Richmond experienced bread riots, but the North experienced far more serious draft riots; the worst, in New York, lasted three days and left over 1,000 dead or wounded. Over 120,000 Northerners evaded the draft and there were 200,000 desertions from the army. A collection of essays on social history during the Civil War has looked at recruitment in the town of Newburyport, Massachusetts, and found, numerically, that the Civil War was not a poor man's fight; that a larger proportion of the sons of skilled labourers enlisted than of unskilled. But this new social history, directing attention away from the battlefield to the home front, is in its infancy and much work remains to be done.

But the North fought for a brighter future as well as for the Union. It was to protect free labour and the future prospect of open and upward social mobility that Northern soldiers took up arms in the first place. As Lincoln memorably put it on Independence Day 1861:

> This is essentially a people's contest. On the one side of the Union, it is a struggle for maintaining in the world that form and substance of government whose leading objective is to elevate the condition of men – to lift artificial weights from all shoulders; to clear the paths of laudable pursuit for all; to afford all an unfettered start, and a fair chance, in the race of life.[19]

And this spirit of enterprise embraced the military as well as the civilian. Unlike the Confederate leadership, which remained fairly static and unchanged, young ambitious unknowns at the start of the war, like Grant and Sheridan, were able to prove themselves and rise rapidly through the ranks to supreme command.

George Frederickson has argued persuasively that this energising, entrepreneurial spirit helped win the war for the North with 'the capacity of Northern society to produce men of talent and initiative who could deal with the unprecedented problems of a total war'. Lincoln grasped this reality in the early stages of the war: 'The dogmas of the quiet past are inadequate for the stormy present. The occasion is piled high with difficulty and we must rise with the occasion. As our case is new, we must think anew. We must disenthrall ourselves, and then we shall save our country.' Grant also grasped the point and acted upon it, for 'war is progressive, because all the instruments and elements of war are progressive'.[20] Northern civilians also grasped it. With enlistment and labour shortages increasing, use was made of mechanical reapers which actually increased the output of grain during the war.

William Hesseltine, in his *Lincoln and the War Governors* (1948), was among the first to discern the strong centripetal forces operating in the North: during the war states lost power increasingly to the federal centre. Lincoln himself had stated that the war was being fought on the principle of whether one can conform peacefully to elections or attempt to overturn the results by treasonable secession, and David Potter suggested that the continued operation of two-party democratic politics in the North helped rather than hindered the war effort. Eric McKitrick took up this suggestion and in an influential essay, 'Party politics and the Union and Confederate war efforts', argued that a powerfully centralising Republican party, at both state and federal level, unified the North while finding that it could keep the Democratic opposition in tow only by making acceptable concessions to them. A two-party system operated in wartime was a safety valve for discontent short of treason. Lincoln had the advantage of a Republican party Cabinet, while Jefferson Davis's Cabinet was deeply divided. This led, McKitrick says, to 'a certain pallor and lack of muscle tone' in the South, and the diffuse opposition to Davis in Congress 'was far more toxic, an undifferentiated bickering resistance, an unspecified something that seeped in from everywhere to soften the very will of confederacy'. But recent research by Mark Neely Jr has questioned this conclusion, and he writes, commonsensically enough, that 'nearly everyone at the time who voiced an opinion believed what few historians believe now, that a two-party system was at best inconvenient during a great war'.[21] J.G. Randall, and T. Harry Williams in his *Lincoln and the Radicals* (1941), stressed the divisions in the Republican ranks between moderates and radicals. Hans Trefousse's *Radical Republicans: Lincoln's Vanguard for Racial Justice* (1969) and David Donald in *Lincoln Reconsidered* have, in turn, suggested that Williams has greatly exaggerated the fissures within Northern party ranks. It was Lincoln, not the historian, who had to deal with this radical wing and perhaps it is he who gets the balance right: 'They are nearer to me than the other side, in thought and sentiment, though utterly hostile to me personally. They are utterly lawless and the unhandiest devils in the world to deal with – but after all their faces are set Zionwards.'[22] What broadly held them together was dedication to racial equality and opposition to Democrats who sought peace through compromising with the South on the issue of race.

What the Northern Democrats opposed, in turn, was an Emancipation Proclamation and a black army fighting for the Union. To which Lincoln replied: 'You say you will not fight to free Negroes. Some of them seem willing to fight for you; but, no matter. Fight you, then, exclusively to save the Union.' Lincoln made it abundantly clear at the beginning of the conflict that the war was for Unionism and not for the abolition of slavery. Lincoln was forced to change his mind by the exigencies of war. Fremont's freeing of slaves in Missouri was rescinded by Lincoln. He moved towards emancipation from both practical and idealistic motives. The practical question revolved around what to do with the black population, some 500,000, which was escaping behind the lines of the Union troops moving ever Southwards. The Emancipation Proclamation of 1 January 1863 was justified in terms of 'military necessity' as well as being termed 'just'. While slaves were freed in territory under Confederate control, their not being freed in territory under Unionist control was a means of containing this vast floating population. Lincoln was also wary of the constitutional propriety of freeing slaves in Unionist areas. It was these practical aspects which led the London *Spectator* to comment: 'The principle asserted is not that a human being cannot own another, but that he cannot own him unless he is loyal to the United States.' Richard Hofstadter in his *American Political Tradition* refers to the proclamation as possessing 'all the moral grandeur of a bill of lading', and Kenneth Stampp judged that if it became Lincoln's destiny to be the great emancipator he embraced the title with extreme reluctance, but Hofstadter and Stampp had been influenced by the revisionist writings of Randall, who placed great emphasis on Lincoln's caution on the subject of race. Lincoln personally loathed slavery: if slavery was right, he suggested, then nothing could be wrong. But Lincoln also appreciated that the vast white majority of his Northern constituency did not believe the black to be their equal. And if Lincoln moved cautiously it was because he represented this constituency. More recently Stephen Oates in his biography of Lincoln, *With Malice towards None*, and La Wanda Cox, perceive a far more radical politican emerging from the crucible of war and looking to long-term racial equality: 'He who would *be* no slave,' Lincoln commented, 'must consent to *have* no slave. Those who deny freedom to others, deserve it not for themselves.' And again: 'Why should they give their lives to us, with full notice of our purpose to betray them?'[23]

The black was now a soldier serving the Union cause. Reaction to the racially inspired New York draft riots and the heroic stand of Robert Gould Shaw's black 54th Massachusetts Regiment at Fort Wagner assisted the transformation. Lincoln quickly grasped the practical consequences of this policy, writing to Grant in 1863: 'I believe it is a resource which, if vigorously applied now, will soon close the contest. It works doubly, weakening the enemy and strengthening us.'[24] Benjamin Quarles and James McPherson have both written excellent studies of the blacks' military contribution to the federal cause. In all, 200,000 blacks served in the army, making up 166 black regiments, fighting in forty major battles, and a further 10,000 served in the navy. They entered the army just when Northern forces were becoming dangerously depleted and by the end of the war constituted over 10 per cent of the entire Union forces.

Lincoln's reputation is now so towering and unquestioned that it seems impossible to imagine that many contemporary Americans were condescending and denigrating towards him, calling him variously 'Simple Susan', 'the baboon', 'gorilla', 'ape' and 'Illinois beast'. For Count Leo Tolstoy he was 'a Christ in miniature, a saint of humanity', while Emerson dismissed him thus: 'You cannot refine Lincoln's taste, extend his horizon, or clear his judgement; he will not walk dignifiedly through the traditional path of the President of America.'[25] Early biographies of the martyred President tended to depict him, oversimplistically, either as the rustic rail splitter from the west or as the great emancipator. The Lincoln literature is immense. In 1943 Jay Monaghan's *Lincoln Bibliography (1839–1939)* listed some 3,958 books and pamphlets, since which time thousands more have appeared.

Lincoln emerges as a consummate politician, capable of boldness and tact, pragmatism and high idealism. He could strike decisively when the situation required it: impose martial law, suspend the writ of *habeas corpus* for 14,000 civilians and suppress over 300 Northern newspapers. Lincoln's policy was simple enough: he was willing to violate a tenth of the Constitution in order to preserve the rest of it along with the Union. Yet he wooed the vital border states with consummate tact. This section contained almost half the Southern population, two-thirds of its white population and three-quarters of its industrial capacity. When Kentucky declared itself neutral at the outbreak of war, Lincoln, diplomatically, did not point out that no state could remain neutral in obeying the orders of the federal government, and did not send troops into that state until the Confederacy did. Lincoln had also endlessly to neutralise, conciliate and unify a heterogeneous party and a Cabinet made up of such egocentric rivals as Edwin Stanton, William Seward and Salmon Chase. He had also to submit himself, unlike his Confederate counterpart, to re-election in the midst of unparalleled crisis. No incumbent President had been renominated since 1840 and no President re-elected since Jackson in 1832. Yet Lincoln pulled it off with a popular majority of 500,000 and carried a large number of Republican Congressmen on his coat tails.

It could be argued that Sherman's capture of Atlanta guaranteed Lincoln's electoral victory, but then Lincoln, as commander-in-chief, had provided the necessary military support for Sherman's victory. To consummate politician can be added the title of consummate military leader. In 1860 Lincoln knew nothing of military strategy, save for a few days' farcical engagement in the local Black Hawk war against the Indians in 1830 but, by the end, historians as various as James Ford Rhodes, T. Harry Williams, Kenneth Williams and David Potter consider him to have been a brilliant strategist. He grasped, long before many of his generals did, the cardinal importance of decisively attacking the enemy head-on rather than taking cities and territories. Again he could be bold. When appointing Burnside he made it perfectly clear that he would risk the threat of that general's becoming a dictator if only he could procure Union military successes. While Lincoln's relations with McClellan were difficult those with Grant were excellent, for Grant was a man of action rather than of words. It is impossible to study the Civil War era without coming away from it with enhanced admiration for this remarkable man.

John Nicolay and John Hay were personal secretaries to the President during the war, and wrote the first comprehensive life of Lincoln in ten volumes (up to 1890). Their study is highly eulogistic but, as they had full access to the Lincoln papers, is a treasure trove of primary material, all the more important because Lincoln's son, Robert Todd Lincoln, locked his father's archives away and would not allow them to be opened until 1947. John Hay wrote to Robert Todd Lincoln upon the completion of the biography: 'I need not tell you that every line has been written in a spirit of reverence and regard ... We are Lincoln men all through.' The hagiographical intent tends to play down the caution of the emancipator and there is a distinct bias against Democrats and 'copperheads' as well as incompetent generals like McClellan, of whom Hay wrote privately to Nicolay: 'I think I have left the impression of his mutinous imbecility; and I have done it in a perfectly courteous manner ... It is of the utmost moment that we should seem fair to him, while we are destroying him.' Lincoln is depicted in respectable garb; his marriage to the well-to-do-family of Mary Todd turned him into a solid Whig, where he stood out politically against the vulgar Jacksonianism of the Illinois masses. More especially they had to counter the writings of William Herndon, Lincoln's one-time law partner, who had suggested that the President was probably born out of wedlock; that Lincoln had contracted syphilis as a young man, enjoyed raunchy stories and the infidel writings of Thomas Paine; that his great love, Ann Rutledge, having died young soon after Lincoln began to woo her, plunged Lincoln into depression and left Mary deserted at the altar first time round. Herndon had sold this sensational material to Ward Hill Lania, whose life of Lincoln, ghosted by Chaucey Black, appeared in 1872. Herndon's own *Life* appeared in 1889. In response Hay wrote to Nicolay: 'God-fearing men make up the reading public. They want a model for all the good little boys to follow, and Billy Herndon's model won't do.'[26]

For James Ford Rhodes, Lincoln was the decisive figure of the era: 'Lacking him the North would have abandoned the contest. His love of country and abnegation of self make him a worthy leader.' And again: 'The preponderating asset of the North proved to be Lincoln.'[27] Lord Charnwood wrote a solid one-volume life, and Senator Albert Beveridge of Ohio, after a long political career, embarked on a multi-volume life of Lincoln which remained incomplete at his death in 1927. But Senator Douglas was as much Beveridge's hero as Lincoln and, as an imperialist and progressive, Beveridge deplored Lincoln's Whig opposition to the Mexican war when he was in the House of Representatives.

The poet Carl Sandburg (1878–1967), the 'Peepul's Poet', as a journalistic colleague, Ben Hecht, called him, tended in his massive six-volume *Prairie Years* (1926) and *War Years* (1939), to return to the earlier myth of the rugged frontiersman. Sandburg was himself a son of the Mid West, born in Galesburg, Illinois, who spent his middle years writing journalism and poetry in Chicago. His identification with Lincoln was strong, for, 'like him, I am a son of the prairie, a poor boy who wandered over the land to find himself and his mission in life'. Writing of Lincoln he could self-indulgently write about himself: 'He grew as hickory grows, the torso lengthening and toughening. The sap mounted, the branches spread, leaves came with wind clamour in them' ... etc. But the volumes, despite winning their author the Pulitzer Prize, are loose, baggy, gaseous stuff, the worst thing to happen to Lincoln, Edmund Wilson waspishly commented, since being shot by John Wilkes Booth. All sorts of hoary myths were revived and poeticised, for Sandburg was no scholar. He refers constantly to Lincoln as 'Abe', an abbreviation the President detested, and resurrected the story, for which there is no foundation, of Lincoln the New Salem clerk walking six miles to return a few cents to a customer who had mistakenly overspent on his bill.

In 1928 Ellery Sedgwick, editor of the prestigious *Atlantic Monthly*, received a package from a Miss Wilma Minor of California, enclosing copies of Ann Rutledge's letters to the young Lincoln. These were authenticated by Sandburg and Ida Tarbell, a famous muck-raking journalist. Sedgwick printed them before Randall and the academic community generally pointed out that the letters were patent forgeries. Miss Minor was a misguided spiritualist who had convinced herself that she communed with the dead Ann Rutledge, rather than a blatant forger looking for monetary rewards, but none of this stopped Sandburg's typical stylistic overkill. 'Abe' and Ann are together: 'A trembling took his body and vast waves ran through him sometimes when she spoke so simple a thing as, "The corn is getting high, isn't it?"' To which Edmund Wilson added: 'The corn is getting high indeed.'[28]

J.G. Randall's four-volume biography reflected the anti-radical bias of the revisionist school. This bias is specially undisguised in his *Lincoln and the Radicals*, where Randall lists their main characteristics as 'anti-slavery zeal as a political instrument, moralising unction, rebel-baiting tolerance and hunger for power'. Randall was born in Indianapolis in 1881 and, after a spell at the University of Chicago working under the Southern historian Edward Dodd, worked for Woodrow Wilson's League ideal during the First World War. News of German atrocities put Lincoln's own unconstitutional acts during the Civil War into perspective. In retrospect he wrote to a friend concerning his *Constitutional Problems under Lincoln* (1926) that 'I may have gone too far in justifying the extreme war powers. My real convictions are ... that many dangers lurk in the war power theory. Possibly my admiration for Lincoln has carried me too far.'

But far more important in shaping his biography, still the standard work on the subject, is its pro-Southern, anti-radical bias. Randall seems to have identified the radical Republicans with the nationalist senators of 1919 and 1920, Henry Cabot Lodge in particular, who eventually destroyed Wilson's internationalist ideals. Randall's Lincoln was always 'moderate, temperate and far seeing'. The President was especially cautious on the question of slavery, though here Randall had to play down the incendiary implications of Lincoln's 'House divided' speech of 1858. For Randall the Emancipation Proclamation was a 'limping freedom' forced upon him by military necessity and radical demands.

In an appendix to his second volume Randall sifted the Ann Rutledge evidence and found the case unproven, and he believed that Herndon had inflated the story in order to belittle Lincoln's wife, whom Herndon disliked. Randall's own wife, Ruth, had written a biography of Mary Todd Lincoln and depicted an essentially happy marriage. An appendix to Volume III discussed the opening of the Lincoln papers in the Library of Congress. There had been vague stories of skeletons being hidden in cupboards, even of some of the papers being burnt. But such was not the case. The 41,000 separate items in 194 volumes offered no instant sensations for eager journalists, only a more rounded portrait of the man and 'the sense of being part of that age, living with Lincoln, handling the very papers he handled, sharing his deep concern over events and issues, noting his patience when complaints poured in, hearing a Lincolnian laugh, feeling a cumulative sense of unending presidential burdens and of hope deferred'.[29]

The image of a cautious, conservative Lincoln is replicated in Benjamin Thomas's one-volume biography published in 1952, in whose index there is no reference to 'Douglass', 'black', 'race' or 'racism'.

Then, with the civil rights movement, came the search for a more committed and *engagé* President. Stephen Oates, a radical historian who had already written biographies of John Brown and Martin Luther King, unveiled a more radical Lincoln in *With Malice towards None* (1977) and King himself crowned his career by delivering his 'I have a dream' speech in 1963, 100 years after the Emancipation Proclamation and in front of its author's monument in Washington, D.C.

The South

Turning to Southern strategy, it would seem, initially, that the South might have succeeded in its bid for independence. As W. Birkbeck Wood and Brigadier General Sir James Edmonds put it in their *Civil War in the United States* (1937), 'The conquest of such a vast expanse of territory, held by a nation in arms, has no parallel in history.' Theoretically the South could have used its size to advantage by retreating further into the sectional heartland, but Southern, like Northern, public opinion demanded a positive strategy and decisive victories. The Southern military was divided over strategy. General Beauregard argued that Davis scuppered the Confederate war effort by being too defensive, while General Joseph Johnston argued, on the contrary, that Southern strategy was dangerously offensive and ultimately self-defeating. This fundamental division has been taken up by armchair military historians, whose conclusions tend to revolve around their attitude to Davis and General Robert E. Lee. One major school holds that Lee threw victory away by going on to the offensive and incurring unacceptable casualties which bled the manpower and morale of the South. This opinion was reinforced by Fuller and Liddell Hart. McPherson suggested that Lee's bravura won battles but lost the war when a more cautious strategy could have afforded to lose a few battles but still win the war. More recently, however, Gary Gallagher suggests that the joint strategy Davis and Lee pursued, which was a subtle combination of offensive and defensive, was the best for the South to pursue and almost paid off. Thus Lee's two raids into enemy territory in 1863 were high-risk but worth a try. The battle of Gettysburg was a close-run affair and, if Lee had been able to hold Cemetery Hill, and if Jeb Stuart and Longstreet's reinforcements had arrived in time, a victory for the Confederacy would have undermined Lincoln's bid for re-election in 1864. As it was, Lee could temporarily emulate Northern commanders and live off enemy territory.

The offensive *v.* defensive debate is also tied up with another imponderable, about which historians argue endlessly; namely, whether the South should have concentrated its efforts in the eastern or in the western theatre of combat. The territory between the two capitals of Washington and Richmond was the main killing field of the war, where the two armies slogged it out. Though vulnerable, Richmond was offered the geographical protection of westward-to-eastward-flowing rivers, while the Shenandoah valley exposed the federal capital to Confederate assault. If the Confederate President was obsessed with the Mississippi valley, his home turf, and Lee with Virginia, an influential faction including Braxton Bragg, Johnston and Beauregard demanded concentration on the western theatre. Thomas Connelly and Archer Jones have supported this choice in *The Politics of Command*. Unfortunately for the South, the North's most able commanders began their duty in the west, while the level of Confederate performance under Bragg, Hood and

Johnston was poor. This failure in the west tends to be blamed on Davis, who did not reinforce the Tennessee area until September 1863, or on Lee's parochial concern with Virginia and a general ignorance of the west. Lee, for example, was convinced that the climate would render it impossible for Grant to break the siege at Vicksburg, much as difficult terrain would make it impossible for Sherman to bring Atlanta to heel. Nevertheless, the general historical consensus is that, while victory in the west would have helped, the Confederacy had to win in the east, and this, finally, it failed to do.

The decentralised departmental system of the South, the military equivalent of states' rights, made it difficult if not impossible to move troops flexibly and concentrate forces. But Connelly and Jones suggest that, militarily, this localism, while inflexible, served the South well in its overall strategy of protecting as much Southern territory against the invader as possible.

Much has been made of the martial superiority of the South, and Southerners at the time certainly considered themselves superior 'cavaliers' in contrast to the unmanly, materialistic 'Yankees'. So much so that Mark Twain was convinced, not entirely unseriously, that the Civil War was a direct result of too many Southerners reading the historical romances of Sir Walter Scott. Though America's prime military academy, West Point, was in New York state, Virginia and South Carolina could boast their own military academies and Virginia especially, having produced Washington, Harrison, Winfield Scott, Zachary Taylor, Jeb Stuart, Stonewall Jackson, Joseph Johnston and Lee, could justifiably call itself the 'mother of generals'. Samuel Huntingdon in his *The Soldier and the State* (1957) argued that continual warfare with Indians on the frontier, the permanent threat of slave revolts, the Southern culture of romantic chivalry and an agrarian environment all made Southerners expert horse riders and marksmen, which prepared the South better for battle. Grady McWhiney and Perry Jamieson in *Attack and Die* (1982) suggested that a predominantly Celtic Southern culture laid emphasis on the martial arts and inculcated a culture of honour, duelling and manliness which led it to favour an offensive strategy: 'The Confederates favoured offensive warfare because the Celtic charge was an integral part of their heritage.'[30] In his *Our*

Masters the Rebels: A Speculation on Union Military Failure in the East, 1861–1865 (1965) Michael Adams does not concede this Southern martial superiority but suggests, instead, that the North believed it to be so and that their unconscious sense of inferiority undermined and crippled their operations in the east.

The British historian, Marcus Cunliffe, in his *Soldiers and Civilians* (1968) has questioned many of these assumptions. The violent culture of lynching and vigilantism was, he insisted, far more a western than a uniquely Southern phenomenon, and if an agrarian society fostered martial skills those qualities would apply as much to an agrarian North as to an agrarian South: indeed, many Southerners looked upon the Northern urban centres as the seats of disorder and violence. Quantitatively it was assumed that more Southerners graduated from West Point, and in 1863 Senator Lane of Kansas had actually demanded the abolition of the Academy as a hotbed of pro-slavery, secessionist views. But Cunliffe points out that the number of Southerners graduating from the Academy is different from those admitted and that Southerners had a higher overall fall-out rate. Computing graduation from West Point between 1802 and 1861, he found 1,133 Northerners graduating as against 627 from the South, which roughly reflects the sectional balance of the population. Here, however, McPherson takes issue with Cunliffe and argues that the South did have a higher percentage of West Point graduates, if one takes only the Southern white population into account. In general terms it is difficult to accept such Northern and Southern stereotypes. John Brown, for example, was a quintessential Northern Calvinist and abolitionist and could hardly be called unmanly, and no one in New England could have been more puritanical and Cromwellian than the South's great military hero, Stonewall Jackson. Indeed, if the North was as effete and materialistic as some theories suggest, one begins to wonder why the South lost the war after a long, protracted struggle.

It has been argued that, even after Lee's formal surrender, continuation of the conflict by means of guerrilla warfare would have rendered the South invincible. Naturally this hypothesis gained serious attention during America's disastrous involvement in Vietnam. If Mao Zedong, Che Guevara and Ho Chi Minh could win, why not the embattled Confederacy likewise? Robert

Kerby suggested just such a possibility in the *Review of Politics* in July 1973, but both James McPherson and Gary Gallagher dismissed this out of hand. There had already been guerrilla warfare in Missouri and the consequences were so appalling that no one, North or South, wished it to be repeated on a grander scale. The mountainous inland piedmont might provide a retreat for such bandits, but it was precisely these areas that were predominantly Unionist and anti-slave. Southern military traditions, civilian expectations and, most important, the continued surveillance of the slave system made it all but impossible. Gallagher concludes that 'Except as an academic exercise in applying twentieth century lessons to a nineteenth century example, debate over the merits of a "people's war" had scant relevance to the Confederacy.'[31]

Gary Gallagher's stimulating *The Confederate War* (1997) turns the tables on most writing on the period by asking, not why the South finally collapsed, but, rather, why it fought so long against seemingly insuperable odds. Gallagher does not discern a demoralised Southern army or resentment on the part of poor soldiers fighting a rich men's war. Instead dedication and morale ran high, even after the disastrous summer of 1863. If Lee was criticised in the South, it was not because of the high casualty figures but because he was seen initially as being too cautious. Lee was right to adopt an offensive strategy which frequently paid off, rather than a defensive posture which yielded little success. The North's superior numbers usually brought them final victory when they undertook sieges. Gallagher cites the example of the fall of Forts Donelson and Henry, along with 16,000–17,500 troops rendered prisoners of war, as a far greater loss to the South than its total casualties at the battle of Chancellorsville. As long as Lee and the Army of Northern Virginia stood firm, so did the South. When Lee surrendered the Confederacy came to an end. Pride in Lee and the level of sacrifice his army was willing to make were both astonishing. Three-quarters of all Southerners of military age were conscripted into the army. A quarter of these were killed in combat, another quarter seriously wounded.

A large number of historians has devoted a huge amount of time to assessing civilian morale as a factor in Confederate defeat. After all, secession began in a wave of euphoria and enemy invasion of their homeland should have united Southerners and reinforced their determination to fight. Charles Wesley's *The Collapse of the Confederacy* (1937) and Charles Ramsdell's *Behind the Lines in the Confederacy* (1944) both indicated that collapsing civilian morale, the result of inflation, poverty, conscription and impressment, all sapped the military effort from behind the battle lines. Frank Owsley's *Plain Folk of the Old South* (1949) insisted that there were not three Southern classes – planter, slave and poor white – but middle-class yeoman farmers too, who were estranged by the administration's deference to the slave-owning class, in particular the exemption from military service for those owning twenty or more slaves. In his *State Rights in the Confederacy* (1925) Owsley came up with his own explanation for internal collapse: 'There was an old saying that the seeds of death are sown at our birth. This was true of the Southern Confederacy, and the seeds of death were state rights.' Doctrinal decentralisation and aversion to co-operation hampered the South from the very beginning. Even by 1862, 100,000 militia were still serving in their individual states rather than coming together into one central army. State governors were tenacious of their powers and quarrelsome. Brown of Georgia was especially culpable, first refusing to allow his state militia to be drafted, then, when this was deemed unconstitutional by the Georgian Supreme Court, exploiting every possible loophole. He rapidly appointed 2,000 public officials and militia officers to avoid the draft. In 1864, when Sherman was invading the state, Georgia's 10,000 state militia remained separate from Johnston's army. Owsley concludes that 'the local defence organisations [had] grown up and multiplied until, like the barnacles on the hulk of a floundering ship, they threatened to drag the Confederacy down to destruction'. But recent military historians such as Yearns in *The Confederate Governors* (1984) and Richard Beringer *et al.* in *Why the South Lost* (1986) have rejected Owsley's thesis. Where Owsley sees Jefferson Davis and Brown at loggerheads over conscription Beringer interprets Brown's actions as a way of avoiding any confusion over current jurisdiction between state and central government in conscripting men. Rather than hampering the war effort Brown of Georgia, Zebulon Vance of North Carolina and others met state welfare needs and strengthened the overall war effort by protecting their own states and keeping them strong. 'On balance,' Beringer concludes, 'state contributions to the war effort far outweighed any unnecessary diversion of resources to local defence.'[32]

David Donald insisted that the South died of too much democracy, a variation on Frank Owsley's theory that state rights killed the Confederacy. 'The Southern soldier was,' Donald wrote, 'a democratic, liberty-loving individualist; his Union counterpart became a cog in a vast machine.'[33] But James McPherson has taken strong issue with this. The South imposed the draft, the first in US history, a year before the Union, had a larger percentage of those of military age enlisted, and for a longer period suspended *habeas corpus* and civil liberties and ruthlessly suppressed Unionists in eastern Tennessee and the North Carolina piedmont. Indeed, McPherson has argued against all these advocates of internal explanations and quotes instead the pivotal remark of a Confederate veteran as to why the South lost: he thought it might have something to do with the Yankees. External, not internal, factors, military failure, not low civilian morale, led to the Confederacy's final defeat.

Kenneth Stampp has postulated yet another theory concerning the internal collapse of morale. In his 'Southern road to Appomattox', reprinted in *The Imperiled Union* (1980), he attempted to argue that, almost unbeknown to themselves, the Confederacy willed defeat because of feelings of guilt concerning slavery. Stampp was not the first to raise this matter. Wilbur Cash in his *Mind of the South*, Bell Wiley in his various writings and Charles Sellars in an essay 'The travail of slavery' in a collection entitled *The Southerner as American* (1960) had also raised the question. Stampp obviously felt somewhat concerned about finding evidence for his guilt theory, admitting that it would 'take some explaining' and 'my hypothesis is not subject to definitive proof; but I think it can be established as circumstantially plausible, because it is a reasonable explanation for a certain amount of empirical evidence'.

But is it plausible? Stampp had himself written a great deal about secession being triggered off by the South's desire to maintain its peculiar institution against Northern threat, and war and sacrifice tend to intensify rather than dissipate strongly held feel-

ings. And, despite his promise, Stampp provides very little empirical evidence to justify his case, which is unsurprising, given that
the root of his thesis revolves around unconscious and unspoken
guilt. And those few contemporary quotations he does give tend
to undermine rather than buttress his thesis. One witness was
Herschel Johnson of Georgia, who wrote in 1862 that 'the first
gun at Sumter tolled [slavery's] funeral dirge. I have a sort of
undefined notion that God ... is permitting us by our own folly
to work out the emancipation of our slaves.' But there is not the
slightest hint of guilt here, only a realisation, similar to that of
Alexander Stephens, that by seceding the South was likely, 'by
our own folly', to bring the destruction of slavery upon itself.
Another contemporary quotation was from a letter by Frederick
Porcher of South Carolina to Judah Benjamin, the Secretary for
War, in 1864: 'Is it not manifest that it is this chasm [slavery]
which has withheld from us the sympathy and co-operation of the
great powers of Europe? Are we not fighting against the moral
sense of the world? Can we hope to succeed in such a struggle?'
But here, again, there was no expression of guilt, only practical
recognition that the defence of slavery had stopped European
intervention on behalf of the Confederation, and made a successful outcome – independence and the continuation of slavery –
unlikely. Again, Stampp quotes from Mary Chesnut's voluminous
diary: 'Ours,' she wrote, for example, 'is a monstrous system, a
wrong and iniquity.' But what Mrs Chesnut is specifically referring to here are the consequences of slavery for white women of
the South: the unadmitted presence of their husbands' mistresses
and their mulatto offspring.

Because Stampp is exploring unspoken assumptions it is as
difficult conclusively to prove him wrong as it is impossible for
Stampp to clinch his argument. But Stampp attempts to overcome
the problem by suggesting that aggressive pro-Southern propaganda, by dint of its very vehemence, is evidence of guilt. Now
Stampp has a watertight case based almost entirely on the absence
of empirical evidence: if Southerners do not speak of guilt they
must feel guilty; if they argue, in turn, that slavery is a positive
good, this too bespeaks guilt. Stampp's ace card, the universal
acceptance of emancipation, with the coming of defeat, is not an
ace card at all. For the South had been defeated, and if it were to

win the forthcoming battle over reconstruction minimum concessions had to be made. The successful outcome of Reconstruction
for Southern white supremacists would tend to suggest that the
strategy paid off. Frank Vandiver, for one, was unable to accept
Stampp's thesis because it smacked of present-mindedness.
Gallagher has recently argued that the South fought so long and
so successfully precisely because of its determination to hold on
to slavery; George Frederickson wondered how one could have
convinced Northern soldiers who fought at Shiloh and Antietam
that the South really wanted to lose those battles, and concludes:
'A commitment to slavery as a source of prosperity and a security
for racial hegemony was undoubtedly at the root of Southern
nationalism.'[34]

Earlier writers had sought the roots of Southern defeat and
found it in the absence of a true sense of nationalism. A section of
the Union was, suddenly and artificially, transformed into a separate nation state and, faced by setbacks and disasters, withered
away. Richard Beringer and his co-authors considered that this
impalpable factor predominantly explained military failure; that,
although a government, the Confederacy had no emotional, spiritual or mystical bonds holding it together. But others have argued
that in 1860 the Confederates saw themselves as true nationalists,
the direct and undeviating inheritors of the revolution of 1776,
and the North as deviant betrayers of that tradition. Emory
Thomas in *The Confederacy as a Revolutionary Experience* (1977)
and *The Confederate Nation* (1979) has argued forcefully that,
although the South began as a section, it became a real nation, for
'the Confederacy had become for many Southerners an end in
itself. The war experience had moulded Southerners and defined
them as a people.' Indeed, Thomas, perhaps exaggeratedly, sees
the emergence of a remarkable state socialism during the war. A
cohesive and sustaining nationalism is also critical to Gallagher's
thesis, who suggests that historians have hitherto neglected this
nationalism because, being tied irrevocably to slavery, it carries
with it 'the aroma of moral disapprobation'.[35]

North and South, as Lincoln observed, prayed to the same
God, and Beringer has suggested that prolonged military defeat
led the South to believe that God was passing judgement on it for
its wickedness. But religion can serve as solace as well as damning

judgement, and helps sustain spirits during times of military reversal and general despair. Faith, that is, could sustain morale, and military setbacks could be interpreted as God testing the will and the perseverance of Southerners in their righteous cause.

Notoriously the Confederacy hoped to play the 'King Cotton' card: deliberately to starve Europe, and Britain in particular, of cotton in the hope that Britain would break the Northern blockade, compel the North to mediate or even enter the war on behalf of the South. No such event occurred, although there was a major incident when the North captured two Confederate agents, Mason and Slidell, on board the *Trent* in 1861 on their way to England and at first refused to release them. A number of historians have cited King Cotton as a major contribution to Southern defeat, that the South's chief embargo on its chief export deprived the South of much needed revenue, and gave Europe the mistaken impression that the Northern blockade was working effectively.

E.D. Adams's *Great Britain and the American Civil War* (1925) was a solid diplomatic history which was probably too pro-British but which, along with Jordan and Pratt's *Europe and the American Civil War* (1931), rejected the myth that Britain was predominantly anti-democratic and pro-Southern. Frank Owsley in his *King Cotton Diplomacy* was markedly anti-British. Rejecting the argument that Britain would rather sacrifice the textile workers of Lancashire than intervene in the war, or that Britain's demand for Northern wheat was a more important economic consideration than Southern cotton, Owsley argued that Britain's so-called wheat famine was mere British and Yankee propaganda and 'it is proposed to substitute a much more sinister term for wheat – "war profits"'. Rather than suffering, Lancashire textile manufacturers had a large contingency supply of raw cotton and when it ran out and supplies became scarce they were able to raise both prices and profits, as well as obtain fresh supplies from Egypt and India. Munition manufacturers also made substantial profits, arming both sides; most significant of all, Britain's greatest rival, the US merchant marine, was largely destroyed by the conflict. As ever, Owsley was influenced by current concerns: 'Those who are at all familiar with the war profits in the more recent war ought not to have any great difficulty in grasping the role England played of war profiteer, and the powerful influence upon government of her war profiteers, especially when all, even the small operatives, were prosperous as a result of the war.' Thus, rather ignobly, Britain did not intervene, but reaped profits and waited for the South to gain its independence, thereby destabilising the North American continent and allowing Palmerstonian balance of power politics full play: 'England never doubted until it was too late that the South would win its independence and the roast pigeon would then fly into the open mouth of the British lion without any other effort than the opening of his jaws.'[36]

Later historians have taken issue with this thesis. While Britain did inevitably profit, there were other, more powerful factors arguing against intervention. There was a genuine wheat famine: Europe had suffered a series of bad harvests and Britain imported 50 per cent of its grain from the United States. Furthermore Britain had far greater interests at stake in the Union – trade, railways, banking and mining investments – which led it to be cautious. But anyhow Britain's diplomatic eye was fastened far more on Europe. There Bismarck was expanding Prussia and Palmerston was exercised over the Schleswig-Holstein question. He was also very wary of his duplicitous rival, Napoleon III, who was dabbling in the troubled waters of Mexico. The Russian government supported the Union as a counterweight to Britain's naval supremacy, and in North America itself Palmerston wished for stability, not instability, for Canada was highly vulnerable and Confederate success might unleash all sorts of imperial ventures deleterious to Britain's hemispheric interests.

It was these predominantly diplomatic considerations, not war profits, D.P. Crook insists in *The North, the South and the Powers* (1974), which dictated Britain's neutral stance. Mary Ellison in *Support for Secession: Lancashire and the American Civil War* (1972) questioned the myth of overwhelming working-class support for the Union, and Joseph Hurnon Jr argues that there were strong anti-Northern, anti-democratic and pro-Southern currents in Britain. Hurnon also questions the high moral stand taken by Gladstone. In a famous speech delivered at Newcastle in 1861 he had declared that Jefferson Davis had created a new nation. Only defeat in his Oxford University seat in

July 1865 and a new South Lancashire constituency brought about a rapid conversion to a pro-Union stance. In the most recent comprehensive study, *Britain and the War for the Union* (1980) by Brian Jenkins, a sensible balance is struck. There was persistent pro-Southern sentiment in Britain, but honour, Europe and the empire dominated considerations, and foreign policy was 'motivated throughout by a cool calculation of benefits to Great Britain'.[37]

It was only towards the end of the war, when engaged in the gigantic clash in the eastern theatre, Grant versus Lee, the Army of the Potomac versus the Army of Northern Virginia, that Lee achieved universal fame. Prior to that, Joseph Johnston and Beauregard and, pre-eminently, Stonewall Jackson, were the darlings of the South, and Lee was refererred to as 'Granny Lee'. To Beauregard 'Lee was a solemn hypocrite; he used the garb of religion to mask his sins, but his iniquities were known'; to Edward Ruffin, Lee was 'too much of a red-tapist' and to Governor Pickens of Virginia 'too quiet and retiring ... His reserve is construed disadvantageously.'[38]

Lee's dignified surrender at Appomattox, his assumption of the presidency of Washington University (later Washington and Lee) in Lexington, Virginia, his refusal to praise or blame in public or to get involved in the controversy of Reconstruction, all aided his rehabilitation. But the shedding of ink by irascible Southern generals continued apace. Longstreet provided Swinton with anti-Lee material for his biography of Lee, arguing that Longstreet was not solely responsible for the defeat at Gettysburg, and Major Dabney's uncritical life of Stonewall Jackson followed Swinton's *Lee*. Longstreet also published his own *History of the Civil War* to counter Braxton Bragg's claims, while Jubal Early burst into print to attack Longstreet and defend Lee. Joseph Johnston's *Narrative of Military Operations* of 1874 was aimed at Hood and Jefferson Davis, to which John Hood responded in *Advance and Retreat*, while Beauregard, in his ghosted *Military Operations of Beauregard* of 1883, asserted that just about everyone had contrived to destroy the Confederacy, and that he alone, deprived of full powers by Davis in the west, could have saved matters. It was left to the eminent military historian, Douglas Freeman, to comment on this bloody battlefield of books that 'to the South it was humiliating to have two old soldiers [Hood and Beauregard] disputing over a battle concerning which, two decades before, each had sought to outdo the other's compliments'.[39]

General Robert E. Lee doubted whether the Confederacy would ever gain its independence without the aid of foreign intervention, and after Appomattox he was to become the central figure in the myth of the lost cause and the predominant symbol of reconciliation following the war, so much so that T. Harry Williams recalls a girl at Sunday school who never could remember whether he appeared in the Old or the New Testament. But, as we have seen, it had not always been so. In the early stages of the war Lee was criticised for his slowness and caution. Generals Beauregard and Stonewall Jackson were initially the military idols of the besieged South. Lee, not Longstreet, was blamed for the narrow defeat at Gettysburg and Jackson hailed as the victor of Chancellorsville. It was the final struggle between Lee and Grant in the Virginia theatre that transformed his reputation. That, and the careful collaboration with his lieutenant, Jubal Early, in rewriting history based on the premise of a glorious but ultimately vain struggle against Grant's overwhelmingly superior forces. As Early wrote to Lee: 'The worst that is left to us is the history of our struggle, and I think that ought to be accurately written. We lost nearly everything but honour, and that should be religiously guarded.' It was, and the sanctification of Lee began. 'Our beloved chief stands,' Early wrote, 'like some lofty column which rears its head among the highest, in grandeur, simple, pure and sublime, needing no borrowed lustre, and his is all our own.' Woodrow Wilson considered Lee 'unapproachable in the history of our country'. In an article entitled 'The soldier who walked with God' Owsley deified the old Southern agrarian order which was personified in Lee, who 'felt he must preserve without stain the family altar and household gods. He was the most convincing evidence in support of an agrarian aristocracy. No other environment or ancestry could have produced such a man.'[40] Lee attained his historical apotheosis in Douglas Freeman's four-volume study, which won him the Pulitzer Prize in 1934. Freeman was not only a brilliant military historian but also a very fine stylist whose prose flows in magisterial fashion. The opening paragraph of chapter XI of Volume 4, entitled 'The sword and Robert E. Lee', captures the flavour of the book:

> Amid the deep shadows of some of the old tombs in European cathedrals the observant traveller occasionally sees a sword that bears the marks of actual combat. Hacks and gaps there still remain, not made, like Falstaff's, to adorn a tale of pretended valour, but won in war when the furious blade met challenging steel. No scratch was on the sword that General Lee laid away that April day in Richmond on his return from Appomattox. His weapon had never been raised except in salute. Rarely had it even been drawn from its scabbard. Yet it was a symbol of a four-year war, the symbol of an army and of a cause. Where it had been, the red banners of the South had flown. About it all the battles of the Army of North Virginia had surged.[41]

These volumes, and the complementary three-volume *Lee's Lieutenants* (1942–44), are, cumulatively, a sustained exercise in hero worship. Lee was daring but not reckless, a brilliant strategist with an outstanding flair for outmanoeuvring the enemy, his greatest virtue – his gentlemanly consideration for others – his one vice as a soldier. But, above everything, there was the extraordinary simplicity of the man: 'Robert Lee was one of the small company of great men in whom there is no inconsistency to be explained, no enigma to be solved. What he seemed he was – a wholly human gentleman, the essential elements of whose positive character were two, and only two, simplicity and spirituality.' Freeman canonised Lee but the influential writings of Fuller and Liddell Hart were to elevate Grant and Sherman at Lee's expense. In the hard professional and mechanised warfare of the twentieth century, Lee's dashing nobility and old world charm seemed anachronistic. Liddell Hart accused him of foolishly ignoring 'the bullet that forbids assault' and singularly failing to adapt to new conditions. Frank Vandiver told his own student, Emory Thomas, that 'Douglas Freeman is God', but another Southerner, T. Harry Williams, was critical both of Freeman and of Lee. Williams found Freeman too worshipful, approaching his idol on his knees, incapable of admitting that, possibly, Lee more than met his match in Grant. Following the Seven Days' battle and Lee's failure to pursue the retreating Union forces, Freeman offered excuses: maps were inadequate, artillery was weak and the quality of his staff poor. But, Williams insists, Freeman goes on to show that Lee did nothing to eradicate any of these weaknesses. Furthermore Lee's biographer was as shortsighted as his hero. Here, for example, was Freeman on Lee's learning of McClellan's replacement by Burnside: 'He was sorry ... that a man who had always conducted operations with science and humanity was supplanted by one whose respect for principles he had no means of determining until Burnside should begin field operations.'[42] That is to say, both Lee and Freeman were conservatives, looking backwards rather than forwards. Richard Beringer, Archer Jones and Bruce Catton extended the assault by arguing that Lee concentrated excessively on the eastern theatre at the expense of the western. Nolan held that Lee's strategy not only bled the South dry but extended the war unnecessarily. McPherson disagrees, insisting that there was still much for the South to play for after Gettysburg, but McPherson, in turn, accused Lee of contributing to the 'Virgin birth' Southern myth that the war was fought for state rights and not to preserve slavery.

In 1977 Thomas Connelly's highly revisionist *Robert E. Lee: The Marble Man* appeared and concentrated on the psychology of the Southern commander. Far from depicting Lee as Freeman had, as simple and serene, Connelly discovered a far more complex and interesting individual. Lee's father, 'Light Horse Harry', had served under Washington but in 1813, when Robert was only six, fell into debt, deserted his family, and sailed for the West Indies, where he died five years later. Shame and poverty fell like a blight upon the family. Robert married an invalid with whom relations were cool and distant, and he made frustratingly slow process in his chosen army career. Far from Freeman's 'marble man', we have here a repressed, cold individual, masking a sense of shame and inadequacy, acting out the Southern code of duty and honour, hollowly but to perfection, and finding emotional relief only in the heat of battle. Lee had once said revealingly, 'It is well that war is so terrible – we would grow too fond of it.' And Connelly concludes that Lee's life 'was replete with frustration, self-doubt, and a feeling of failure. All these were hidden behind his legendary reserve and his credo of duty and self-control.'[43] What finally emerges here is an inscrutable and enigmatic figure not dissimilar to his great adversary, Grant. Connelly's revisionist zeal may have gone too far, and Emory

Thomas's biography (1995) is more balanced, but it is no longer possible to return to the grand simplicities of Jubal Early and Freeman.

Gallagher has re-established Lee's military credentials, and made him a central figure in the South's prolonged determination to fight on to the bitter end. Gallagher has also argued that historians' excessive emphasis on low Southern morale stems from their concentration on Davis's presidency rather than Lee's army. Lee had been a brilliant strategist, and yet the South still lost. Many blamed Jefferson Davis for the defeat. This was the general opinion at the time, and it has continued to be held by a majority of historians writing on the brief years of the Confederacy. Ironically Jefferson Davis, unlike Lincoln, was pre-eminently prepared to be the South's commander-in-chief. Educated at West Point, a dazzling campaigner during the Mexican war, and President Pierce's Secretary of War, Davis was appointed President of the new found Confederacy and seemed to be everybody's choice. But then the carping began.

One of his chief political opponents, Robert Barnwell Rhett of Georgia, dismissed him as 'a mean-born man, utterly unworthy and unfit for his great office'. Beauregard held Davis responsible for pursuing a strategy disastrous to the South: 'The passive, defensive policy may make a long agony, but can never win the war.' Even Grant in his *Memoirs* did not avoid a damaging reference to this one-time general in the Mexican war and Secretary for War: 'On several occasions he came to the relief of the Union army by means of his superior military genius.'[44]

The Vice-president, Alexander Stephens of Georgia, was even more stinging in his attacks on his president, dismissing him in private as 'an unprincipled, untruthful, unreliable bad man ... a weak, shy, hypocritical, aspiring knave'. In public Stephens concluded that 'the disasters attending the conflict are chargeable ... to the men in authority, and to no one is it more attributable than to Mr. Davis himself'. Here Stephens conveniently forgot that he was, himself, part of that chargeable authority. To some it seemed unfair that the President should carry all the opprobrium of defeat. Mary Chesnut, for one, in her diary remarked, 'How they dump the obloquy on Jeff Davis.' The President's second wife, Verena, penned a eulogy for her husband in 1890 but her praise sometimes, unwittingly, revealed essential flaws in his character. When she wrote that 'he did not know the arts of the politician, and would not practise them if understood' she was making a point which many of his critics, both then and later, would use against him.[45]

Stung by these criticisms, short of money, and enraged by Joseph Johnston's accusation that he stole $2 million of Confederate money when escaping from Richmond, Davis wrote his *Rise and Fall of the Confederate Government*. After Appomattox and with the South in ruins he had attempted to flee to Mississippi to continue the fight in May 1865. The apocryphal story that the ex-President had attempted to escape Union troops in the guise of a woman added an air of absurdity to that of defeat. But his two years' stay in prison, and the general desire to heal sectional wounds, encouraged Davis to attempt a vindication.

The resulting volumes are dry and lack political and social perspective, for he was a notoriously unsociable animal outside his close family circle, but the general aim of the writing is abundantly clear. 'I have argued,' he wrote, 'against leaving history to posterity.' 'The incentive to undertake the work now offered to the public was the desire to correct misapprehensions created by industriously circulated misrepresentations as to the acts and purposes of the people and the General Government of the Confederate States.'[46] These misapprehensions concerned, especially, the constitutional right of the South to secede, and those who questioned his military handling of the conflict. In this apologia no one is spared the lash on either side, not Johnston nor Beauregard, Grant nor Sherman. The book is arid, prolix and entirely self-serving.

Davis was regarded by his Southern contemporaries as too stiff, dry and intransigent. He concentrated all military decisions in himself and acted as a military dictator. His strategies were all wrong. He was too offensive; no, others insisted, he was too defensive. He was sensitive and neurotic and took offence easily. His personal animosity towards Beauregard and Johnston was fatal to the Confederacy's cause. He could not get on with people: he was rigid, formal, unfriendly and unapproachable. He was impossible to work with, getting through six Secretaries of

War during the conflict. He was jealous of Lee and did not give him overall command until February 1865, when it was too late. He would not, could not, delegate: he went through 7,500 promotion forms personally. Major strategic decisons were made in Richmond, and not in the field where the military realities could be more readily grasped. He had incompetent favourites who continued to wreak havoc – Braxton Bragg, General Pemberton and the disastrous Commissary General, Lucius Northrop – because they enjoyed the personal protection of the President.

This, in general terms, is the bill of indictment, though at times, as Clement Eaton has suggested, it seemed impossible for Davis to win. If he acts decisively he is a military dictator; if he acts with caution he is feeble and vacillating; if he appoints army professionals he is accused of excessive 'West Pointism'; if he makes non-professional appointments, such as Robert Toombs of Georgia, or Henry Wise of Virginia, he is indulging in political patronage. When he acts boldly and decisively, by sending Lee off into Maryland, he is accused of abandoning the west and rendering Richmond vulnerable to enemy attack.

Nevertheless there was a general consensus among historians that Davis contributed decisively to the South's defeat. James Ford Rhodes wrote that: 'Manifestly superior as had been Davis's advantages in family, breeding, training and experience, he fell far below Lincoln as a compeller of men.' Bell Wiley was harsh, as was Allan Nevins, who spoke of him as 'too much of a martinet, too moody and too metaphysical'. Owsley's verdict was typically extreme: 'One of the pettiest men who ever held high place ... a martinet for red tape and military punctilio.' Davis squandered Lee's talents by pinning him down to the defence of Richmond and Petersburg, and his dismissal of Johnston from the Army of Tennessee gave Sherman a free hand to march into the Southern heartland. Fuller was trenchant about the President, who 'breathed the air of the cloister, and his soul had grown stiff as the parchment it had fed upon'. E. Merton Coulter made invidious comparisons: 'The American revolution had its Washington. The Southern revolution had its Davis. Therein lay in part the historical fact that the one succeeded and the other failed.' Paul Escott in his *Jefferson Davis and the Failure of Confederate*

Nationalism (1978) repeated the accusation that Davis's fatal error was to ignore the problems of the common people. Frank Vandiver was somewhat more ambivalent: 'He was leader of a revolution, yet he had a legal mind. Revolution and strict legality were somehow incompatible.' Yet was not Davis representative of the Confederacy, and did they not share in his common failings? Vandiver continues: 'Label him wrong in many things; say he was a paradox; call him guilty of frequent misplaced confidences and missed opportunities; say that in the final analysis he was too enmeshed in tradition to be a successful leader of the Confederate war effort – but credit him with nerve. Jefferson Davis was much like his country.'[47]

A minority of historians has argued strongly in Davis's defence. Rembert Patrick in his *Jefferson Davis and his Cabinet* (1944) concludes that 'Davis's claim to conspicuous ability as a leader is incontestable'. Hudson Strode in his exhaustive three-volume *Jefferson Davis: Confederate President* (1955–64) also made a strong case for him and Shelby Foote, a fellow Civil War authority, wrote to Strode that 'it is as if a gigantic conspiracy has been formed for the purpose of misrepresenting Davis so as to hide his true nature from the world'. Gallagher's study places Davis's brilliant handling of the war along with Lee's. There was, instead, an absence of capable subordinates to carry through their audacious joint strategy. I will leave the final verdict to David Potter: 'If the Union and the Confederacy had exchanged presidents, one with another, the Confederacy might have won its independence.'[48]

Notes

1 Lee quoted in Thomas Connelly, *The Marble Man: Robert E. Lee and his Image in American Society* (New York, 1977), p. 213.
2 Quoted in James McPherson, *Drawn with the Sword* (New York, 1996), p. 117.
3 Grant quoted in Marcus Cunliffe, *Soldiers and Civilians* (London, 1969), p. 335; and Lee in McPherson, *Drawn with the Sword*, p. 115.
4 Charles Roland in Grady McWhiney (ed.), *Grant, Lee, Lincoln and the Radicals* (Evanston, Ill., 1964), p. 32. Luraghi quoted in Richard Beringer *et al.* (eds), *Why the South lost the Civil War* (Athens, Ga., 1986), p. 59.
5 Stanley Lebergott, 'Why the South Lost', *Journal of American History* (69, 1983), p. 73.

6 Grant's *Memoirs* (New York, 1990), pp. 634, 735, 741, 769–70.

7 Sherman's *Memoirs* (New York, 1990), p. 5.

8 *Ibid.*, pp. 207, 705, 813.

9 McClellan quoted in Warren Hassler Jr, *Commanders of the Army of the Potomac* (Baton Rouge, 1962), p. 48; and McClellan's letter to Lincoln, 7 July 1862, in Henry Steele Commager (ed.), *Documents of American History*, I (New York, 1968), p. 414.

10 McClellan quoted in Hassler, *Commanders of the Army of the Potomac*, p. 95; in McPherson, *Drawn with the Sword*, p. 147; and Lincoln in McPherson, *Battle Cry of Freedom* (Harmondsworth, 1988), p. 533.

11 Halleck quoted in T. Harry Williams, *Lincoln and his Generals* (London, 1952), p. 209; Lincoln in McPherson, *Battle Cry of Freedom*, pp. 414, 638; Grant in Brian Holden Reid, *J.F.C. Fuller: Military Thinker* (London, 1987), p. 120; Sherman in Hassler, *Commanders of the Army of the Potomac*, p. 195.

12 Jay Luvass (ed.), *The Civil War: A Soldier's View: A Collection of Civil War Writings by Col. G.F.R. Henderson* (Chicago, 1958).

13 J.F.C. Fuller, *The Generalship of Ulysses S. Grant* (Bloomington, Ind., 1929), pp. xi, 361.

14 Reid, *Fuller*, p. 100. Grant quoted in J.F.C. Fuller, *Grant and Lee: A Study in Personality and Generalship* (London, 1933), pp. 82, 62.

15 Fuller quoted in Brian Bond, *Liddell Hart* (London, 1977), p. 63 n. 24.

16 Sherman quoted in Williams, *Lincoln and his Generals*, p. 166, and Edmund Wilson, *Patriotic Gore* (New York, 1962), p. 192.

17 Emily Dickinson quoted in Philip Paludan, *A People's Contest* (New York, 1988), p. 366; Melville in George Frederickson, *The Inner Civil War: Northern Intellectuals and the Crisis of the Union* (New York, 1965), p. 185.

18 Holmes quoted in Frederickson, *The Inner Civil War*, p. 219.

19 Lincoln quoted in Commager, *Documents of American History*, I, p. 395.

20 Fuller, *The Generalship of Grant*, pp. xi, 361.

21 Eric McKitrick, 'Party politics and the Union and Confederate war effort', reprinted in Frank Gatell *et al.* (eds), *The Growth of American Politics*, I (London, 1972), pp. 427, 440; and Mark Neely Jr in James McPherson, *We Cannot Escape History* (Urbana, 1995), p. 88.

22 Lincoln quoted in McPherson (ed.), *We Cannot Escape History*, p. 70.

23 Lincoln quoted in Williams, *Lincoln and his Generals*, p. 212; Hofstadter, 'Lincoln', in *The American Political Tradition* (London, 1967), p. 131; Lincoln quoted in James McPherson, *Abraham Lincoln and the Second American Revolution* (Oxford, 1991), p. 54; and McPherson, *Battle Cry of Freedom*, p. 769.

24 Lincoln quoted in Gabor Boritt (ed.), *Why the Confederacy Lost* (Oxford, 1992), p. 161.

25 Tolstoy quoted in McPherson, *Drawn with the Sword*, p. 376; and Emerson in Cunliffe, *Soldiers and Civilians*, p. 376.

26 Hay quoted in Paul Angle (ed.), *Hay and Nicolay's Life of Abraham Lincoln* (Chicago, 1966), p. xiv; and in Merrill Peterson, *Lincoln in American Memory* (Oxford, 1994), p. 118.

27 James Ford Rhodes, *History of the Civil War* (New York, 1917), p. 438; and quoted in Boritt, *Why the Confederacy Lost*, p. 37.

28 Sandburg quoted in Stephen Oates, *Our Fiery Trial* (Amherst, Mass., 1979), p. 102; and Peterson, *Lincoln in American Memory*, pp. 276–7; and Wilson, *Patriotic Gore*, p. 116.

29 Randall quoted in Mark Neely Jr, *The Fate of Liberty: Abraham Lincoln and Civil Liberties* (Oxford, 1991), p. 12; Peterson, *Lincoln in American Memory*, pp. 302, 309; and Randall, *Lincoln the President*, III (London, 1952), p. 436.

30 Gary Gallagher, *The Confederate War* (Cambridge, Mass., 1997), p. 121.

31 *Ibid.*, p. 141.

32 Frank Owsley, *State Rights in the Confederacy* (Chicago, 1925), p. 10; and Harriet Owsley (ed.), *The South: Old and New Frontiers* (Athens, Ga., 1969), p. 82; Beringer *et al.*, *Why the South lost the Civil War*, p. 249.

33 David Donald (ed.), *Why the North won the Civil War* (London, 1960), p. 84.

34 Kenneth Stampp, *The Imperiled Union* (Oxford, 1980), pp. 246–69; Gallagher, *The Confederate War*, p. 46; George Frederickson, *Blue Over Gray* (Indianapolis, 1950), p. 60.

35 Thomas quoted in Gallagher, *The Confederate War*, p. 66; *ibid.*, p. 70.

36 Frank Owsley, 'Why Europe did not intervene', reprinted in Owsley, *The South*, pp. 114, 121; Owsley quoted in Brian Jenkins, *Britain and the War for the Union*, II (Montreal, 1980), p. 393.

37 Jenkins, *Britain and the War for the Union*, p. 393.

38 Beauregard quoted in Thomas Connelly and Archer Jones, *The Politics of Command: Factions and Ideas in Confederate Strategy* (Baton Rouge, 1973), p. 183. Ruffin and Pickens quoted in Emory Thomas, *Robert E. Lee* (New York, 1995), p. 213.

39 Freeman quoted in Arthur Link and Rembert Patrick, *Writing Southern History* (Baton Rouge, 1965), p. 279.

40 Early quoted in Gallagher, *The Confederate War*, pp. 169, 170–1. Wilson quoted in Alan Nolan, *Lee Considered* (Chapel Hill, 1991), p. 5. Owsley, *The South*, p. 235.

41 Douglas Freeman, *Robert E. Lee: A Biography*, IV (New York, 1935), p. 165; and Freeman quoted in Thomas, *Robert E. Lee*, p. 13.

42 Liddell Hart quoted in Kirkwood Mitchell, 'Lee and the bullet of the Civil War', *William and Mary Quarterly* (2nd Series, 10:1, 1930), p. 26. Vandiver quoted in Thomas, *Robert E. Lee*, p. 13. Freeman quoted in T. Harry Williams, *The Selected Essays* (Baton Rouge, 1983), pp. 191–2.

43 Lee quoted in Connelly, *The Marble Man*, pp. xiv, 207.

44 Rhett quoted in Bell Wiley's foreword to Jefferson Davis, *The Rise and Fall of the Confederate Government* (New York, 1958). Beauregard quoted in Fuller, *The Generalship of Ulysses S. Grant*, p. 30; and Grant quoted in his *Memoirs* (New York, 1990), p. 480.

45 Stephens quoted in Link and Patrick, *Writing Southern History*, p. 255; and in James Rabin, 'Alexander Stephens and Jefferson Davis', *American Historical Review* (64, 1959), p. 320.

46 Davis quoted in Bell Wiley's foreword to Davis, *Rise and Fall of the Confederate Government*.

47 Rhodes, *History of the Civil War*, p. 429. Owsley in *The South*, p. 220. Fuller, *Grant and Lee*, pp. 27–8. Coulter quoted in Donald Sheehan and Harold Syrett (eds), *Essays in American Historiography* (New York, 1960), p. 28. Frank Vandiver, *Rebel Brass* (Baton Rouge, 1956), pp. 27, 42.

48 Rembert Patrick, *Jefferson Davis and his Cabinet* (Baton Rouge, 1944), p. 44. Hudson Strode, *Jefferson Davis: Confederate President* (New York, 1959), p. xii. David Potter in Donald, *Why the North won the Civil War*, p. 109.

Selective bibliography

Aaron, Daniel, *The Unwritten War: American Writers and the Civil War* (Oxford, 1973).

Adams, E.D., *Great Britain and the American Civil War* (2 vols, New York, 1925).

Beringer, Richard, Hattaway, Herman, Jones, Archer, and Still, William, Jr, *Why the South lost the Civil War* (Athens, Ga., 1986).

Bond, Brian, *Liddell Hart* (London, 1977).

Boritt, Gabor (ed.) *War Comes Again* (New York, 1995).

Boritt, Gabor (ed.), *The Historian's Lincoln* (Urbana, 1988).

Boritt, Gabor (ed.), *Why the Confederacy Lost* (Oxford, 1992).

Collins, Bruce, 'The Southern military tradition' in Brian Holden Reid and John White (eds), *American Studies: Essays in Honor of Marcus Cunliffe* (London, 1991).

Connelly, Thomas, *The Marble Man: Robert E. Lee and his Image in American Society* (New York, 1977).

Connelly, Thomas, and Jones, Archer, *The Politics of Command: Factions and Ideas in Confederate Strategy* (Baton Rouge, 1973).

Coulter, E. Merton, *The Confederate States of America* (Baton Rouge, 1980).

Crook, D.P., *The North, the South and the Powers* (New York, 1974).

Cunliffe, Marcus, *Soldiers and Civilians* (London, 1969).

Current, Richard, *The Lincoln Nobody Knows* (New York, 1988).

Davis, Cullom, Strozier, Charles, Veach, Rebecca, and Ward, Geoffrey (eds), *The Public and Private Lincoln* (Carbondale, Ill., 1979).

Davis, Jefferson, *The Rise and Fall of the Confederate Government* (2 vols, New York, 1988).

Donald, David (ed.), *Why the North won the Civil War* (London, 1960).

Donald, David, *Lincoln Reconsidered* (New York, 1969).

Donald, David, *Lincoln* (London, 1995).

Eaton, Clement, *Jefferson Davis* (New York, 1977).

Ellison, Mary, *Support for Secession: Lancashire and the American Civil War* (Chicago, 1972).

Escott, Paul, *After Secession: Jefferson Davis and the Failure of Confederate Nationalism* (Baton Rouge, 1978).

Fehrenbacher, Don, *Prelude to Greatness: Lincoln in the 1850s* (Stanford, 1962).

Fehrenbacher, Don, *Lincoln in Text and Context* (Stanford, 1987).

Förster, Stig, and Nageler, Jurg (eds), *On the Road to Total War* (Cambridge, 1997).

Franklin, John Hope, *The Emancipation Proclamation* (New York, 1963).

Frederickson, George, *The Inner Civil War: Northern Intellectuals and the Crisis of the Union* (New York, 1965).

Freeman, Douglas, *Robert E. Lee: A Biography* (New York, 1934–35).

Freeman, Douglas, *Lee's Lieutenants: A Study in Command* (3 vols, New York, 1942).

Fuller, J.F.C., *The Generalship of Ulysses S. Grant* (Bloomington, Ind., 1929).

Fuller, J.F.C., *Grant and Lee: A Study in Personality and Generalship* (London, 1933).

Gallagher, Gerry, *The Confederate War* (Cambridge, Mass., 1997).

Gatell, Frank, Goodman, Paul, and Weinstein, Allen (eds), *The Growth of American Politics*, I (London, 1972).

Grant, General Ulysses S., *Memoirs* (Library of America edition, New York, 1990).

Hart, Basil Liddell, *Sherman: Soldier, Realist, American* (London, 1929).

Hassler Jr, Warren, *Commanders of the Army of the Potomac* (Baton Rouge, 1962).

Hattaway, Herman, and Jones, Archer, *How the North Won* (Urbana, 1983).

Hofstadter, Richard, 'Lincoln' in his *The American Political Tradition* (London, 1967).

Hyman, Harold (ed.), *Heard Round the World: The Impact of the Civil War* (New York, 1968).

Jenkins, Brian, *Britain and the War for the Union* (2 vols, Montreal, 1980).

Jones, Archer, *Confederate Strategy from Shiloh to Vicksburg* (Baton Rouge, 1961).

Jordan, H.D., and Pratt, Edwin, *Europe and the American Civil War* (London, 1931).

Lebergott, Stanley, 'Why the South lost: commercial purpose in the Confederacy, 1861–1865', *Journal of American History* (69, 1983).

Linderman, Gerald, *Embattled Courage* (New York, 1987).

Luvass, Jay (ed.), *The Civil War: A Soldier's View: A Collection of Civil War Writings by Col. G.F.R. Henderson* (Chicago, 1958).

Luvass, Jay, *The Military Legacy of the Civil War* (Chicago, 1989).

Malthiessen, F.O., *American Renaissance: Art and Expression in the Age of Emerson and Whitman* (Oxford, 1941).

McPherson, James, *The Struggle for Equality: Abolitionists and the Negro in the Civil War and Reconstruction* (Princeton, 1964).

McPherson, James, *The Negro's Civil War* (New York, 1965).

McPherson, James, *Ordeal by Fire* (New York, 1982).

McPherson, James, *Abraham Lincoln and the Second American Revolution* (Oxford, 1991).

McPherson, James, *What They Fought For* (New York, 1994).

McPherson, James, *For Cause and Comrade* (New York, 1995).

McPherson, James, 'Lee dissected' in his *Drawn with the Sword* (Oxford, 1996).

McWhiney, Grady (ed.), *Grant, Lee, Lincoln and the Radicals* (Evanston, Ill., 1964).

McWhiney, Grady, *Southerners and other Americans* (New York, 1973).

Neely Jr, Mark, *The Fate of Liberty: Abraham Lincoln and Civil Liberties* (Oxford, 1991).

Neely Jr, Mark, 'The Civil War and the two party system' in James McPherson (ed.), *We Cannot Escape History* (Urbana, 1995).

Nicolay, John, and Hay, John, *Life of Lincoln* (Chicago, 1966; condensed).

Nolan, Alan, *Lee Considered* (Chapel Hill, 1991).

Oates, Stephen, *With Malice towards None* (New York, 1977).

Owsley, Frank, *State Rights in the Confederacy* (Chicago, 1925).

Owsley, Frank, *King Cotton Diplomacy* (Chicago, 1931).

Paludan, Philip, *A People's Contest* (New York, 1988).

Peterson, Merrill, *Lincoln in American Memory* (Oxford, 1994).

Quarles, Benjamin, *The Negro in the Civil War* (Boston, Mass., 1953).

Ramsdell, Charles, *Behind the Lines in the Southern Confederacy* (Baton Rouge, 1944).

Randall, J.R., *Lincoln: The President* (4 vols, completed by Richard Current, London, 1945–55).

Reid, Brian Holden, *J.F.C. Fuller: Military Thinker* (London, 1987).

Richardson, Heather, *The Greatest Nation of the Earth* (Cambridge, Mass., 1997),

Roland, Charles, *The Confederacy* (Chicago, 1960).

Sherman, General Tucumseh, *Memoirs* (Library of America edition, New York, 1990).

Sklar, Kathryn Kish, 'Victorian women and domestic life' in Cullom Davis, Charles Strozier, Rebecca Veach and Geoffrey Ward (eds), *The Public and Private Lincoln* (Carbondale, Ill., 1979).

Stampp, Kenneth, 'The Southern road to Appomattox' in his *The Imperiled Union* (Oxford, 1980).

Stephens, Alexander, extracts from 'A Constititutional View of the late War between the States' in Edwin Rozwenc (ed.), *The Causes of the American Civil War* (Boston, Mass., 1961) and Kenneth Stampp (ed.), *The Causes of the Civil War* (Englewood Cliffs, N.J., 1963).

Strode, Hudson, *Jefferson Davis* (3 vols, 1955–64).

Thomas, Benjamin, *Abraham Lincoln* (New York, 1952).

Thomas, Emory, *The Confederacy as a Revolutionary Experience* (Columbia, S. Ca., 1971).

Thomas, Emory, *Robert E. Lee* (New York, 1995).

Thomas, Emory, *The Confederate Nation, 1861–1865* (New York, 1979).

Vandiver, Frank, *Rebel Brass* (Baton Rouge, 1956).

Vinovski, Mavris (ed.), *Towards a Social History of the American Civil War* (Cambridge, 1990).

Williams, Kenneth, *Lincoln Finds a General* (5 vols, New York, 1949–59).

Williams, T. Harry, *Lincoln and his Generals* (London, 1952).

Williams, T. Harry, 'Freeman: historian of the Civil War: an appraisal' in his *The Selected Essays* (Baton Rouge, 1983).

Wilson, Edmund, *Patriotic Gore* (New York, 1962).

6

Reconstruction

Reconstruction provides an especially clear litmus test of historians' preconceptions and assumptions. Here, however briefly, there was a revolutionary experiment in race relations when large numbers of black citizens were enfranchised and many of their erstwhile white masters disfranchised. What would happen when the freedman was no longer politically invisible? Ironically, white supremacist historians had to emphasise black domination in the South during reconstruction in order to practically demonstrate black political incapacity. Reconstruction created a large number of popular myths and stereotypes which, after 'redemption' in 1877, were taken up by professional historians, embroidered upon endlessly with footnotes and given the full imprint of serious scholarship. Progress in the historiography of reconstruction has been a matter of slowly shedding the stubborn, self-serving mythologies which clung so tenaciously about this period, and reinstating the Northern 'carpetbagger', Southern 'scalawag' and freedmen into a truer and more complex role in the drama of this period. Replacing the bland simplifications is a subtler analysis which is more human, more moving; heroic and tragic at the same time. In the words of Du Bois: 'the slave went free; stood a brief moment in the sun; then moved back again toward slavery'.[1]

Henry Wilson's *History of the Rise and Fall of the Slave Power in America* appeared in 1877, the same year 'home rule' was granted to the South. In this book Wilson exempted himself, his President and the Republican party for the failure of Reconstruction and firmly blamed white violence and intransigence. 'On the one side were those who would do justice to the black man, . . . on the other were those who brought to the discussion the still dominating influence of caste, belittling the negro and his wants, and, with cruel insensibility, resisting his claims upon either their sympathy, their humanity, or their sense of justice'.[2] There was a good deal of truth in this summary, but it is also disingenuous in its exculpation of the Republican party record. Grant had campaigned in 1868 on a mandate to bring peace between North and South which boded ill for the freedman, who depended so entirely upon the continued military support and sustained commitment of the Republican party. If modern research is showing Grant to have been more dedicated to black freedom than was previously thought, intractable political facts limited his freedom of action. Republican voters were predominantly Northern voters, and Northern voters were growing tired of the everlasting black question. Further assistance to the Southern black led to a Northern white backlash. This sea change can be chartered in the editorials of the influential *New York Nation*, edited by E.L. Godkin. This newspaper, the chosen broadsheet of America's intellectual elite, had been born during the heady ante-bellum years of abolitionism and the growing threat of the slave interest. Like Lincoln, the *Nation* had slowly adopted emancipation as a war aim along with a restored Union. With the ending of the war, it continued to advocate radical Reconstruction and the cause of the freedmen, but increasingly events closer to home gained its attention. An essentially conservative and mugwump paper, it panicked in its reaction to mass immigration into America's already crowded Northern city centres. Poor, propertyless, ignorant and usually Democratic voters, these aliens threatened the security of property and government by a wise WASP elite. Now the North had its own ethnic problem and a movement to restrict immigration arose which was strikingly similar to the white supremacist phenomenon in the South. The new immigrant also fuelled the growth of corruption. Instead of a purged and purified post-bellum republic, the nation's very integrity was now threatened by the politics of the 'pork barrel' and the ward bosses who bought and sold votes in the political market place. New York City had its own major scandal when Boss Tweed of Tammany Hall and his ring were exposed for mass corruption in 1871. President Grant's Cabinet was also deeply involved in graft when the Whiskey Ring was exposed. Increasingly the *New York Nation*'s editorials turned from reconstruction matters to crusade for immigration restrictions, civil service reform and the purification of city politics. This Northern trend towards self-absorption was reinforced by the practical arithmetic of voting blocs. The initial Republican strategy in the South had been to unite Southern unionists and the newly enfranchised freedmen to secure victory against the Democratic party. This strategy had ultimately failed. But meanwhile the economic programme of the Republican party – homesteads, a sound currency, a transcontinental railroad, high tariffs and a stable banking system – had captured the support of the old north-western states such as Ohio, Illinois and Indiana, which meant that it could survive electorally with or without the tenuous Southern vote. The electoral equation followed inexorably. When in 1875 Mississippi was subject to a reign of terror and intimidation Governor Adelbert Ames urgently requested military aid from Grant. Grant refused, for to grant it would have jeopardised the gubernatorial elections in Ohio which it was vital for the Republican party to carry. Henry Wilson's party significantly contributed, then, to the defeat of Reconstruction.

It was left to a black historian to resist an all-enveloping white consensus from which the freedman would be essentially excluded. In 1883 George Washington Williams, who had served in the Union army, published the first serious history of his people in the United States. He avowedly wrote his *History of the Negro Race 1619 to 1880* 'not as a blind panegyrist of my race, nor as a partisan apologist, but for a love for "the truth of history". I have striven to record the truth.' Five years later he published *A History of Negro Troops in the War of Rebellion* which illustrated the decisive role blacks played in their own liberation: some 200,000 had served in the ranks and a further 300,000 indirectly helped sustain the Union military effort. Williams also commented on how badly treated black soldiers were, at times, by their white superiors. Even so, Williams's comment on the failure of Reconstruction was sadly resigned: 'An ignorant majority, without competent leaders, could not rule an intelligent Caucasian minority.'[3]

James Ford Rhode's conciliatory history was not dissimilar to the secret negotiations held between Northern and Southern congressmen in the Wormley Hotel in Washington in 1877, which brokered an acceptable deal between the two hostile sections. The South had been wrong in attempting to hold on to slavery and secede with that purpose in mind. But the South, in turn, had rightly opposed the misguided attempt by the radical Republicans to enfranchise the freedmen and temporarily disfranchise the white Southern elite. As we have seen, Rhodes had come from a wealthy industrial background and had enough money to retire early and devote himself to writing history. Once he had settled in Boston, his politics became increasingly conservative and increasingly smug. Everywhere the genteel mugwump looked he saw a threat to the old stable Republican order: from strange immigrants speaking incomprehensible tongues flooding into Boston; from foreign anarchists fermenting discontent and industrial strife; from ward bosses battening on the city treasury and corrupting the judiciary; from debtor farmers in the west demanding inflation and the debasement of a sound currency. Having done well himself, Rhodes had good reason to feel content with this threatened *status quo*. As a mugwump he held firm to the tenets of rule by an educated elite, the sacredness of property and the benign workings of a *laissez-faire* economic order. Charles Beard caught this conservative side perfectly. 'Mr Rhodes has seen America a part of the time through the windows of a counting house, and the remainder of the time from the windows of the Centennial Club.' William Hesseltine, the Wisconsin historian, was even more direct, 'Rhodes was a damn snob ... There's been too damned much oozy morality spread over the period of reconstruction.'[4] Hesseltine noted that Rhodes used the phrase 'property and intelligence' like a mantra fifteen times in one chapter on Reconstruction alone. It was Rhodes's overwhelming fear of America, his America, being flooded by foreigners, with the concomitant threat of the sequestration of private property, which made him so hostile to Northern attempts at radical Reconstruction in the South. 'What idea,' he asked, 'could barbarism thrust into slavery obtain of the rights of property?' Certain radicals wished not only to free the slave but to give him a vote, confiscate the land of disloyal confederate planters, and to bestow forty acres and a mule on each freedman. The Republican party, instead of working with the Whig Unionist oligarchy of the South, attempted, insanely, to form an alliance with Southern freedmen by granting them a vote. 'No larger policy in our country has ever been so conspicuous a failure as that of forcing universal negro suffrage upon the South ... It pandered to the ignorant negroes, the knavish white natives and the vulturous adventurers who flocked from the North.'[5] Rhodes believed that a limited educational and property franchise for a few freedmen might have been acceptable to the Southern elite, but by forcing black rule on the South at the point of a bayonet, the healing process of restoration was ruined and the 'best men' of the South were driven into the ranks of the Democratic party. This disastrous *dénouement* was a direct result of the radical Republicans' naive assumption that blacks were equal to whites. '3,500,000 persons of one of the most inferior races of mankind had, through the agency of their superiors, been transformed from slavery to freedom.' Rhodes could not help reflecting how much more efficiently Prussia and Britain would have dealt with the problem. As it was, President Johnson foolishly encouraged Southern states to reject the Fourteenth Amendment granting equal civil liberties to the freedman (only Johnson's native state of Tennessee accepted), which resulted in the triumph of the radical wing in Congress, who then proceeded to pass the Reconstruction Acts of 1867. 'No law so unjust in its policy, so direful in its results had passed the American Congress' since the equally catastrophic Kansas–Nebraska Bill. It followed that Rhodes welcomed the 'redemption' of the South every bit as much as Southerners did. Errors had been committed on both sides; each section was indicted for foolish and misguided policies, for which each section suffered the consequences. The scales of justice were once again even, and the distracting sectional conflict could now come to an end. The year 1877 witnessed 'the final triumph of Southern intelligence and character over the ignorance and corruption that so long had thriven under Northern misconcepts'.[6]

So satisfying was this morality play in healing sectional wounds and providing a rationale for the desegregation and disfranchisement laws which followed that its general contours continued to hold sway over the profession well into the twentieth century. The questioning, as ever, came from black historians, deeply dissatisfied with this pro-Southern travesty of the facts. John Lynch was born a slave on a Louisiana plantation in 1847. During Reconstruction he had been appointed a justice of the peace by Governor Ames of Mississippi at the early age of 21. In 1872 he had advanced to the speakership of the Mississippi House of Representatives and in 1875 became the first black, at the age of twenty-six, to enter the US House of Representatives. Having lived through Reconstruction, he knew that Rhodes's narrative was biased and untruthful; 'a compilation of untrue, unreliable and grossly exaggerated statements taken from campaign literature, and the most one sided, biased, partisan and prejudiced historical work'. Lynch set out his counter-case in *The Facts of Reconstruction* (1913). 'I do not hesitate to assert,' he wrote, 'the Southern Republican governments were the best governments those states ever had and ... a fair, just and impartial historian will, someday, write a history covering the Reconstruction period [giving] the actual facts of what took place.'[7]

Du Bois also concentrated his fire on Rhodes. Rhodes's history, he insisted, was full of propaganda and racism and, moreover, Rhodes was almost uniquely disqualified by his character to write about, or understand, the real issues of Reconstruction. He knew nothing of economic history, or of the aspirations of blacks to democratic government, and as an industrialist he remorselessly exploited wage labour in his own factories.

The turn of the century was a time of disfranchisement, Jim Crow laws and lynchings in the South. Social Darwinism was in the ascendant. In the North Social Darwinism immunised business from any form of state or federal regulation and encouraged the growing discrepancies in wealth. In the South it rationalised caste. In also justified a belligerent foreign policy, and in 1898, discarding a long tradition of neutrality and isolation, the United States embarked upon a war with Spain over Cuba. These were the heady years when 'Teddy' Roosevelt charged up San Juan Hill in Cuba with his 'rough riders', when Admiral Dewey defeated an insignificant Spanish fleet in Manila Bay and claimed the Philippines for the United States, and Rudyard Kipling wrote specifically of Americans taking up the white man's burden of trusteeship over lesser races. Theodore Roosevelt succeeded to the presidency on the assassination of McKinley in 1901, and found himself fighting a guerrilla rebellion against American rule in the Philippines. He snapped at those unpatriotic anti-imperialists who opposed America's military rule, likening them to the disloyal draft rioters who had questioned Northern war policy during the Civil War. At home, Roosevelt's White House dinner with the black leader, Booker T. Washington, met with an avalanche of criticism and was never to be repeated. The fortunes of the black race in America reached their nadir.

It was against this background that the influential studies of reconstruction by J.W. Burgess and William A. Dunning appeared. Burgess, born into a slave-holding Unionist family, finally settled in Columbia University in New York City to establish its renowned School of Political Science. A worshipper of German scholarship, Burgess's history was shaped throughout by notions of biological struggle, conquest by the superior race, the defeat, and eventual extinction, of lower forms of humanity. Hence his thesis in *Reconstruction and the Constitution 1866–1876* (1902) was entirely predictable. Reconstruction

> was the most soul-sickening spectacle that Americans have ever been called upon to behold. Every principle of the old American polity was here reversed. In place of government by the most intelligent and virtuous part of the people for the benefit of the governed, here was government by the most ignorant and most vicious part of the population for the benefit, the vulgar, materialistic, brutal benefit of the governing set.

As with Rhodes, Burgess centred his invective upon the granting of the suffrage to the freedman:

> There is no question now that Congress did a monstrous thing and committed a great political error, if not a sin, in the creation of this new electorate. It was a great wrong to civilisation to put the white race of the South under the domination of the negro race. The claim that there is nothing in the colour of the skin from the point of view of political ethics is a great sophism. A black skin means membership in a race of men which has never of itself succeeded in subjecting passion to reason, has never, therefore, created any civilisation of any kind.

For Burgess, radical reconstruction was an explicable aberration, a total reversal of the iron laws of racial distinction and racial advancement. But America's assumption of a new, imperialist burden put the history of reconstruction into scientific perspective.

> And now that the United States has embarked on imperial enterprises under the direction of the Republican party, the great Northern party, the North is learning every day by valuable experience, that there are vast differences in political capacity between the races, and that it is the white man's mission, his duty and his right, to hold the reins of political power in his hands for the civilisation of the world and the welfare of mankind.

To which he added, with specific reference to the acquisition of the Philippines: 'The Republican Party, in its work of imposing the sovereignty of the United States upon eight millions of Asiatics, has changed its views in regard to the political relations of races and has at last virtually accepted the idea of the South upon that subject.'[8]

William Dunning, Burgess's ablest pupil at Columbia, took up the swelling imperial theme and made what was by now the commonplace connection between Asiatic possessions and the lessons of Reconstruction. Adding a passage to his 1901 edition of *Essays on the Civil War and Reconstruction*, he wrote that 'In view of the questions which have been raised by our lately established relations with other races, it seems not improbable that the historian will soon, or ever, have to record a reversal of the conditions [of racial equality] which the undoing of Reconstruction has established.'[9] By this date Dunning enjoyed a towering reputation in the field of Reconstruction history, analogous to that of Phillips on slavery. His postgraduate research had been carried out under the supervision of the great German nationalist historian, Treitschke, in Berlin and, although his name was invariably linked with reconstruction history, his main intellectual focus and area of research were in political theory, on which he wrote three volumes. He was more concerned with the philosophy of Kant and Hegel than with the misdemeanours of Senator Sumner, which may explain his casual approach to historical scholarship. He spent only three days, in all, sifting through the vital Library of Congress archives on Andrew Johnson, relied almost entirely on white sources, and was heavily dependent on his students' dissertations. But Dunning's stature grew predominantly because his writings reflected the culmination of a pro-Southern interpretation of Reconstruction, and because he built a cadre of graduate students, 'the Dunning school', who worked under him, respected him and disseminated his theories throughout the academic community.

The American Historical Association was founded in 1884, the same year as Cleveland's election as President. Cleveland was also the first Democrat President since the Civil War. In 1913 Dunning was elected president of the American Historical Association and the American Political Science Association simultaneously, the same year in which the first Southerner since the Civil War, Woodrow Wilson, entered the White House. Dunning's singular achievement was to take an essentially banal, Southern Democratic view and give it academic respectability.

Dunning's *Reconstruction: Political and Economic 1865–1877* (1907), Volume 22 of the prestigious American Nation series, stated its central and underlying theme unequivocally in its preface: 'few episodes of recorded history more urgently invite thorough analysis and extended reflection than the struggle through which the Southern whites, subjugated by adversaries of their own race, thwarted the scheme which threatened permanent subjugation to another race'. The ante-bellum South's problem was not one of slavery but of race relations, of

> the coexistence in one society of two races so distinct in characteristics as to render coalescence impossible; that slavery had been a *modus vivendi* through which social life was possible; and that, after its disappearance, its place must be taken by some set of conditions which, if more humane and beneficent in incidence, must in essence express the same fact of racial inequality.

Because of this determining fact, Dunning approved of the postwar Black Codes which were interpreted by the Republicans at the time as almost reimposing slave conditions on the freedmen. The codes were, he insisted, 'in the main a conscientious and straightforward attempt to bring some sort of order out the social and economic chaos which a full acceptance of the results of war and emancipation involved'.[10] On this question at least all white Southerners, rich or poor, Republican or Democrat, could agree. There followed a full blown recital of Reconstruction caricatures. Southern scalawags were 'more respectable perhaps in numbers than in social or intellectual position' and were collectively, 'a class who lacked the moral authority to conduct government in the Southern States'. Northern 'carpetbaggers' arrived in the South with 'limited positions and an unstable future'. To hold office and sustain their immoral and untenable position the 'carpetbagger' and scalawag depended on the support of an ignorant black electorate. 'The negro had no pride of race and no aspiration or ideals save to be like the whites. With civil rights and political power, not won, but almost forced upon him, he came gradually to understand and crave those more elusive privileges that constitute political equality,' such as a desire to mix socially with whites and indulge 'in the hideous crime against white womanhood, which now assumed new meaning in the annals of outrage': namely (though too horrendous to name) miscegenation. The 'reckless enfranchisement of the freedmen and their enthronement in power' were an unmitigated disaster. 'To stand the social pyramid on its apex was not the surest way to restore the shattered equilibrium of the South.' As a consequence the freedmen 'exercised an influence in political affairs out of all relation to their intelligence and property', and their leaders 'were very frequently of a type who acquired and practised the tricks of knavery rather than the useful arts of politics, and the vicious courses of these negroes strongly confirmed the prejudices of the whites'.[11]

President Johnson was praised for his astute statesmanship and common sense in seeking a lenient policy of 'restoration' in the South. In his support of the Black Codes, and in his insistence that the South should reject the Fourteenth Amendment, he displayed 'the same integrity of purpose, force of will, and rude intellectual force, which had raised him from the tailor's bench in a mountain hamlet in Tennessee, and sustained him when he confronted the problems of the national administration'. In stark contrast to Johnson's moderation was the 'truculent, vindictive, and cynical' Thaddeus Stevens, who not only wished to enfranchise the black but even urged the confiscation of the planters' lands to give to the freedmen. 'A keen and relentlessly logical mind, an ever-ready gift of biting sarcasm and stinging repartee, and a total lack of scruple as to the means in the pursuit of a legislative end, secured him an ascendancy in the House which none of his party associates ever dreamed of disputing.' Stevens's radical counterpart in the Senate was Charles Sumner.

> His forte was excited moral fervour and humanitarian idealism ... He would shed tears at the bare thought of refusing the Freedmen's rights of which they had no comprehension, but would filibuster to the end of the session to prevent the restoration to the Southern whites of rights which were essential to their whole conception of life. He was the perfect type of that narrow fanaticism which erudition and egotism combined to produce, and to which political crises alone give the opportunity for actual achievement.[12]

When Albert Bushnell Hart, the respected editor of the American Nation series, pencilled out this attack on Sumner, Dunning erased the pencil marks and sent his manuscript back unchanged. Dunning felt utter contempt for the author of civil rights legislation and all those radicals like him, 'the emotionalists', engaged in 'abstract theories of equality' and other 'trite generalisations of the Rights of Man'. Misguided militants, these 'fanatics were more extreme than the Southern fire-eaters who had precipitated the war'. If not motivated by impractical and unscientific idealism, like Sumner, they were moved instead, by unscrupulous party politics and unctuous humbug, such as Henry Wilson, 'whose tears in their flow never for a moment distorted his count of the votes to be gained for his party'. A combination of Yankee cynicism and unworldliness imbued the ethos and actions of the Freedmen's Bureau with 'that mysterious Providence which had inspired its wards with an unbounding confidence in the wonder-working capacity of the power it represented'. One of its misguided aims was to strive 'to create a sense of the sanctity of marriage when such an idea had but a shadowy, if any, existence'. Dunning approved of the mass intimidation and violence which led to the redemption of Mississippi because, he insisted, Governor Ames's 'carpetbagger' regime was eaten up with corruption. If the appalling race riots in New Orleans and Memphis led to black deaths and Northern disgust, that disgust was motivated by hatred of Southern whites: 'That the blacks were being abused was probably of less influence than the thought that the "rebels" were abusing them.' The activities of the Klan were referred to, lightly, in passing, as 'picturesque details'. Dunning's achievement, in short, was to undermine both the aims and the achievements of congressional Reconstruction. As he wrote to a fellow historian, Frederic Bancroft, with an almost audible sigh of self-satisfaction, 'Lord, how the Reconstructers have been Reconstructed.'[13] They had indeed.

Despite his gross bias Dunning had added fresh perspectives to Reconstruction history: the impact of the North and of congressional political and constitutional debates. He even admitted that some Reconstruction state constitutions, such as that of South Carolina, were remarkable experiments in good government, and extended the conventional chronology of the era to encompass populism and the passing of the Jim Crow laws. But his remarkable influence, which extended into the late 1930s, was largely due to the application of his ideas through his students, who went forth and multiplied. Each was given a state and a state archive to work on, and most unerringly followed the moral contours of their supervisor. Charles Ramsdell in his *Reconstruction in Texas* (1910) and J.G. Roulhac Hamilton in *Reconstruction in North Carolina* (1914), for example. Walter Fleming in his *Civil War and Reconstruction in Alabama* (1905) directly linked the debased Southern black with the debased new Northern immigrant.

> The former good manners of the negro were now replaced by impudence and distrust ... Pushing and crowding in public places, on street cars and on the sidewalks, and impudent speeches everywhere marked generally the limit of rudeness. And the negroes were, in this respect, no worse than those European immigrants who act upon the principle that bad manners are a proof of independence.

Fleming was especially influential because he compiled *A Documentary History of Reconstruction* (1907), which was widely used for teaching purposes in universities. Selected documents were provided, with a commentary such as this on the Klan, which 'suited the negroes, made life and property safe, gave protection to women, stopped burnings ... and started the whites on the way to gain political supremacy'. There were exceptions among the Dunning school. Mildred Thompson's study of Georgia showed uncommon sympathy for the freedmen's political aspirations and gave a more rounded and balanced interpretation of that state's troubled years. James Garner's *Reconstruction in Mississippi* (1901) praised the 'carpetbag' Governor Adelbert Ames for his personal integrity before going on to reprimand him for bias against Southern whites and 'overconfidence in the mental and moral ability of the black race'.[14]

The Dunning school dominated the academic world. The fictional trilogy written by Thomas Dixon had a far more profound impact on general opinion, all the more so because the second novel in the series, *The Clansman: The Historical Romance of the Ku Klux Klan* (1905) was made into one of the first great epics of American cinema, D.W. Griffith's *Birth of a Nation* (1915). Dixon, born in North Carolina in 1864, had studied at Johns Hopkins alongside a fellow Southerner, Woodrow Wilson, before becoming a Baptist clergyman in New York City. The leitmotif of his fictional trilogy was blatantly clear. The Klan, the heroic invisible empire, saves the South and white womanhood from the chaos and degradation of black domination and miscegenation. Racial mixing and sex obsessively and neurotically haunt its author. Miscegenation, as Dixon wrote in *The Leopard's Spots*, would destroy 'the foundation of racial life and of civilisation. The South must guard with flaming sword every avenue of approach to this holy of holies.' For 'one drop of negro blood makes a negro. It kinks the hair, flattens the nose, thickens the lip, puts out the light of intellect, and lights the fire of brutal passions. The beginning of negro equality as a vital fact is the beginning of the end of this nation's life. There is enough negro blood here to make mulatto the whole Republic.'[15] The dark hidden fears, which Dunning only gingerly hinted at, here become explicit.

The film director, Griffith, was born in Kentucky in 1875 into an aristocratic family ruined by the Civil War. But *The Birth of a Nation* was not merely personal revenge carried out by the son of a Confederate colonel, and was not hugely popular with the cinema-going public simply because of its innovative cinematic techniques. It also probed the white psyche's unease and fear of race and sex. Lincoln is depicted as the 'Great Heart' of conciliation who pardons the Confederacy's 'little Colonel' with the words 'I shall deal with [the Southerners] as if they had never been away.' Austin Stoneman, the Thaddeus Stevens character, is depicted as sexually desiring his mulatto housekeeper, Lydia Brown, 'the great leader's weakness that is to blight a nation'. With Lincoln's assassination, Lydia tells Stoneman, 'You are now the greatest power in America.' In the South another mulatto, Gus, parallels the Northern theme of miscegenation and illicit lust, by desiring Flora Cameron. In a graphic, climactic scene, Gus chases Flora, who, to save her honour, leaps to her death from a cliff. 'For her who had learned the stern lesson of honour we should not grieve that she found sweeter the opal gates of death.'[16]

Flora's brother, Ben, a leading Klansman, vows revenge. Hooded in the Klan uniform and carrying a Confederate flag, Ben calls the Klan to arms. 'Brethren, this flag bears the red stain of the life of a Southern woman, a priceless sacrifice on the altar of an outraged civilisation.'[17] In a scene edited out of the final version Gus is mutilated and castrated for his crime. The film ends with a ringing vindication of the Klan and the symbolic reunification of North and South in a marriage between the Stoneman and Cameron families. The two personifications of evil in the film are mulattoes, the depraved offspring of miscegenation, but in filming Griffith gave these parts to white actors, while black actors who played minor parts received no credits. On the sets, too, Southern actors refused to don Union uniforms.

The impact of the film on its audience was electric. As Woodrow Wilson exclaimed after a private screening in the White House: 'It is like writing history with lightning. And my only regret is that it is all so terribly true.'[18] Chief Justice Edward White, himself a Klansman when young, organised his own private showing for a select group of senators, justices and congressmen. Riots occurred in cinemas throughout the country. The film's patent racism was attacked by the black dean of Howard University, by Moorefield Storey (president of the American Bar Association), by Villard, Jane Addams, Booker T. Washington and others. As a concession to this outrage, Griffith added a reel depicting black workers at the Hampton Institute (permission was granted by its white president) but both Dixon and Griffith publicly and repeatedly attested to the historical authenticity of the film. Why then was Thaddeus Stevens, incorrectly, given a wife and children? And his relations with his mulatto housekeeper were mere unsubstantiated gossip. But both author and director, in claiming historical accuracy, appealed to Woodrow Wilson's *History of the American People* (1901), which threw an approving glow over the Klan and also accused Stevens of putting the white South under the heel of the black. Here seemingly pure, disinterested scholarship contributed to the climate of racial hysteria.

Following the example set by Dunning, the late 1920s saw a rash of strongly pro-Johnson biographies. If, as was now the consensus, radical Reconstruction was profoundly flawed in its aims and assumptions, it followed that Andrew Johnson's struggle against Congress and his fight for a conciliatory policy of restoration was a wise and heroic one which led to his being impeached by a vindictive Congress. Robert Winston's *Andrew Johnson: Plebeian and Patriot* (1928), Lloyd Stryker's *Andrew Johnson: A Study in Courage* (1929) and George Milton's *The Age of Hate: Andrew Johnson and the Radicals* (1930) were variations on this common theme, which culminated in Claude Bower's *The Tragic Era* (1929). This last was the work of a journalist whose graphic style gained it special selection by the Literary Guild of America and a huge reading public. It followed an exaggerated, and by now clichéd scenario: the Northern radicals 'the emissaries of hate'; the freedmen planning 'lustful assaults' on Southern womanhood. The conclusion: 'Never have American public men, in responsible positions, directing the destiny of the Nation, been so brutal, hypocritical and corrupt, ... the Southern people literally were put to the torture.'[19] No matter that this highly influential book was written by a partisan Democrat exploiting history for campaign propaganda purposes and aiming indirectly at the current enemies of the Democratic presidential candidate, Al Smith. The book popularised and disseminated the Dunning line, and, moreover, won Bowers the American embassy in Spain, an appointment bestowed by a grateful President Roosevelt in 1933.

W.E.B. Du Bois stood out against this overwhelming white

historical consensus. Born in Massachussets in 1868, he first encountered the race problem at Fisk University, in Nashville, Tennessee, where segregation and discrimination were widespread. Moderate and fairly conservative at first, Du Bois grew increasingly radical over the years. While Booker T. Washington became identified with the politics of accommodation and the attempt by blacks to try to attain and be judged by white standards, Du Bois, who played a major role in founding the National Association for the Advancement of Colored People, strove increasingly to spearhead Afro-America's 'talented tenth', to celebrate racial pride and a degree of racial separatism. Centred at the University of Atlanta in Georgia from 1897 to 1910 and again after 1932, he organised a series of Pan-African conferences calling for the independence of African colonies. In 1961 he joined the Communist party and, totally disenchanted with American racism, emigrated to Ghana, where he died in 1963.

In 1903 in his *Souls of Black Folk* he identified the problem of the twentieth century as being the problem of the colour line. He also identified the unique and tragic dualism of the black in America. 'One ever feels his twoness – an American, a Negro; two souls, two thoughts, two unreconciled strivings; two warring ideals in one dark body, whose dogged strength alone keeps it from being torn asunder.'[20] Du Bois's crucial historical contribution, culminating in his *Black Reconstruction in America 1860–80* (1935), was to return to the black race its rightful and active role in the making of the Civil War era; to argue that slavery was the fundamental cause of the Civil War, and that the black, rather than being a passive tool, actively sought to earn his freedom, and played a critical role in the failed attempt to reorder race relations during the Reconstruction era.

Du Bois's Marxist training enabled him to grasp the underlying economic struggle which followed upon emancipation. Reconstruction could be interpreted in terms of class as well as racial struggle. Access to capital, land, economic choice, the enjoyment of the fruit of one's own labour, were of the essence, and the struggle for economic control went hand in hand with the struggle for political influence. 'It was,' he wrote, 'the far more fundamental question of whom this wealth was to belong to and for whose interests laborers were to work.'[21] In the ante-bellum

South 7 per cent of Southerners dominated 5 million whites, owned 4 million slaves and collaborated with Northern business in industrialising agriculture in the South by means of slave labour. Emancipation was achieved, in part, because black labour and black soldiers actively sought freedom and, deserting the plantations, went on a 'general strike' and joined the swelling ranks behind the Union army's advance. One seminal chapter in the book was initially entitled 'The dictatorship of the black proletariat in Southern Carolina'. He dropped the opening 'Dictatorship of' only because South Carolina's revolutionary experiment fell short of expropriating private property in the form of land. Yet the chapter does amply illustrate the revolutionary collaboration of black and white in that state, which imposed taxation on property and administered it, however briefly, for the benefit of black and white labour alike. Chapter 14, entitled 'The counter-revolution of property', traces the unravelling of this revolutionary achievement and the economic consequences of Southern 'redemption'.

Du Bois's revisionist intent is patent in the very title of an essay published in the *American Historical Review* in 1910 – 'Reconstruction and its benefits'. This determinedly upbeat article points to the emergence of democratic government, free public schooling and new social legislation in the period. Through the agencies of black churches, schools and the Freedmen's Bureau, blacks and the Republican party began to transform the South and make its society more equitable. Able black politicians such as John Lynch, speaker of the Mississippi House of Representatives, and Cardozo, treasurer of South Carolina, effectively mobilised the black vote to bring about radical social improvements. There had been an overall increase of taxation in the South after the war, but it was not the result generally of large-scale corruption and peculation. The state legislature that voted itself gold spittoons, or voted for compensating its speaker after he lost money on the race course, was a colourful exception. 'There was one thing the white South feared more than negro dishonesty, ignorance and incompetence,' Du Bois wrote, 'and that was negro honesty, knowledge and efficiency.' Taxes had increased, because, for the first time, the tax system was spread more fairly, and revenue was needed to make up for the ravages of war and lay the foundations of a progressive social infrastructure. Du Bois submitted a new article on 'Reconstruction' to the *Encyclopaedia Britannica* which the editor refused to print because of such judgements as the following.

> White historians have ascribed the faults and failures of Reconstruction to negro ignorance and corruption. But the negro insists that it was negro loyalty, and the negro vote alone, that restored the South to the Union; established the new democracy, both for white and black, and instituted the public schools.[22]

Instead, the fourteenth edition of the *Encyclopaedia Britannica* carried the usual depiction of a black saturnalia of corruption and jobbery written by Frederick Jackson Turner.

Du Bois depicted the Freedmen's Bureau as a noble and enlightened attempt to assist the black race practically. Though desperately overstretched and underfunded, it brought relief to social suffering, overseeing the change to free labour, buying and selling land, establishing black schools, offering financial assistance to the needy and administering justice in an often hostile environment. The Black Codes, justified by Dunning, were seen in a new and harsher perspective, for they indicated only too clearly what the South proposed to do to the emancipated negro, unless constrained by the nation. Though forced, to some extent, to rely upon the writings of his historical opponents, Du Bois in a vituperative chapter, 'The propaganda of history', traced the distortions of Reconstruction history through the highly selective use of primary materials. Black eye witnesses, like most poor whites, were systematically excluded, as were the records of the Freedmen's Bureau, the papers of the Congressional Committee on Reconstruction, and the radical legislative record of the Thirty-ninth Congress. Northern observers sympathetic to black aspiration and radical reconstruction such as Nicolay and Hay, Georges Clemenceau, George Julian, Carl Schurz and John Sherman were also deliberately ignored. Du Bois's secondary bibliography was sharply divided into 'Standard anti-negro', 'Propaganda', 'Historians fair or indifferent', 'Sympathetic' and 'Negro historians' and Du Bois was withering on the racial bias of Rhodes, Burgess and Dunning.

Du Bois was generally ostracised by the historical profession during his life, since which time opinions have varied. David Donald wrote of Du Bois's history being 'marred by a quasi-Marxist bias'; T. Harry Williams criticised his dubious contention of class unity between black and white labour; Kenneth Stampp found him naive and disappointing; Willie Lee Rose found him brilliant and beautiful and inconsistent; Peter Kolchin referred to *Black Reconstruction* as 'a passionate work of radical scholarship'; Eric Foner called it 'a frustrating, flawed, but monumental study'. Foner, in particularly, stressed Du Bois's seminal insights as having shaped his own and contemporary concerns about reconstruction. Dedicating his Walter Lynwood Fleming lectures delivered at Louisiana State University in 1982 to the memory of Du Bois, he writes of this 'towering figure of modern American life'. His *Black Reconstruction* 'is replete with insights, revolutionary in its implications for the scholarship of the 1930s, that have become almost commonplace today'.[23] This is a fine vindication of Du Bois's once neglected reputation.

Du Bois was incapable of toppling the entrenched fortress of historical orthodoxy singlehanded. While adopting a similar Marxist framework to Du Bois, Charles Beard did not question this orthodoxy. On the contrary, his progressivist strategy of replacing political and ideological man with economically motivated man emptied Reconstruction entirely of its moral content. As Du Bois put it, one came away from reading Beard with 'the comfortable feeling that nothing right or wrong is involved', only the impersonal working out of predetermined economic forces. While Beard did recognise the Civil War as a 'Second American Revolution', that revolution was measured in terms of property and wealth, and confiscation, rather than of human beings. Reconstruction was revolutionary because it expropriated property in the form of slaves, 'the most stupendous act of sequestration in the history of Anglo-Saxon jurisprudence', as Beard put it, to the tune of $4 billion ($3 trillion by 1990 standards), and because the Fourteenth Amendment, under the guise of granting black equality, established a powerful protection for the interests of Northern trusts.[24] Because the war had been ignited by economic interests it followed that the Reconstruction period had to be a consolidation of those same guiding economic interests. The real Civil War struggle was only superficially fought out on its battlefields: the underlying struggle resulted in a conquest of King Cotton by Northern industrial capital. It was the triumphant culmination of a Federalist–Whig tradition which riveted high protective tariffs, a national banking system, a sound gold-based currency and internal improvements – all highly beneficial to big business and capitalist entrepreneurs – on to the republic. Beard's historical battleground was singularly unheroic. The 'due process' clause of the Fourteenth Amendment, written by John Bingham, congressman and Ohio railroad lawyer, deliberately personalised and protected all business organisations from state or federal intervention, and swept away Jacksonian egalitarianism.

The revisionist school was, theoretically, diametrically opposed to the progressive school. Where Beard saw inevitability everywhere the revisionists saw only chance, political manipulation and unrestrained fanaticism. If the Civil War was a terrible mistake then Reconstruction, the direct consequence of the Civil War crusade, had also to be a terrible error. The revisionist attack on militant abolitionists was shifted on to the radical Republicans. Fanatical humanitarianism, misplaced philanthropy were, in both cases, the cause of unnecessary agitation. Throughout his biography of Lincoln, J.G. Randall consistently targets the radical Republicans, not copperheads, McClellan or Democrats, as the President's chief enemies in the North. With Northern victory 'the triumph of the Union was spoilt by the manner in which victory was used', Randall wrote. Instead of Lincoln's moderate policy of malice towards none, the radicals – 'a more unlovely knot of politicians would be hard to find' – 'pursued anti-slavery zeal as a political instrument, with moralising unction, rebel-baiting intolerance and hunger for power'.[25] The revisionist school served to buttress the Dunningite edifice.

But cracks were beginning to appear in that edifice. In 1939 Francis Simkins from Virginia called for a fresh, unbiased look at the period, and William Hesseltine followed Du Bois in seeing class as an issue in the reconstruction struggle. In 1939 Vernon Wharton's *The Negro in Mississippi 1865–1890* found conditions nothing like as bleak in that state as the Dunning school had argued. Taxes and state expenditure did rise, but the circumstances were exceptional and provision for blacks had hitherto been non-existent. There was not excessive theft and inefficiency; indeed, the restoration governments which followed were far more corrupt.

Howard Beale in *The Critical Year: 1866* (1930), and in an important article 'On rewriting Reconstruction history' of 1940, contributed to this change of focus. Influenced by Beard and the politics of the Great Depression and the New Deal, Beale emphasised biracial class divisions in the South and economic motives. 'Textiles, coal, iron and steel, tobacco factories, railroads, and mill villages were as important as loyal leagues, klans and black codes'. Most political speeches of the period were 'claptrap' 'pure show' and 'mere shibboleths'. The economic intent of the Reconstruction Acts was to get high tariffs, congenial to the North, passed before the South and the Democratic party regained power and influence. Like Beard, Beale stressed economics and class, New England versus South and West: 'An industrialised North East, dominated by business principles that were to create the machine-made America of today, faced an agrarian South and West contending for those time-honored principles of frontier individualism and plantation aristocracy which had dominated an America that was passing.'[26] Beale contributed to the rehabilitation of the 'statesmanlike' Johnson because Johnson stood up for the old Jeffersonian order against the predominant business ethos of his own party. But within this limiting Beardian framework there was fresh thinking. Beale insisted that the traditional racial pejoratives should be dropped for good; that Reconstruction history was American, and not exclusively Southern, history; that Northern business was as willing to support Southern white supremacy as Northern politicians were willing to wave the bloody flag; that the radical wing of the Republican party sincerely attempted to assist the poor of the South and that, opposed to the wealthy Bourbon Democratic restoration, biracial coalitions sprang up and founded the Granger movement in the 1870s and 1880s.

But the Bourbons of the historical profession continued to fight a rearguard action against these radical implications. In 1942, for example, Albert Moore of the University of Alabama delivered his presidential address to the Southern Historical Association. He spoke feelingly of the South being treated economically, psychologically, politically and culturally as a colony of the North; he said that James Ford Rhodes's contention that the South was treated mildly after the war ignored the confiscation of slave property and the mental torture – 'the crucifixion of the South' – which followed. The radical Republicans were excoriated for pampering the blacks, raising false hopes, and pursuing a fanatical vendetta against the South.

In 1948 E. Merton Coulter published his *South during Reconstruction* in the prestigious History of the South series, of which he was joint editor. Reviewing it, Frank Owsley averred that 'there are few historians today whose approach is more impartial and unemotional than Coulter's'.[27] T. Harry Williams, a Northerner who had recently gained tenure at Louisiana State University, wrote privately to his former teacher, William Hesseltine, 'it's a crying shame the way the profession has reviewed Coulter's godawful book on Reconstruction. Isn't someone going to have the courage to say it's based on race prejudice and distortion of the sources?'[28] The young John Hope Franklin did have the courage to review Coulter in the *Journal of Negro Education* and found it to be both partial and emotional. When Coulter wrote in his introduction that 'No amount of revision can write away the grievous mistakes made in this abnormal period of American history,' he meant that blacks holding state offices was 'diabolical and to be remembered, shuddered at, and execrated', and that radicals behaved in a manner akin to fascists.[29] One such radical, Carl Schurz, was denigrated for lacking common sense – that is, supporting black emancipation – and for his unpatriotic non-American origins (he was a German who had escaped from the political reaction following the 1848 revolutions). Blacks in general were spendthrift, gullible, excessively emotional and heavy drinkers. Coulter defended the codes which excluded blacks from jury service and excluded black testimony against white defendants in court, but then went on to say that his opinion on this matter was purely academic because the codes were never enforced. Franklin provided evidence which showed that they were, and went on to undermine Coulter's limited and selective use of sources. Rather than examining the minutes of state constitutional conventions, Coulter quoted from white opponents of the conventions in the press. Black voices and the Freedmen's Bureau reports were neglected while Coulter would quote liberally from Little Rock's *Weekly Arkansas Gazette*.

At times the bias could be subtle and devious. Coulter spoke of the mulatto Louisiana State Superintendent of Education, Edward King, as so abysmally ignorant and careless in his duties that he did not know how many schools there were in his state. Coulter had quoted from King's *The Great South* and, when Franklin checked the source, he discovered an explicit statement by King on the immense and frustrating difficulty of getting returns from distant interior districts in a time of great disruption and that he received yearly reports tardily or not at all. At other times Coulter relied on supposition rather than evidence. He insisted that when black officials were pitched out of South Carolina's state government in 1877 they returned to their humble employment as street sweepers, waiters or field hands. Franklin carefully followed up the careers of these officials and found Coulter's assertion to be simply untrue, and gave four specific individual examples to prove his case.[30]

But Coulter was among the last of a doomed historical order. As David Potter wrote: 'For two generations after Appomattox, the compulsive memories of the Lost Cause had held the Southern mind in thrall; myth had grown like ivy over the brick and mortar of Southern historical experience; sentimentality and veneration had inhibited realism.'[31] Now all that was to change and Reconstruction history witnessed a period of rampant revisionism. The revolution began quietly enough. In 1961 John Hope Franklin published his own history of Reconstruction in the Chicago History of American Civilization series. With great tact and subtlety, in a chapter entitled 'The South's new leaders', he restored the neglected black contribution to the period. In 1965 Kenneth Stampp reversed the previous assumption that Reconstruction was tragic because it was attempted by roundly asserting that Reconstruction's tragedy lay in its ultimate failure. In 1969, along with Leon Litwack, Stampp edited an excellent collection of revisionist essays on the period.

As early as 1947 Vernon Wharton had rejected the myth of black domination and corruption in his *Negro in Mississippi*. In 1965 Joel Williamson in *After Slavery*, which dealt with freedmen in South Carolina, James Richardson in *The Negro in the Reconstruction of Florida*, and John Blassingame in his *Black New Orleans 1860–1880* (1973) painted a far more positive picture of the black's contribution to Reconstruction. The once despised radicals were now rehabilitated and a stream of biographies – Ralph Korngold and Fawn Brodie on Thaddeus Stevens (1955 and 1959 respectively), Benjamin Thomas and Harold Hyman in their *Stanton*, Hans Trefousse in his studies of Benjamin Butler and Benjamin Franklin Wade – depicted men of principle. In a sensitive study of the Port Royal experiment, where confiscated land on the South Carolina islands was given to freedmen to culti-vate, Willie Lee Rose presented the Freedmen's Bureau and New England schoolmistresses in a sympathetic light. In contrast Andrew Johnson, in studies by Eric McKitrick, La Wanda and John Cox, Hans Trefousse and William Brock, received a far more critical examination.

Computers and the new political history came to the aid of this reassessment. In *The Politics of Reconstruction* (1965) David Donald searched for 'objective behaviour patterns' and 'quantifi-ably measurable forces' and found them in politicians seeking re-election or aspiring to higher office.[32] His analysis of congres-sional roll calls found radicals Sumner, Stevens and George Julian hailing from solid and safe Republican constituencies, while conservatives came from electorally marginal areas. If Donald concluded from this that Republican politicians were less bold and less idealistic than had previously been thought, it also followed that radicals were tapping a Northern constituency which was concerned with securing civil liberties for the freed-men. Edward Gambill's analysis of the critical Thirty-ninth Congress measured how Republicans voted rather than what they said and found that radicals, no less cohesive than the moderates, were more unified than conservatives in the Republican or Democratic ranks. Glenn Linden and the Coxes used quantifica-tion techniques to measure the balance of idealism and expediency in Republican motivation and came down finally on the side of idealism.

Vann Woodward in his *Reunion and Reaction: Origins of the New South*, and a biography of Tom Watson, found evidence of a biracial alliance, albeit temporary, emerging in the South, though he was sceptical of radical motives, which included a wish to keep freedmen in the South and avoid mass northward migration. He saw Reconstruction and the post-Reconstruction era not simply as a struggle between North and South but as a continuing war within the South itself, between the jostling orders of poor whites and freedmen, the old planter regime and the Whiggish industrial order which was attempting to bring about the regeneration of the Southern economy. In an article, 'Beyond the realm of social consensus' (1981), Armistead Robinson also discovered fresh evidence of a biracial coalition in Georgia and resurrected part of Du Bois's class thesis.

The ante-bellum class tension between piedmont yeoman farmers and tidewater plantation owners continued unabated after the Civil War. As cotton production became more commercialised and subject to international markets, and as cotton prices fell precipitously following the slump of 1873, an increasing number of impoverished yeomen became landless tenants and sought a biracial class coalition within the Republican party against the Democrats. But this nascent co-operation was brief, for Governor Joseph Brown of Georgia was a moderate who still looked to the old planter elite for support, and incited racial hatred to break up a potentially radical alliance of the poor. 'Racism,' Robinson concludes, 'did not overwhelm class; racism became an organising principle for social strata fearful of class-based political action.'[33]

Meanwhile George Frederickson, Eric Foner and others had embarked on comparative studies which yielded new, exciting insights. They revealed Southern Reconstruction to have been in many ways unique. Russia and Britain paid financial compensation to serf and slave owners; abolition in the British empire, Brazil and Cuba was gradual; abolition in the United States, as in Haiti, came in war and rebellion. Only in the United States was abolitionism accompanied by civil rights and rapid political enfranchisement – 'a remarkable political and social mobilisation of the black community', as Frederickson put it.

Eric Foner, in the tradition of Du Bois, has also given much greater emphasis to the revolutionary nature of Reconstruction. Even in the 1960s and 1970s historians tended to interpret Reconstruction in negative, conservative, fatalistic terms. Thus

Eric McKitrick, though critical of Johnson, believed moderate Reconstruction was preferable to radical, congressional reconstruction. William McFeely in his biography of General Oliver Howard, head of the Freedmen's Bureau, tended to depict that agency essentially as organising and disciplining black labour for the benefit of its erstwhile masters. Vann Woodward and Stampp both placed emphasis on the limitations and restrictions of Reconstruction. Harold Hyman and Michael Les Benedict argued for the constitutional conservatism of the period and the continued deference to states' rights against federal interventionism.

In his *Reconstruction* and *Nothing but Freedom* Foner has stressed, instead, the extraordinary innovativeness and experimentation of the period. There was a revolution, the work of a new political class of freedmen backed by a newly empowered nation state determined to bring about sweeping changes. Where others saw the semi-peonage of sharecropping as a defeat, Foner sees it as a practical compromise. True, the freedman regarded cotton as a slave crop: it could not be drunk and it could not be eaten. Ideally the freedman wished for his own forty acres and a mule, but in most cases they were unobtainable. The Southern white master class hoped to establish a labour system as analogous to slavery as possible. The North wished the freedman to buckle down to wage labour. No group got its own way entirely. Sharecropping was a form of grudging compromise, much as Genovese's slave prised concessions from his master's paternalism. The freedmen became heavily mortgaged to local merchants and the whites to whom they had contracted. But the system did give the blacks some independence and enabled them to work at their own pace during the varying seasons, which they preferred to a flat hourly wage. Foner quotes tellingly from General Robert Richardson, the treasurer of the American Cotton Planters' Association: 'The emancipated slaves own nothing, because nothing but freedom has been given to them.' To which Foner replies: freedom is a good deal more than nothing. 'The struggle unleashed by emancipation, for equality in social relations, access to the resources of the earth, and the fruits of its labour, still continues.'[34] If Foner was inspired by Du Bois, McPherson borrowed Beard's concept of a second revolution, to measure change not in tangibles, but rather in human terms: as an experiment in race relations backed by a committed federal government.

Today each and every tenet of the Dunning interpretation has collapsed. The first tenet was that of a vindictive North imposing a harsh peace on a prostrate South. Not so. As James Ford Rhodes had insisted, reconstruction was the mildest punishment ever inflicted by victor upon vanquished, and it was the South which initially refused to accept the consequences of defeat. South Carolina, for example, refused to repudiate its Confederate debt, Mississippi to accept the Thirteenth Amendment, and Florida and Georgia refused to repeal the ordinances of secession. Only one Confederate, Wirtz, was executed for war crimes, as a consequence of the suffering of soldiers under him in the Andersonville prisoner-of-war camp. The ex-Confederate President Jefferson Davis was imprisoned for two years, but one of the supposedly most vindictive radicals, Thaddeus Stevens, actually argued against Davis's trial and conviction, and historians such as Franklin and Stampp have shown that the freedmen, rather than insisting upon the disfranchisement of disloyal whites, attempted to get such disabilities removed. Such Northern harshness as there was stemmed from the white South's refusal to accept blacks' civil rights and the legitimacy of congressional prerogatives.

Another myth, asserted by Jefferson Davis and converted into a major thesis by Beard and Owsley, was that the aim of the North, both during and after the war, was to turn the South into a colony of Northern capitalism. In an article, 'New England business and radical reconstruction: an examination', which appeared in the *Mississippi Valley Historical Review* in 1959, Stanley Coben refuted this assumption.[35] There were few Republican party connections with big business; there was initially very little New York financial interest in investment in the South because the South was unstable and investment there was highly risky, while the west offered a far more lucrative and safer field for financial returns. In so far as business concerned itself with the politics of Reconstruction, it sought a quick return to normal – that is, the business community tended to support Johnson's Reconstruction plan rather than radical congressional plans which threatened further economic instability. Kolchin's analysis of fourteen business journals found only one, *Iron Age*, radical in its political allegiance. In California two of the state's railroad magnates, E.D. Croker and Leland Stanford, were pro-radical, but a third, Collis Huntington, was anti-radical. The radicals were supposed to be spearheading the economic take-over of the South under the guise of concern for the freedmen. But Glenn Linden's analysis of forty-seven Senate roll calls between 1873 and 1877 revealed no alignment between political and economic questions; indeed, the radicals were totally split on economic questions. For example, Stevens, a Pennsylvania iron manufacturer, feared competition from cheap Nova Scotia coal and English iron and steel manufacturers, and advocated high tariffs and mild inflation to keep the economy buoyant, while Senator Sumner, from Massachusetts, represented cotton and woollen manufacture, an industry which was highly competitive and required the importation of cheap raw materials: he advocated free trade and a sound currency through the resumption of special payment. The Republican party did become increasingly identified with business interests when ideology yielded to organisation, but this came after the end of Reconstruction. Empirical research reveals that the thesis of a collective conspiracy to enslave the South economically was non-existent. Indeed, the figure who best fits the stereotype of Northern capitalism at the time is none other than the wealthy New York corporation lawyer Sam Tilden, and he, of course, was the Democratic party presidential candidate in the disputed election of 1876.

The Dunningites depicted President Johnson as an honourable statesman, pursuing a policy of wise restoration and protecting whites against the africanisation of the South. From the Southern Democratic point of view this interpretation was sound. A poor white from the border state of Tennessee, Johnson began as a states' rights Democrat whom Lincoln rewarded with the vice-presidency for his loyalty to the Union during the war. Certainly his negrophobe opinions chimed perfectly with Democratic and Southern sentiments. After receiving a delegation led by Frederick Douglass petitioning for black enfranchisement, he expressed his opinion in private. 'Those damned sons of bitches thought they had me in a trap! I know that damned Douglass; he's just like any nigger, and he would sooner cut a white man's throat than not.'[36] There was a certain irony in Johnson's strategy. Obsessed by class and by his humble origins, loathing the wealthy planter class, he feared an emerging post-war alliance of planters and freedmen against the white yeoman class. But his intransigence ultimately allied him to that very planter caste he despised. Hitherto historians had treated him kindly because of the personal humiliation he had suffered under congressional impeachment, and because, in retrospect, his policy of restoration seemed wiser than the continued disruption of Congress. McKitrick's study of 1960 depicted him as a prickly perennial outsider, but McKitrick's anti-radical stance tended towards kindness. Kenneth Stampp was less sympathetic: stubborn, recalcitrant, the last Jacksonian, Johnson was largely responsible for the grave constitutional crisis which led to his impeachment. La Wanda and John Cox and William Brock also depicted a floundering President fatally vetoing reconstruction legislation and forcing moderates such as Lyman Trumball and John Sherman into the radical ranks. David Donald, in contrast, depicts Johnson as a virtuoso politician, attempting to cobble together enough white Unionist votes to sustain his presidency. But there is the rub. At most, Johnson was willing to concede a limited extension of the franchise to blacks who held property, were literate or had served in the Union army. The bulk of his party insisted that the badge of slavery remained as long as the freedman suffered from civil disabilities. Hence the President's support of the Black Codes and his veto of the Freedmen's Bureau and Civil Rights Bill were disastrous for the cause of moderation.

Surprisingly Grant's presidency, which covered two-thirds of reconstruction, has received far less attention; his military reputation offset by the encroaching charges of corruption which bedevilled his administration. Yet a recent study by Arthur Zilversmit, entitled *Grant and the Freedmen*, depicts a failed young man voting for Buchanan in 1856 and for Douglas in 1860, but slowly coming to terms with the implications of the Fourteenth Amendment and, unlike Johnson, approving, as far as possible, the Republican strategy of sustaining the black vote against Klan violence and intimidation.

The Dunningites placed much emphasis upon the wise,

constitutional conservatism of the American polity. Radical demands were aberrant: the North ultimately respected states' rights and limited the area of federal intervention. Recent studies by Phillip Paludan, Harold Hyman and Michael Les Benedict have reiterated this point and quote Thomas Carlyle's aphorism of America as benignly ruled by 'anarchy plus a street constable'.[37] But this is very much a matter of perspective along the lines of whether a wineglass is half full or half empty. The Dunningites made much of the temporary overreaching of federal powers and the relative ease with which the Fourteenth and Fifteenth Amendments were informally undermined. The Supreme Court was indeed conservative in its doubts concerning the constitutionality of Lincoln's suspension of *habeas corpus*. Its decision in *ex parte Milligan* (1866), which concerned the unconstitutional arrest and imprisonment of a civilian by a military court, undermined the constitutionality of the Freedmen's Bureau. Similarly the Supreme Court's decisions in the *Slaughterhouse* and *Civil rights* cases undermined the federal commitment to civil liberties. But the Freedmen's Bureau was, in itself, and for its time, a highly innovative extension of federal power, however poorly funded and manned. The radicals also exploited Article 4, section 4, of the Constitution, which guaranteed a republican form of government in the states, to enlarge equality before the law and insist upon the consent of all who were governed, black as well as white. James McPherson, for one, sees the wineglass as half full, and has argued that one of the revolutionary consequences of the Civil War and Republican eras was a decisive swing towards greater federal intervention. In his book *The Second American Revolution* he notes that, while eleven of the first twelve amendments acted to limit federal authority, those which followed, beginning with the three Civil War amendments, extended national authority, and that this change can also be detected in Lincoln's change of language from 'Unionism' to 'nationhood' as the war developed a mystic sense of the nation state.

If Reconstruction historiography is a perfect litmus test of racial assumptions, the Fifteenth Amendment is an excellent yardstick for measuring Republican party motivation. In a study of the passage of the Fifteenth Amendment in 1903 Allen Braxton asserted unequivocally that the principal motive was party opportunism, and, of course, Dunning agreed. It was simply inconceivable, Dunning wrote, that 'rational men of the North should seriously approve of suffrage *per se*': there had to be a self-serving purpose.[38] In 1965 William Gillette argued that the principal motive was to secure Northern black votes for the Republican party, and Vann Woodward, in a sceptical essay entitled 'The political legacy of reconstruction' pointed out the hypocrisy of a North which sought to impose black suffrage on the South when only five Northern states had black suffrage themselves. Vann Woodward concluded that 'One is left to wonder how much Radical Reconstruction was really concerned with the South and how much with the party needs of the Republicans in the North'.[39]

In many ways the matter is complicated. First, disentangling motives is often difficult and politicians especially are prone to do the right thing for the wrong reason. Secondly, the issue becomes almost tautological. As Stevens made perfectly clear, party and policy went together, and without the Republican party there would be no genuine Reconstruction. Democrats would rapidly return to power. Urging his radical plans in the House of Representatives, Stevens admitted that 'Another good reason is that it would assure the ascendancy of the Union [Republican] Party. "Do you avow the party purpose?" exclaims some horror-stricken demagogue. I do. For I believe on my conscience, that on the continued ascendancy of that party depends the safety of this great nation.'[40] Thirdly, with emancipation, the ending of the three-fifths rule increased Southern representation in the House by twelve or thirteen seats. Briefly, under the Reconstruction Act there were 703,000 black voters, as against 627,000 whites in the South, and part of the Republican party strategy was to consolidate its ascendancy by means of the Fifteenth Amendment.

If, as Gillette suggests, the party aim was to garner Northern black votes, the pickings were thin. Representing only 1 per cent of the Northern electorate, even those states with the largest number of black votes, New Jersey and Ohio, could muster only 3.4 per cent and 2.4 per cent of the state electorate respectively. In their 'Negro suffrage and reconstruction politics: the problem of motivation and reconstruction historiography', the Coxes approached this vexed question by analysing not political rhetoric but the practical electoral consequences which followed upon enfranchising the black. They insist that the North had become the power base of the Republican party and, as such, the South was electorally less important. The old rural 'copperhead' North-west had become industrialised, and, with the Homestead Acts and veterans' pensions, gave increasing allegiance to the Republican party. Apart from the contested presidential election of 1876 the black vote was not vital to overall Republican victory. Nevertheless the granting of the black franchise did result in a white racist backlash in the North. The Coxes provide ample evidence. In 1867, for example, Governor Rutherford Hayes of Ohio held a referendum on black suffrage which resulted in only 46 per cent of the state voting in favour, the Democrats gaining control of both Houses, and the popular governor himself holding on to office by a majority of only 0.4 per cent. New York State, having officially ratified the Fifteenth Amendment, returned a Democratic majority of twenty and rescinded its ratifi-cation. Indeed, all the crucial, pivotal states the party had to hold to cling on to power – New York, Indiana, Pennsylvania, Ohio, Illinois – were opposed to black suffrage.

The Coxes observed a consistent pattern of support for blacks, from the granting of black suffrage in Washington D.C. (116 Republicans voting for, fifteen against and ten abstaining) which remained firm up to the passing and ratification of the Fifteenth Amendment in 1870. Their voting analysis confirmed McPherson's thesis that since the early days of abolitionism the Republican party had remained committed to the black cause, for altruistic as well as for party reasons. The Coxes concluded circumspectly that

> Analysis of ballots in the 1870s and 1880s does not confirm the reasonableness of expectations for a succession of Republicans in the White House as the result of negro enfranchisement. The motives of Congressmen doubtless were mixed, but in the period of national crisis when the issue of equality was basic to political contention, it is just possible that party advantage was subordinate to principle.[41]

The image of the corrupt Northern 'carpetbagger', vital to the Dunningite myth, has been systematically undermined by modern scholars such as Richard Current, George Frederickson and John Hope Franklin. Dunningites invariably used the term pejoratively but, far from being the dregs of Northern society moving South to exploit the area economically with the support of federal bayonets, most were well educated and from a professional background. In his analysis of ten carpetbag governors Current found seven of them to have been college-educated (D.H. Chamberlain, one-time governor of South Carolina, was educated at both Harvard and Yale), and nine of them were Union veterans, the exception, Harrison Reed in Florida, having been too old to serve. The majority had settled in the South before the Reconstruction Acts and hoped to make their future in the South, much as many Southerners went North after the Civil War to make their fortunes. Four did settle permanently in the South and four others spent at least a decade there. Political involvement, Current insists, was not their original intention. Two had come to the South on military duty, two were businessmen and four became cotton planters. The image of carpetbagger dominance is pure myth.

In an analysis of Southern state conventions of 1867–68, Franklin revealed carpetbaggers as in a minority in every state except Mississippi. He also revealed a far higher Southern white representation, twice as many as Northern carpetbaggers, as had hitherto been assumed. None arrived penniless, though some became impoverished after failed business ventures in the South. Indeed, many turned to political office and Republican party patronage (as Lawrence Powell argues, in *The Politics of Livelihood: Carpetbaggers in the Deep South*) as a means of surviving economically as cotton prices fell catastrophically throughout the rest of the century. Six ex-Confederate states had no carpetbag governors, and those that did, such as Arkansas, Mississippi, Louisiana, Florida and South Carolina, experienced only brief Republican rule before the ban on ex-Confederate leaders holding office ended in 1872.

Some went South for idealistic reasons. One such, Albion Tourgee, moved from Ohio to North Carolina in 1865 to set up a nursery business and crusade on behalf of the freedmen. Becoming a state judge, he battled heroically on behalf of black power and against the intimidation of the Klan before admitting defeat and retiring back to the North in 1879. Many of the governors, such as Ames of Mississippi and D.H. Chamberlain of South Carolina, were impeccably honest, while others, such as Henry Warmoth of Louisiana and Robert Scott of South Carolina, did make profits though without breaking the law. Given the turbulent and unstable conditions of the time, Current suggests, Louisiana corrupted Warmoth rather than the other way round. And Warmoth was exceptional: most carpetbaggers, if they left the South, left it deep in debt. The major carpetbag crime, both at the time and in the eyes of the Dunningite school, was to support black suffrage, although even this generalisation is misleading, for Warmoth and Chamberlain's experience left them deeply conservative and negrophobe.[42]

The rehabilitation of the 'scalawags', or 'white negroes' as they were pejoratively referred to by Southern Democrats, has accompanied that of the carpetbagger. In an analysis of white Mississippi Republicans, David Donald found not the stereotypical rednecks but a wealthy and educated elite who were conservative by nature, as opposed to the secessionists as they were to the radicalism of congressional Reconstruction. Allan Trelease found Unionism most vital among up-country farmers, who had no more reason to be well disposed towards the old planter class than the freedmen but were now willing to vote along with the enfranchised black as long as the blacks were junior partners and did not push for social equality. In essence the scalawags' one sin was loyalty to the Union. Franklin concludes that 'They hardly deserved the name [of 'scalawag'], nor did they deserve the numerous other opprobrious labels pinned on them by hostile critics.'[43]

The Dunningite school insisted that the Northern carpetbagger and Southern 'scalawag' joined together in unholy alliance to enthrone the freedman. There was, in fact, no black domination, nor a black majority in both Houses, in any state. There were, briefly, two black senators in Washington. There were 600 black legislators in total who held a temporary majority in the two states which had a black majority, South Carolina and Mississippi, and black politicians constituted a majority (of seventy-six to forty-eight) in the South Carolina state constitutional convention, which ensured such progressive legislation as universal male suffrage, the abolition of property qualifications for the holding of office and the removal of presidential elections from the state legislature to the state's voters. But none of this remotely amounts to black domination.

Dunningites insisted that the primary aim of the Republicans was to empty the coffers of the Southern states in an orgy of corruption. There was undoubtedly a great deal of poverty in the South following the disruption of war. The South's share of the nation's wealth fell from 30 per cent to 12 per cent between 1860 and 1870, but this was not the consequence of legislative corruption. Hitherto the South had hardly been taxed at all – the land tax in Mississippi had been only 0.1 per cent, for example – and what taxes there were, such as the poll tax, were regressive. Complaints about extravagance and peculation resulted from the introduction of a more progressive taxation system levied on personal property in land, and the launching of welfare provisions. South Carolina, for example, doubled its budget between 1860 and 1873, but, overwhelmingly, the money was spent on education, health care and improved communications. This is not to deny the existence of corruption, merely to deny that it was endemic in the South, and to assert that it pales into insignificance besides the rampant corruption of the North.

The Dunningites managed, in a somewhat contradictory manner, to suggest both short-term black dominance and long-term black passivity. This view too has changed. Granted a vote for the first time, 700,000 freedmen were organised into Union Leagues and the turn-out was often as high as 90 per cent. 'The entry of negroes into the political arena,' as Franklin observes, 'was a most revolutionary aspect of the Reconstruction programme.'[44] Unfortunately the protracted opposition of most Southern whites, combined with the fact that the Republican black vote was guaranteed and did not have to be actively wooed, made it a short-term phenomenon. The sharecropping system that evolved in the South was a compromise between white demands for greater efficiency and black desire for a greater degree of personal autonomy in their labour. The system shifted income distribution to the freedman from 22 per cent to 56 per cent, the greatest redistribution of income in American history, McPherson insists. Once having gained the vote the freedmen voted overwhelmingly for education. The black population spent something in the order of $1 million in order to be able to read the Bible and the word of God for themselves. In 1860 90 per cent of blacks were illiterate. By 1880 the figure had fallen to 70 per cent and by 1900 to 50 per cent, with over 34 per cent of blacks in school. The schools were segregated, but segregated schools were infinitely preferable to no schools at all, and the education achievement, given all the vicissitudes of the time, was immense. Du Bois was right to refer to Reconstruction as 'The dawn of freedom' when the silent slave was given a voice at last.

Next to education the blacks desired land. A few radicals such as Stevens and George Julian advocated the confiscation and redistribution of land, but such an assault on property was deemed far too revolutionary, and this failure has been considered one of the major tragedies of reconstruction. Here the problem was not one of land shortage. Even without confiscation, large tracts of Louisiana and Mississippi (over 10 per cent) remained unsettled. The Freedmen's Bureau directly controlled 850,000 acres, the Southern Homestead Act of 1862 was aimed specifically at providing land for poor blacks as well as whites, and General Sherman's Order No. 15 allowed 40,000 freedmen to settle on a vast swathe of confiscated land beyond Charleston. One of President Johnson's first acts was to rescind Sherman's order and return the land to whites. But even the land policy was not a total failure. By 1880, 1–5 per cent of land was owned by freedmen, and by 1910 the figure had reached 25 per cent. Comparative studies by Foner, Kolchin and others suggest, furthermore, that land ownership was not, by itself, enough. Land had been granted in Haiti, Jamaica and Russia, but the emancipated serfs, for example, were given plots too small to work profitably; they were crippled by redemption payments, and usually ended working the land for their former owners. It was the lack of political control, as Wendell Phillips suggested at the time, which hampered economic emancipation. Without political power freedmen were unable to obtain cheap credit, avoid crippling taxes, get adequate supplies of seed and fertiliser or gain access to open markets. As one freedman remarked in 1871, 'The white people's arms are longer than ours.'[45]

Reconstruction revisionism has now come full circle. The

Dunningites have been revised, and the assumption that Reconstruction was a tragedy because it was attempted has been replaced by the belief that the tragedy of Reconstruction lay in its ultimate failure. The more positive assessment of recent years has interpreted Reconstruction as a genuine revolution in race relations and strikingly experimental, despite its flaws. Dunningite mendacity has at last been finally laid to rest. As one eighty-eight-year-old former slave put it: 'I know folks think the books tell the truth, but they shure don't.' Eric Foner, in his magnificent *Reconstruction* of 1988, has offered a professional apology. 'This rewriting of Reconstruction history [by the Dunningite school] was accorded scholarly legitimacy – to its overwhelming shame – by the nation's fraternity of professional historians.'[46] Now atonement has been made.

Notes

1 Du Bois quoted in Eric Foner, *Reconstruction: America's Unfinished Revolution, 1863–1877* (New York, 1988), p. 602.
2 Wilson quoted in Arthur Link and Rembert Patrick (eds), *Writing Southern History* (Baton Rouge, 1965), p. 314.
3 Williams quoted in John Hope Franklin, *Race and History* (Baton Rouge, 1989), p. 44; and in Franklin's biography of *George Washington Williams* (Chicago, 1985), p. 112.
4 Beard quoted in Thomas Pressly, *Americans Interpret their Civil War* (New York, 1962), p. 332; and Hesseltine in Peter Novick, *That Noble Dream* (Cambridge, 1988), p. 233.
5 Rhodes quoted in John Hope Franklin, *Reconstruction* (Chicago, 1961), p. 433; and Kenneth Stampp, *The Era of Reconstruction* (London, 1965), pp. 5–6.
6 Rhodes quoted in Harvey Wish, *The American Historian* (New York, 1960), pp. 222–3; and in Link and Patrick, *Writing Southern History*, p. 307.
7 Lynch quoted in Link and Patrick, *Writing Southern History*, p. 309; in Franklin's *Race and History*, p. 388; and in Foner's *Reconstruction*, p. 610.
8 Burgess quoted in Grady McWhiney, *Southerners and other Americans* (New York, 1973), p. 128; in Harold Hyman (ed.), *The Radical Republicans and Reconstruction, 1861–1870* (Indianapolis, 1967), pp. xxix–xxx; in Wish, *The American Historian*, p. 230; and Novick, *That Noble Dream*, p. 76.
9 Dunning quoted in Thomas Pressly, 'Racial attitudes, scholarship and Reconstruction: a review essay', *Journal of Southern History* (32, 1966), p. 91.
10 William Dunning, *Reconstruction: Political and Economic, 1865–1877* (New York, 1907), p. 1. Quoted in Wish, *The American Historian*, p. 232. Dunning, *Reconstruction*, p. 58.

11 Dunning, *Reconstruction*, pp. 14, 121, 213, 214. William Dunning, *Essays on the Civil War and Reconstruction* (New York, 1965), p. xii; and quoted in Pressly, 'Racial attitudes', p. 89.

12 Dunning, *Reconstruction*, pp. 19, 86–7.

13 Dunning quoted in Pressly, 'Racial attitudes', p. 90. Dunning, *Essays on the Civil War*, p. ix. Dunning, *Reconstruction*, pp. 87–8, 46, 32, 80–1. Dunning to Bancroft quoted in Hyman, *The Radical Republicans and Reconstruction*, p. xxx.

14 Fleming quoted in Link and Patrick, *Writing Southern History*, p. 301; and in Charles Sellers Jr, *The Southerner as American* (Chapel Hill, 1960), pp. 11–12. Garner quoted in Richard Current, *Three Carpetbag Governors* (Baton Rouge, 1967), p. 95.

15 Dixon quoted in Robert Lang (ed.), *The Birth of A Nation: D.W. Griffith, Director* (New Brunswick, N.J., 1994), pp. 279, 285.

16 Lang, *The Birth of a Nation*, pp. 271, 19, 23, 123.

17 *Ibid.*, p. 17.

18 Wilson quoted in Franklin, *Race and History*, p. 16.

19 Bowers quoted in Gerald Grob and George Billias (eds), *Interpretations of American History*, I (New York, 1972), p. 482.

20 Du Bois quoted in John Hope Franklin and August Meier (eds), *Black Leaders of the Twentieth Century* (Urbana, 1982), p. 64.

21 Du Bois quoted in Eric Foner, *Nothing But Freedom* (Baton Rouge, 1983), p. 71.

22 Du Bois quoted in Rayford Logan (ed.), *W.E.B. Du Bois: A Profile* (New York, 1971), pp. 249, 273.

23 David Donald, *The Politics of Reconstruction* (Cambridge, Mass., 1984), p. 367; Peter Kolchin, *American Slavery* (Harmondsworth, 1993), p. 285; Eric Foner, in Stanley Elkins and Eric McKitrick (eds), *The Hofstadter Aegis* (New York, 1974), p. 183; Foner, *Nothing but Freedom*, p. 5.

24 Du Bois quoted in Logan, *Du Bois*, p. 256. Charles and Mary Beard, *The Rise of American Civilization* (New York, 1930), p. 100.

25 Randall quoted in Grob and Billias, *Interpretations of American History*, p. 464. Randall quoted in Don Fehrenbacher, *Lincoln in Text and Context* (Stanford, 1987), p. 192; and in Donald, *The Politics of Reconstruction*, p. 2.

26 Howard Beale, 'On rewriting reconstruction history', *American Historical Review* (46, 1940), pp. 807–7. Beale quoted in Marcus Cunliffe and Robin Winks (eds), *Past Masters* (New York, 1969), p. 379.

27 Moore quoted in Grob and Billias, *Interpretations of American History*, p. 498. Owsley quoted in Franklin, *Race and History*, p. 25.

28 Williams quoted in Novick, *That Noble Dream*, p. 349 n. 45.

29 Coulter quoted in Franklin, *Race and History*, p. 26; and in Foner, *Reconstruction*, p. xx.

30 Franklin's review of Coulter is reprinted in Franklin, *Race and History*.

31 Potter quoted in Cunliffe and Winks, *Past Masters*, pp. 375–6.

32 Donald quoted in Frank Gatell and Allen Weinstein (eds), *American Themes* (London, 1968), p. 342.

33 Armistead Robinson, 'Beyond the realm of social consensus', *Journal of American History* (68, 1881), p. 285.

34 Foner, *Nothing but Freedom*, pp. 6, 110.
35 Coben's article is reprinted in Seth Schreiner (ed.), *Reconstruction: A Tragic Era* (New York, 1968).
36 Johnson quoted in Kenneth Stampp and Leon Litwack (eds), *Reconstruction: An Anthology of Revisionist Writings* (Baton Rouge, 1969), p. 72.
37 Carlyle quoted in Phillip Paludan, *A Covenant with Death* (Urbana, 1975), p. 15.
38 Dunning quoted in Frank Gatell, Paul Goodman and Allen Weinstein (eds), *The Growth of American Politics*, I (London, 1972), p. 492.
39 Vann Woodward's essay is reprinted in *The Burden of Southern History* (Baton Rouge, 1968).
40 Stevens quoted in Woodward, *The Burden of Southern History*, p. 95.
41 La Wanda and John Cox, *Politics, Principle and Prejudice, 1865–1866* (New York, 1963), p. 225.
42 Richard Current, *Those Terrible Carpetbaggers* (Oxford, 1988).
43 Franklin, *Reconstruction*, p. 101.
44 *Ibid.*, p. 86.
45 Quoted in Eric Foner, *Politics and Ideology in the Age of the Civil War* (Oxford, 1980), p. 120.
46 Foner, *Reconstruction*, pp. 611, 609.

Selective bibliography

Anderson, Eric, and Moss Jr, Alfred (eds), *The Facts of Reconstruction: Essays in Honor of John Hope Franklin* (Baton Rouge, 1991).
Aptheker, Herbert, 'Du Bois the historian' in Rayford Logan (ed.), *W.E.B. Du Bois: A Profile* (New York, 1971).
Beale, Howard, 'On rewriting reconstruction history', *American Historical Review* (46, 1940).
Bogue, Allan, 'Historians and radical reconstruction: a meaning for today', *Journal of American History* (70:1, 1983).
Coben, Stanley, 'New England business and radical reconstruction: an examination', *Mississippi Valley Historical Review* (75, 1989).
Cox, La Wanda and John, *Politics, Principle and Prejudice, 1865–1866: Dilemmas of Reconstruction America* (New York, 1963).
Cox, La Wanda and John, 'Negro suffrage and Republican politics: the problem of motivation in reconstruction historiography' in Frank Gatell and Allen Weinstein (eds), *American Themes: Essays in Historiography* (London, 1968).
Current, Richard (ed.), *Reconstruction* (Englewood Cliffs, N.J., 1965).
Current, Richard, *Three Carpet-bag Governors* (Baton Rouge, 1967).
Current, Richard (ed.), series of articles on Reconstruction, *Reconstruction in Retrospect* (Baton Rouge, 1969; originally in *The Atlantic Monthly*, 1901).
Current, Richard, *Those Terrible Carpetbaggers* (Oxford, 1988).
Donald, David, 'Scalawags in Mississippi Reconstruction', *Journal of Southern History* (10, 1944).
Donald, David, *The Politics of Reconstruction* (Cambridge, Mass., 1984).
Du Bois, W.E.B., 'Of the dawn of freedom', reprinted in Staughton Lynd (ed.), *Reconstruction* (New York, 1967).

Du Bois W.E.B., *Black Reconstruction in America, 1860–1880* (New York, 1969).

Du Bois. W.E.B., 'Reconstruction and its benefits' (1910); reprinted in Staughton Lynd (ed.), *Reconstruction* (New York, 1967).

Dunning, William, *Essays on the Civil War and Reconstruction* (New York, 1965).

Dunning, William, *Reconstruction: Political and Economic, 1865–1877* (1907; reprinted New York, 1962).

Foner, Eric, *Politics and Ideology in the Age of the Civil War* (Oxford, 1980).

Foner, Eric, 'Reconstruction revisited', *Reviews in American History* (10, 1982).

Foner, Eric, *Nothing but Freedom: Emancipation and its Legacy* (Baton Rouge, 1983).

Foner, Eric, *Reconstruction: America's Unfinished Revolution, 1863–1877* (New York, 1988).

Foner, Eric, 'The meaning of freedom in the Age of Emancipation', *Journal of American History* (81:1–2, 1994).

Forster, Gaines, *Ghosts of the Confederacy* (New York, 1987).

Franklin, John Hope, *Reconstruction* (Chicago, 1961).

Franklin, John Hope, *George Washington Williams* (Chicago, 1985).

Hyman, Harold (ed.), *The Radical Republicans and Reconstruction, 1861–1870* (Indianapolis, 1967).

Kincaid, Larry, 'Victims of circumstance: an interpretation of changing attitudes towards Republican policy makers and Reconstruction', *Journal of American History* (49:2, 1962).

Kolchin, Peter, 'The business press and Reconstruction, 1865–1868', *Journal of Southern History* (33, 1967).

Link, Arthur, and Patrick, Rembert (eds), *Writing Southern History* (Baton Rouge, 1965).

Lynd, Staughton (ed.), *Reconstruction* (New York, 1967).

McKitrick, Eric, *Andrew Johnson and Reconstruction* (London, 1960).

Miller, Philip, 'Look back without anger: a reappraisal of William A. Dunning', *Journal of American History* (61, 1974–75).

Paludan, Philip, *A Covenant with Death* (Urbana, 1975).

Peskin, Allan, 'Was there a compromise of 1877?', *Journal of American History* (59, 1973).

Polakoff, Keith, *The Politics of Inertia: The Election of 1876 and the End of Reconstruction* (Baton Rouge, 1973).

Pressly, Thomas, 'Racial attitudes, scholarship and Reconstruction: a review essay', *Journal of Southern History* (32, 1966).

Robinson, Armistead, 'Beyond the realm of social consensus: new meanings of Reconstruction for American history', *Journal of American History* (68, 1981).

Rudwick, Elliott, 'Du Bois' in John Hope Franklin and August Meier (eds), *Black Leaders of the Twentieth Century* (Urbana, 1982).

Simkins, Francis, 'New viewpoints of Southern Reconstruction', *Journal of Southern History* (5, 1939).

Simpson, Brooks, *Let Us Have Peace: Ulysses S. Grant and the Politics of War and Reconstruction, 1861–1868* (Chapel Hill, 1991).

Stampp, Kenneth, *The Era of Reconstruction* (London, 1965).

Stampp, Kenneth, and Litwack, Leon (eds), *Reconstruction: An Anthology of*

Revisionist Writings (Baton Rouge, 1969).

Trefousse, Hans, *Andrew Johnson: A Biography* (New York, 1989).

Trelease, Allan, 'Who were the scalawags?', *Journal of Southern History* (29, 1963).

Weinberg, Meyer (ed.), *W.E.B. Du Bois: A Reader* (New York, 1970).

Weisberger, Bernard, 'The dark and bloody ground of Reconstruction history', *Journal of Southern History* (25, 1959).

Woodward, C. Vann, *Reunion and Reaction: The Compromise of 1877 and the End of Reconstruction* (New York, 1956).

Zilversmit, Arthur, 'Grant and the freedmen', in Robert Abzug and Stephen Märzlich (eds), *New Perspectives on Race and Slavery in America* (Lexington, Ky, 1989).

INDEX